W9-DJN-765

ALLERTON PARK INSTITUTE

Number 16

Papers presented at an Institute
conducted by the
University of Illinois
Graduate School of Library Science

November 2-5, 1969

SERIAL PUBLICATIONS
IN
LARGE LIBRARIES

Edited by
WALTER C. ALLEN

University of Illinois
Graduate School of Library Science
Urbana, Illinois

INTRODUCTION

If ever there was a perplexing area in librarianship, it is the handling of serial publications. It is inconceivable that any library could operate without them. It is equally inconceivable that any library can cope with them without experiencing some sort of trauma. The enormous numbers of them, their endless variety, their lasting qualities (as to both physical properties and content), their arrangement and handling present daily and frequently difficult problems. And, the larger the library, the more these problems emerge to plague the many librarians who have to deal with them. Users face difficulties too, and it is, of course, the aim of the librarians to minimize these.

The planning committee conceived this Allerton Park Institute, the sixteenth in the series annually sponsored by the Graduate School of Library Science of the University of Illinois, as a step by step discussion of the many phases of dealing with serials. From Sunday, November 2, to Wednesday, November 5, 1969, over one hundred speakers and participants met at the University's conference center, Allerton House, a few miles from Monticello, Illinois.

As usual at conferences of this sort, many questions were raised, discussed, sometimes answered and sometimes compounded or left for further consideration during informal periods following the presentations of the papers. Many other discussions went on between and after sessions, during meals, walks and other interludes. Unfortunately, we have no record of any of these informal gatherings.

Theodore Peterson, Dean of the College of Communications of the University, was the keynoter. Long concerned with trends in periodical publications, especially those of a more popular nature, Peterson took a hard look at the magazine world and its fluid nature, and ended by asking more questions than he answered.

It was the feeling of the planning committee that selection and acquisition of serials are two entirely different things. William A. Katz, compiler of "Magazines for Libraries" and frequent contributor to library periodicals *about* periodicals, advocated a general revision of buying policies, especially concerning periodicals which most librarians (and probably more patrons) usually think of as "off-beat" (or worse). Adrenalin rose, and in some cases remained high. A somewhat less controversial area is that of acquisitions, the actual locating, buying and paying for serials. Peter Gellatly also took up questions of agents, duplicates, and spiraling costs, to cite a few specific topics.

Kathryn L. Henderson gallantly stepped into an arena which many catalogers found themselves unable to enter because of various conflicts of assignments, and produced a major paper on the changing approaches to serials cataloging. Her husband, William Henderson, binding librarian for the

the University of Illinois Library, and James Orr, of Hertzberg-New Method, Inc., gave a pair of papers which presented the varying points of view of the librarian and of the professional library binder. It is a source of frustration that the many examples of the binder's art which Orr brought to the Institute cannot be reproduced here.

Probably the largest collection of serials in the country is that of the Library of Congress. Samuel Lazerow of the Serial Record Division reviewed the question of recording information on serial delivery—or non-delivery. Many libraries are experimenting with automated approaches. Donald P. Hammer of Purdue University Libraries presented what was, in effect, a slide talk on various methods of recording such information with the assistance of machines. A few of his illustrations are reproduced here.

Thomas D. Gillies of the Linda Hall Library discussed the peculiar dilemmas of one particular body of serials—those published by the United States government. He also explored a large body of materials—technical reports—which are not exactly serials, but somehow seem to present many of the same problems.

So far, the papers have been concerned with internal questions. What about the user? The final two papers are reflections of the needs of patrons, as well as of staff. Bill M. Woods works closely with questions of bibliographic control; his paper reflects this interest and the changing trends in indexing. Warren B. Kuhn's assignment was to consider various methods of housing and servicing serials, so that they will be of the greatest benefit to the largest number of patrons in a library of some size.

A paper on union lists was planned for the Institute, but unfortunately had to be dropped from the schedule. In its place there was a panel discussion of some of the problems involved. Participants were two of the speakers, Donald P. Hammer and Kathryn L. Henderson, and Mary MacDonald, of the Illinois State Library; the chairman of the Institute planning committee moderated. Essentially, the discussion centered around purposes and, therefore, degrees of inclusiveness; methods of compilation; compatibility of entries so that lists can be consolidated if desired; and methods of updating. Also touched on was the matter of selectivity in the *Union List of Serials* and *New Serials Titles*, and the need for special supplemental lists of serials not included in the major national, regional and state lists. While few, if any, firm conclusions were reached, some patterns of existing lists, needed ones, methods and usages of them did emerge from the discussion.

No conference just happens. It represents the ideas and hard work of many people—planning committee, staff, speakers, and participants. In this case, the planning committee had the benefit of the experience and specialized knowledge of William Huff, serials librarian of the University of Illinois; Rolland E. Stevens, who was closely involved with acquisitions problems for a number of years, and Kathryn L. Henderson, who has long been concerned with questions of serials cataloging. In addition, Herbert Goldhor was able to steer us gently through the perilous waters of conference planning. Other members of the faculty assisted in chairing sessions and welcoming participants.

As in the past, this Allerton Park Institute was planned and conducted with the cooperation of the Division of University Extension. In the early stages Susan Holty was academic coordinator, Extension Library Science, Division of Library Extension. She was succeeded by Mrs. Donna Lenfest, whose excellent handling of details concerning rooms, meals, transportation, and hospitality made the conference a pleasant one. As always, the staff at Allerton House were efficient, helpful, and cordial; they have our thanks.

That more than ninety people should come from all over the country (including Puerto Rico) to hear these papers and take part in the discussions is certainly a sign of interest in the topic. They brought much; we can only hope that they took something away.

Finally, for those who were here, and for those who were not, we present this volume of papers, somewhat edited, but preserving the essence of the ideas of the speakers. Much of the work involved here is the expert copy editing of Barbara Wallen, of the Publications Office of the Graduate School of Library Science.

Walter C. Allen
Chairman, Conference Committee

April 1970

TABLE OF CONTENTS

Theodore Peterson
Dean, College of Communications
University of Illinois
Urbana, Illinois

THE BRIGHT, BLEAK FUTURE
OF AMERICAN MAGAZINES

On Friday, January 19, 1969, Martin S. Ackerman, who professedly had come to the presidency of the Curtis Publishing Company as savior, announced that the *Saturday Evening Post* would cease publication with its February 8, 1969, issue. The mourners came solemnly to the funeral, and there were obituaries and euologies galore.

Since countless clinicians have already performed autopsies on Benjamin Franklin's illegitimate offspring, this is not the occasion to speculate in detail about why the magazine died. Yet if one is to assess the future of American magazines, it does seem important to put the death of the *Saturday Evening Post* in perspective, especially since at its death some people heard the ominous tolling of John Donne's churchbell—tolling not just for the *Post* but for all magazines.

Certainly the death of the *Saturday Evening Post* should remind us of the essential mortality of all magazines. Many of the magazines that led in circulation, advertising and prestige preceded the *Post* in death. And in the same month that the *Post* died, *American Builder* slipped quietly into the grave. Eight years earlier, *American Builder* had been its publisher's number one magazine, and only the previous November it had observed its hundredth anniversary. In April, 1969, *Western Farm Life* died at age seventy-one. In April, too, the Hearst Corporation gave up its attempts to sustain *Eye*, a two-year-old monthly for young swingers. Over the years, death has come with democratic impartiality to the young and old, to the poor and to the once wealthy.

But it has come for different reasons. William Emerson, the last editor of the *Saturday Evening Post,* the man who as much as anyone had kept it alive for its last four years, had this to say when his magazine died:

1

It makes me bitter and angry. This is the end result of misrule. It was not the fault of the editorial product or of the people on the staff. Both were excellent.

This was a business problem. The Post Company is a big, cumbersome, *integrated* publishing organization and in a time of intense competition, this was a handicap. We were the slaves of our own institution.[1]

As Emerson said, the Curtis Publishing Company was a big, cumbersome, integrated organization which, indulging its squirrel-like instincts, acquired forests for making paper, mills for converting forests into paper, printing plants and engraving plants and binderies, subscription agencies and distribution facilities. Burdened by enormous fixed costs, it lacked maneuverability.

Curtis could afford to be acquisitive, for in the days before broadcasting it controlled the major national advertising media in the United States. In the 1920s, its publications took in about $2 of every $5 that advertisers spent on national advertising in magazines. In 1923, the year that Briton Hadden and Henry Luce started Time Inc., the Curtis magazines accounted for 43 percent of national magazine advertising.

Curtis, however, chose to acquire the wrong things. It could have gone into radio, which its officers evidently regarded as a passing fad, and it could have gone into television. It could have gone into paperback book publishing, for which it had all of the ingredients from manuscripts to distribution facilities; instead it banked on the impregnability of print.

With wealth and power came arrogance. In the lush days, competitors will tell you, Curtis advertising salesmen on their trips from Philadelphia to Chicago to sell space took suites in the best hotels and invited advertisers to come place their orders. And once, when Curtis printers were on strike, others will tell you, the company contracted with Cuneo Press to handle its printing until the dispute was settled. After the strike, Cuneo made a bid for the business. The Curtis treasurer discovered that letting Cuneo do the printing would save the company a million dollars a year, so he took Mr. Cuneo to see Cyrus Curtis, who swiftly disposed of the matter. "Mr. Cuneo," he is supposed to have said, "we are not interested in saving a million dollars a year."

My feeling is that the death of the *Saturday Evening Post* reveals more about the long-term management policies of Curtis than it does about the future of magazine publishing. Even so, William Emerson said of its manner of death, "This has done irreparable harm to the whole publishing industry."[1]
Perhaps.

True, *Advertising Age,* a leading trade publication, devoted its October 20, 1969, issue to magazines. Its introduction said:

But now it is magazines . . . which have garnered the attention of the naysayers in the advertising/marketing world. More than anything else, of course, it was the widely reported troubles of the Curtis Publishing Co. and the demise of the *Saturday Evening Post,* once the unquestioned king of advertising media in the United States, which gave impetus to the mournful tolling of the bells.[2]

Other reasons it mentioned are the widespread acceptance of color television and the influence in advertising agencies of a creative generation which was raised on television.

True, a naysayer bent on looking for them can find a number of at least superficial signs that magazines are in trouble. For instance, A. Kent MacDougall, in one of the perceptive pieces about magazine publishing that he writes for the *Wall Street Journal,* [3] noted that Time Inc. had suffered a series of setbacks. His story, which appeared on the eve of the annual meeting of Time Inc. stockholders, reported that *Time* had lost ground to *Newsweek,* although its circulation has continued to rise; that *Life* had lost advertising page volume for nine of the previous twelve years, although its circulation also has continued to grow. Time Inc. had lost heavily on several non-publishing ventures—$5 million on General Learning Corp., its joint venture with General Electric; $6 million on its Selling Areas-Marketing Inc., a subsidiary that sells computerized information on the movement of goods from warehouses to supermarkets; $3 million on a television investment in Venezuela; and $5.2 million on the market value of its stock in Metro-Goldwyn-Mayer. As if to bear out MacDougall, there has been a reshuffling in the higher echelons of Time Inc., and changes have been made in key personnel and in editorial policies of *Time* and *Life.* Yet MacDougall spoke only of temporary setbacks, not imminent death, and it would be premature to predict that a "For Rent" sign will soon appear on the Time-Life Building.

Then there is the *New Yorker.* Recently Douglas Davis came right out in public and said what others had been saying privately: "The *New Yorker* is in trouble. Trouble of a highly qualified, specialized kind, but trouble all the same."[4] He reported that its advertising volume was slipping, as were its profits; that among the advertising agencies it was getting the reputation of being "square" and "out-of-date"; that the lively upstart, *New York* magazine, aiming at the eighteen to thirty-four set, was reaching an important audience and filling an editorial need that the *New Yorker* had chosen to ignore. The facts are that the *New Yorker*'s advertising volume in 1968 was 7 percent below that of 1967, and that in the first nine months of this year its page volume was down by 11 percent, its advertising revenues down by 6 percent. I happen to think that the *New Yorker,* like its audience, has become middle-aged and stuffy; but whether or not it actually is in perilous health is quite another matter.

A couple of months ago when *Look* ran an article linking Mayor Joseph Alioto of San Francisco with the Mafia, the mayor charged, among other things, that the magazine is in bad financial trouble. Editor William Arthur went on a twenty-station hookup in California on September 11 to answer some of the charges, specifically to deny that *Look* has lost $10 million in the past two years and that Standard and Poor's has said that if *Look* does not turn the profit corner soon, Cowles Communications will be in serious trouble. It is no secret that Cowles Communications has lost money in the past couple of years. But a good deal of that loss has come from the *Suffolk Sun,* a daily newspaper that the company started in Long Island in November 1966. How big a financial drain the paper has been, it is hard to say; some outsiders have estimated the losses at $10 million. In any case, the company closed down the newspaper in October 1969, because it saw no prospects for profitable operations in the short term.

What I am trying to suggest by all of this is that one can find gossip, rumor and some hard facts to question the health of magazine publishing. The questioners make a number of points. One is that television has emerged as a major competitor for audience and advertising. Furthermore, a young generation in the advertising agencies has grown up on television, and many of them are more impressed by television than by the printed media when it comes to deciding where to spend their clients' advertising dollars. Another is that magazines have done far too little to bring young people into their audiences. Still another is that in this age of microcards, microfiche, computerized information banks, facsimile, videotape cartridges and other communications marvels, the magazine is obsolescent.

Yet I do not think we have approached the day when libraries should start phasing out their serials departments because magazines are becoming extinct. Magazines will be with us for a long time to come, I think, although not necessarily the same magazines that now crowd our newstands and litter our coffeetables.

Magazine publishing has always been an occupation for gamblers. When Arnold Gingrich and his associates started *Esquire* in 1933, experts quoted them odds of 200 to one against success, and I suspect that the odds have changed little since then. Since the late nineteenth century, magazines have been sensitive to changes in the economy, and they have been especially vulnerable in times of rapidly rising costs because of their curious economics—selling their products to readers at far less than the cost of production and taking their profits from the sale of advertising. Under this system, a large circulation can be either an asset or a terrifying liability. It can be an asset if it attracts a lot of advertising; it can be a liability if it increases faster than advertising rates can be adjusted or if its costs outpace advances in advertising rates. It can be a massive liability if advertising volume drops off.

And a magazine's advertising volume can drop off suddenly. When advertising budgets suffer, as in a recession, so do magazines. An advertiser can cancel his magazine advertising on short notice; he is usually committed for at least thirteen weeks to the advertising he has placed on network television. Moreover, magazine publishing has traditionally been a low-profit industry. Last year, for instance, it is doubtful that the average profit was much more than 3 percent of revenues.

Despite all of this gloomy talk, there are some bright spots. For one thing, magazines at last have learned to live with television, although it took them several years to learn the lesson. At first magazines challenged television in the area of television's greatest strength—audience size. If television could deliver enormous audiences to advertisers, they reasoned, so could magazines, and they charged off after huge circulations at whatever the cost. Now, however, they have begun to exploit their own special strengths, and they are the better for it.

For another thing, the advertising volume of magazines has made respectable advances since the advent of television. True, it is hard to become euphoric over what has happened to advertising page volume. Last year the number of advertising pages—83,406—was only 230 more than in 1957 when television had emerged as a big peril, although the number was a few thousand more than that in 1967, 1966, and 1965. This will be the fifth consecutive year that advertising revenues have exceeded a billion dollars, and they have increased by more than 60 percent since 1957. Last year fifty-seven of the top advertisers spent more money in magazines than they did the previous year. Sears, Roebuck and Company made the biggest increase—$7,701,000. (Incidentally, if you would like to guess which advertiser spends the most money in *Playboy*, here is your answer—Sears.) There is also some reasonably good evidence that the aggregate circulation of magazines has been growing faster than the population for the past twenty years.

Certainly the birth rate of magazines shows little sign of decreasing. The Magazine Publishers Association has listed more than eighty new magazines that were started in the first nine months of 1969, and the list is surely incomplete. Here are some of them: *Afro-American Woman, Apartment Ideas, Family Health, Government Executive, Homemaking with a Flair, Jock/New York, Mid-Atlantic Living, Single, Twenty-Five* and *Washington Monthly*. My guess is then that magazines are not being faced with total extinction. They will have to adapt to a new environment to survive, to be sure, but some of them are already showing an awareness of that necessity.

I will mention just a few of the things that have happened and that are likely to happen. One of the most notable developments during the past couple decades has been the steady drift toward the special-interest magazine—the magazine with a sharply-defined audience and a sharply-defined editorial appeal. In recent years, I think the audiences and the editorial appeals have become increasingly narrowed, something that is reflected in the titles of new magazines during that period: *Yankee Trader, Amateur Rocketeer, Wheels Afield* (about mobile homes and campers), *Scrumdown, Catholic Traveler* (with information about shrines and pilgrimages), *Sports-fishing, Modern Bridge, Bank Equipment News, Chess Forum* and *Private Pilot*.

This pin-pointing of audiences has not been confined to magazines. In varying degrees, all of the mass media have been doing it except television, and I strongly suspect that television will head in that same general direction of specialized audiences in the next few years as a result of videotape cartridges, multiple-set homes, community-antenna systems and other things. Since fragmentation of audience seems a characteristic of our times, I think that the future belongs to the special-interest magazines, which in recent years have shown the greatest health and potential.

Another development has been the growth of regional editions. Magazines with national circulations are giving advertisers the chance to buy space in copies distributed only in some restricted area—a marketing zone, a state, a city, a county. In doing so, they have increased their flexibility as an advertising medium, opened up new sources of potential advertisers, and put themselves in closer competition with the local media. The number of magazines with regional editions has grown from 126 in 1959, to 186 in 1965, to 235 in 1969. These editions have accounted for a growing share of advertising revenues; the $2 million they brought in last year represented about a 40 percent increase over five years ago.

Since publishers began to exploit regional editions in 1959, the geographic regions have become smaller and smaller. Now several magazines sell space in copies going into such cities as Chicago, Los Angeles and New York. *Farm Journal,* which has published more than 125 different editions of a single issue, will sell circulation in any one of the 3,070 counties in the United States.

Publishers are sorting out their audiences for advertisers not just by geographic area but also by demographics—income, home-ownership, job function, and so on. For instance, in early 1968, *Look* introduced what it calls its Top/Spot edition. Using computers and census data, it discovered the zip code postal zones with the highest median incomes. Now an advertiser can buy space in the copies going only to the 1.1 million affluent readers in those zones instead of in all of the copies of *Look. Esquire* will sell advertisers access to just the half-million of its subscribers living in zip code areas with an average of 70 percent owner-occupied homes. About a year ago *Fortune* began publishing a special edition going to 120,000 computer-selected subscribers who are associated with manufacturing concerns. *Time* has had editions for physicians, educators, and students, and the *Reader's Digest* has had one for pupils in grades seven through twelve and their teachers.

So far most of this experimentation has been for the benefit of the advertiser. But Carroll Streeter of *Farm Journal* has predicted that a decade from now automation might enable his magazine to be tailored to the concerns of individual subscribers. Each subscriber would indicate the subjects he is especially interested in, and they would be programmed. As the magazine moved down the assembly line of the bindery, content matching the special interests of each subscriber would be bound into his individualized copy. Printing technology is not yet sophisticated enough for this sort of thing; in a decade perhaps it might be.

In the 1970s I would not be surprised if two other things did become fairly common. One is free distribution of some consumer magazines to carefully chosen lists of readers. For years, trade and technical magazines have practiced free distribution under the euphemism "controlled circulation." Recently a few new consumer magazines have tried it without notable success, but they have been essentially coupon-books for housewives, and I doubt that they were a fair test. Another is a break with traditional publishing schedules. Nothing in the nature of magazines requires that they appear weekly or fortnightly or monthly; that frequency is simply a convention. I would not be surprised if magazines, abandoning that convention, came to adjust their appearances to the patterns of living of their audiences and to the marketing patterns of their advertisers rather than to some rigid schedule.

To me one of the biggest changes in magazines has been in content. I believe that in the past half-dozen years magazine content has become more sophisticated in approach, has tackled more significant problems and issues, and has been blessed with more experimentation than at any time in the forty years I have been reading periodicals. Let us grant that magazines were too slow in taking up such subjects as civil rights, poverty and the Vietnam War. They have taken them up, and they have covered them from every imaginable angle. My generalization does not apply to every magazine, of course, but it does apply to some of several types—mass-circulation magazines, religious magazines, trade and technical magazines, among others.

Just as significantly, magazines have begun to experiment with reporting techniques. They have been the fount of the so-called "new journalism," which at its best brings the vision of the artist upon people, conditions and events and which uses the devices of literature to report actual happenings.

Television was, I believe, an important force in improving magazine content. On the one hand, television is the entertainment medium par excellence; on the other hand, it has made people aware of things that had not previously concerned them. Magazines began to leave outright amusement to television and to explore the widening range of interests that television helped to make possible.

The new forms of communication—computerized information banks, video-tape cartridges and all the rest—will probably have a similar influence on magazine content. In order to survive, magazines will turn to the tasks that they can do more effectively and efficiently than other forms of communication—reporting and assessing underlying social conditions, for instance, and perhaps providing a refuge for the browser.

Those that can adapt will survive, I think, and we are joined to both their past and their future. Let me elaborate on that cryptic sentence. If librarians want to rank alongside Albert Schweitzer and Jonas Salk as great humanitarians, they can earn that seat of glory by keeping a balanced, representative collection of magazines as the documents of our age. Magazines can tell us a great deal about the world we live in, the goals we seek, the values we cherish. They are a good primary source for the historian concerned with American civilization and for the scholar interested in popular culture. And if we are unaware of the zealousness with which scholars have been putting popular culture up for examination in the past decade or so, we are missing out on one of the phenomena of the times.

Let me give a couple quick illustrations of the value of magazines. It is quite well accepted now that the true confession magazines provide their readers with guides to daily living. As middle-class housewives turn to factual articles in *McCall's* and *Ladies' Home Journal* for ideas about child rearing or advice on coping with family problems, some blue-collar housewives turn to the narratives in *True Story* and *True Confessions.* In the experiences of others, they hope to find answers to some of the questions that perplex them. What sort of help do they get? What rules of conduct are implicitly prescribed by the confession magazines? What values do they prize? How have all of those things changed over the years? To answer questions of that sort, one obviously needs access to a good file of confession magazines. Take another type of question. How have the mass-circulation magazines portrayed the Negro over the years? Did their portrayal reflect an unthinking racism that may have perpetuated the status quo? Is it true that the Negro magazines themselves subtly enforced the status quo? Again, the answers lie in the right collection of magazines. Magazines are sources of factual material as well. In the days of silent movies, for instance, *Photoplay,* a movie fan magazine, carried a good deal of significant information about the motion picture industry that is not available anywhere else.

I had always naively assumed that in those gloomy library stacks the files of magazines were there. I had assumed that if one wanted a copy of *Photoplay* for March 1923, or *True Story* for April 1927, or *True Detective* for May 1929, or *Confidential* for June 1958, a library would be a more likely place to look than someone's attic. Then a few years ago I discovered how very wrong I was. I was thinking about writing a book about the wonderful world of the pulp magazines of the 1920s and 1930s and the fascinating characters who populated it. When I started looking for runs of *Black Mask, Dime Detective, Blue Book, Argosy, Spicy Western, Rangeland Love, Battle Aces* and some of their fellows, I was astonished to discover that virtually no libraries have them. Of the enormous outpouring of pulp magazines that sustained Max Brand and other writers at a penny a word, only a tiny fraction, alas, has survived. I was even more astonished three years ago to discover that only two libraries in the United States profess to have complete runs of *Playboy* and only four more to have any bound volumes at all—this even though *Playboy,* whatever one may think of it, has been a remarkable reflection of and significant influence on the change in manners and morals of the past decade.

So I did some rudimentary checking on other magazines that have illuminated various aspects of life and culture in the U.S. over the past half-century or so. I was surprised to find how rarely some of them turn up on library shelves. Some, in fact, seem available only from the Library of Congress; a few evidently are not even available there. Among them were *Down Beat,* which has covered the jazz scene since 1934; *Amazing Stories,* which was started in 1926 as one of the first science fiction magazines; *Hot Rod,* which came along in 1948 to capitalize on and stimulate the craze for souped-up automobiles; *Ballyhoo,* which was started in 1931 as a fortnightly of broad satire and which ran up a newstand sale of two million, an incredible record for the time; *Mad,* which is a contempory version of *Ballyhoo; Abbott's Monthly,* which had a short life as a pioneer magazine for Negroes; *Fate,* which for the past twenty years has served readers interested in reincarnation, predictive dreams, extrasensory perception, and other aspects of the occult; *Black Mask,* which H. L. Mencken and George Jean Nathan started in 1920 to run manuscripts they could not publish in *Smart Set; Saucy Stories,* which was also a product of Mencken and Nathan; *Salute,* which was addressed to World War II veterans and which drew on *Yank,* the army weekly, for some of its talent; *College Humor,* which in the 1920s and 1930s portrayed a John Held Jr., version of college life; *Dude, Gent* and *Nugget,* which were all imitators of *Playboy;* and *Capt. Billy's Whiz Bang,* which was a monthly of smoking-car humor that became the foundation of today's Fawcett Publications.

Altogether I listed a hundred magazines under such headings as confession magazines; fact detective magazines; pulps; hobbies and leisure; humor and satire; action-adventure; and sex, shock and sensation. Selfishly, I am concerned that runs of some of them—*Dime Western, Fifteen Range Romances,* and *Detective Story* for instance—are mouldering in publishers' warehouses in Brooklyn, if indeed they are not already beyond recall. I urged University Microfilms of Ann Arbor to start microfilming the hundred titles as an American Civilization/Popular Culture series, and I recently heard that the project was getting under way.

Most of those magazines are seldom found in libraries, and I think that I know the reasons, excluding budget limitations. One reason is that librarians are not specialists in magazines. Given their other duties, they can scarcely be blamed for not keeping track of all the new magazines that pop up. Even if they had a budget as large as President Nixon's investment in real estate, they would find it impractical to subscribe to a magazine until it has demonstrated its worth and staying power. One test of whether or not libraries subscribe to a magazine, I suspect, is whether or not it is listed in the right indexes. And one test of whether or not a magazine is listed in the right indexes, I further suspect, is whether or not libraries subscribe to it. *Esquire,* as I recall, was a long time in earning beatification by the indexes. *Playboy,* which nowadays is quoted by the clergy almost as often as Genesis, still has not made the indexes.

That leads to another reason. Librarians are eminently respectable; many of the magazines that tell us a great deal about our century do not seem to be respectable. *Night and Day, Dude, Clyde, Eros, Sir, Modern Romances, Dime Western, Doc Savage*—they seem shabby companions to share library shelves with such upright citizens of the magazine world as the *National Geographic* and *Reader's Digest.*

Moreover, people, librarians included, form mental images of some magazines without bothering to read them. Those images, whether or not they have a basis in reality, linger on in perpetuity. I still encounter people who think of *Esquire*—which is surely one of the best magazines in the U.S.—as something to be read furtively in barbershops. I still encounter people who think of *Playboy* as the greatest threat to the moral fiber of the nation since the abolition of the 72-hour work week.

Serial librarians have the beneficent task of selecting the magazines that best disseminate current knowledge and of preserving some of the most representative aspects of our subcultures. Their task is already a big one, and I am afraid that it will not get easier. If my guess is right, magazines will be around for some time, and the gamblers among us will be bringing out new ones at no less a rate than in the recent past. From the fifty or sixty or eighty. new magazines that appear each year, which ones should the serial librarian choose for their current use and value? Which ones to represent these times to a later generation? And as I have said, magazines have been becoming more and more specialized. As they continue to restrict their editorial appeal, I should imagine that the serial librarian will find it increasingly difficult to decide on which ones to spend his not-unlimited funds to get the most effective representation. Should he have *Girl Talk? Vertical World? Gap,* which seeks to bridge the generation you-know-what? *Flying Yankee? Fund Raising Management? Gambling Illustrated? Weight Watchers?*

And so we end, not with a band, but with a question.

References

1. Emerson, William. "What's New and What's Next," *Media/Scope,* 13:9, Feb. 1969.

2. "Print is Alive and Well . . . But," *Advertising Age,* 40:49, Oct. 20, 1969.

3. MacDougall, A. Kent. "Time Inc.'s Trials: Big Publisher Pledges New Projects Despite a Series of Setbacks," *Wall Street Journal,* 49:1, April 15, 1969.

4. Davis, Douglas. "The New Yorker Seeks a New Look," *National Observer,* 8:1, Feb. 17, 1969.

William A. Katz
Professor, School of Library Science
State University of New York
Albany

SERIALS SELECTION

This paper will consider some relatively unorthodox, fairly bibliographically free aspects of magazine selection—an approach in the worst tradition of the essentially fact-for-fact oriented library literature. However, anyone seeking orthodox information about indexes, abstracts or access to bibliographical information on magazines is referred to Winchell's *Guide to Reference Books* where it is all put precisely and accurately. In a more discursive readable fashion, William Huff has achieved much the same thing in his exellent article "Periodicals" in the January 1967, issue of *Library Trends*. Also, in my book, *Magazines for Libraries,* one will find a relatively exhaustive general and subject bibliography to the field.

Discussing what he terms a psychograph of adolescent rebellion, Bruno Bettelheim states that today's youth are frustrated "because modern technology has made them *obsolete*—they have become socially irrelevant and, as persons, insignificant."[1] Much the same might be said of the present art of magazine selection. Technology, from the "until forbidden" order to reliance on indexes and computerized records apparently has made much of the process obsolete. Large libraries, at any rate, now no longer select as much as collect. In so doing, it seems to me, they have made the magazine socially irrelevant, at least to all but a small, highly selected segment of the community.

In the words of Bob Dylan, "The Times They are a Changing." Particularly in larger libraries there is a recognition that somehow, in some way, the library must re-establish contact with those living outside of mid-cult suburbia. Public libraries are moving back to the streets, and academic libraries are studying ways to serve the so-called disadvantaged student, usually an euphemism for the Black. A cursory glance at the literature and a visit to almost any local, regional or national meeting confirm the suspicion that the

11

old values, the values based on the best for a few, are giving way to a more relative, realistic idea of service and selection. It is not surprising that the National Advisory Committee on Libraries concluded its report with a statement that a library can be understood only as it enhances a socially valuable function.[2] In the spirit of this statement is the newly organized American Library Association Social Responsibilities Round Table which demands that ALA take a social, humanistic stand on issues other than cataloging rules.

Almost all of this paper is devoted to the humanistic side of librarianship, primarily because I subscribe to a position stated succinctly by Christopher Lasch and Eugene Genovese:

> The arts and humanities must be rescued from their present degraded, essentially ornamental postion and established on an equal footing with science, as studies that make their own contribution to the understanding of the objective world. Unless these things are done, the working class and the American people as a whole will have no defense against a technological anti-culture that perpetrates one atrocity after another against people of other nations while it ruins its own environment and increasingly reduces its citizens to insecurity and anxiety.[3]

I do not wish to suggest there is no place for technology in libraries, but on the other hand, I am not overly impressed with what has been done—as compared to what has been published—to date. I think the real danger, at least in terms of magazine selection, is that the librarian who becomes involved with the shortcuts of record keeping and ordering offered by automation is apt to forget what the machine is really doing in his garden. In addition to the commendable notion that technology can make the library more efficient, it has given many justifications for employing the magic term "science" in library science.

Technology is no help in finding material in magazine selection. There is little to find. Librarians apparently consider it of minor importance. A survey of the early 1960s found that in sixty-five representative larger libraries, only five have written statements of their magazine selection policies.[4] The sludge of book selection is fulsome. Magazines are mentioned in three recent publications,[5] but only as a footnote or minor consideration. Somehow the magazine rarely rates its own selection discussion. The reason is not difficult to ascertain.

In most libraries, big or small, public or college, the magazine may be a major housekeeping chore, a joy for solve-it-all-with-a-computer administrators or a trauma for the reader who seeks the one copy which is either "now at the bindery," stolen, or otherwise missing, but in terms of quantity (or often quality) they are of little significance. Admittedly in special and large libraries, magazines may constitute from 50 to 75 percent of the current reference sources, but for collections excluding Yale, Harvard and fifty to 100 university and public libraries, the holdings normally are limited to what is ordained permissible by such basic Wilson indexes as *Reader's Guide to Periodical Literature, Social Sciences and Humanities Index* and possibly *Applied Science and Technology Index.* Numerous surveys indicate that the normal college library will be fortunate to subscribe to 400 periodicals, and better school and public libraries will average less than one-half that number. The budget for magazines in many libraries is even smaller than for janitorial services—a generalization which is not supported by empirical evidence, only by a cynic's suspicion.

The fascinating aspects of all this are that while no more than 10 to 20 percent of Americans read books, at least 80 to 90 percent read magazines. If the library is concerned with reading *per se*, more attention might be given to the attraction of *True Story* and the *Reader's Digest* as compared to the average book. Put another way, the average reader is more interested in fun than intellectual pursuits. Fritz Machlup found that almost 40 percent of the readers' dollars was used to purchase "pastime knowledge," while only some 20 percent was involved with "intellectual knowledge." The rest was divided between religion and works on practical knowledge.[6]

Regardless of the type and number of magazines a library has, it takes no survey to make one point—the collection is geared toward education and job-oriented aids rather than toward recreation and entertainment. If anything, in larger libraries the stress is on serials indexed in *Chemical Abstracts* or *Biological Abstracts*, to name only two of the close to 300 indexing and abstracting services directed to science and technology in the United States. In any discussion of magazines, sooner or later the discussion swings to and stays at a dead pragmatic center. I have yet to discover even an article which supports what Machlup and the American reader know; that is, magazines of entertainment and joy are of more importance to the majority than are titles of the learned societies, organizations and universities. The possible exception may be the really small library where emphasis is on such gems as *Good Housekeeping* and *McCall's*, but even here it is assumed that when it comes to recreational reading, the middle class *hausfrau* is the only one who counts.

Is seems irrelevant whether the librarian subscribes personally to the puritan, Calvinistic ethic that joy is sin or to the hippie, turned-on mystique that joy is love. The point is that in terms of magazine selection, the librarian, in his zeal to collect rather than to select, tends to be purer than Calvin, forgetful that somewhere out there an audience has been lost, or at least partially turned off by the magazines he has selected. Granted, there is no evidence to prove that magazines devoted to recreation and fun provide major and moving experiences for readers. Still, their absence may indirectly prevent would-be readers from becoming involved in any library experience at all.

Let me try to support my contention that libraries often overlook the obvious. A journey to the Newport Folk Festival in 1969, followed by thirty-six hours at the Woodstock festivities alerted me to something which many librarians probably are aware of; that is, when it comes to reading magazines, the turned-on college man has taken up comic books. If Tolkien was once the "in thing," now the student who can give the genealogy and history of Super-boy or Batman is much more celebrated. More sophisticated members of the community go even a step further in following the activities of pornographic, socially irreverent characters in comic strips which appear in underground newspapers such as *Screw, Kiss* and *Pleasure*. Admittedly this is a trifle super-fluous, tangential to education, but is it any more ridiculous than the scholar who wants line and verse from an article in the *PMLA*? Both are extremes, yet while the library gladly serves the eccentricities of the elder, it assiduously avoids the more humorous, more human needs of the younger. I am not necessarily suggesting librarians put in a stock of comic books, but, then again, why not? And I do not mean for future social studies. If nothing else, the gesture, which would be inexpensive enough, might do something to humanize the library. Out of curiousity I asked a number of comic book fans if they had ever seen their favored fare in a college or university library. The consensus: "Come off it, dad, you must be kidding." Well, I am not kidding, and the tragedy is that some of the best minds of our younger generation must resort to comics as a mark of defiance against the establishment, sadly represented in this case as much by the library as by the oldsters.

At one time, particularly in the 1930s, effort was made to relate reader preferences to the library, but this rings oddly now. We have largely given up the attempt. Along with the rest of America, librarians have tended to ignore the presence of large groups of potential readers—groups which are excluded from libraries because they are superfluous. If the times are changing, it is primarily because the library along with other public institutions may break up unless the needs of the subordinate members of the society are considered.

Libraries have to give up the traditional emphasis on quality and adopt a more realistic selection policy based on relevance—relevance not only of the magazine *per se,* but relevance of the magazine to the community it serves. If one subscribes to the notion that good, better and best are only relative, if the library is for every man, why should it not be just as much for the housewife or for the working girl who enjoys *True Story* as much as for the better educated suburban matron who gets a similar treat from *McCall's* or *Ladies' Home Journal*? Admittedly, the support of entertainment as well as education as a goal for magazine selection is debatable. Also debatable is the controversial magazine, and while space does not permit a justification of a comic book in a library, perhaps an analysis of controversial magazines is applicable.

Let me begin with that old standby *Playboy.* While I do not consider it even mildly controversial in terms of content, it is a useful example on two counts. First, it has attracted more debate in libraries during the past decade than possibly any other mazagine except *Evergreen Review.* Second, it is illustrative of the misguided overemphasis on deleting a magazine because it causes a high reading on too many librarians' personal shock meters. One might just as well register the polemic *Realist* or the right wing *American Opinion* or the Communist-oriented *Worker*—all drive the shock meter up to the danger mark. However, sex always appears a trifle more interesting than politics, so consider *Playboy.*

While it is questionable (to paraphrase policy statements) that *Playboy* either contributes "to the reform of manners in general," or helps the individual "to grow intellectually and spiritually," its publisher claims it assists five million under-thirty readers to "enjoy life more fully." In the words of the Public Library Association in *Minimum Standards for Public Library Systems,* it provides "wholesome recreation and constructive use of leisure time."[7] It also provides a look at what is up front which upsets and disturbs—in one way or another—a good many librarians. The librarian may rightfully question its moral and social values, but in the wake of its dedicated five million readers, this a pretty weak argument.   Also, it is difficult to argue with the Harvard Business School which thinks publisher Hugh Hefner's experiences are a lesson for its pupils. The librarian solves it by a tendency to cop out. The favored argument runs that it may serve some needs, but there is not enough money in the budget for such magazines. The dollars are better spent on an indexed item such as *Reader's Digest* or the *Ladies' Home Journal*. Well, this may or may not be true, but the confusion between moral policy on the one hand and pragmatic considerations on the other satisfies no one. The *Playboy* reader stays away from the library, the librarian dutifully continues to study methods of learning about community needs, and the selection policy remains a moribund monument to bias.

While there is no accurate count of how many small, medium-sized or large libraries take *Playboy* (either issue by issue or on less exciting microfilm), a survey of school libraries is instructive. In any discussion of large libraries, elementary and high schools seem to be forgotten. Just why, I am not quite sure, but I suspect it is because they offer only elementary science courses and certainly do not boast Nobel Prize winners or potential grant grabbers on the faculty. Still, it seems to me they are relatively important, and a survey of a few years ago is instructive for all libraries.

Comparing the selection policies of school libraries with the demands of the students, James R. Squire observed: "There is no close correlation between magazines available in school libraries and those the students read frequently . . . more throughtful periodicals are seldom selected by students. *Mad Magazine*, in fact, accounted for forty more readers in the survey than either *Harper's* or *Atlantic Monthly*."[8] Squire also discovered that the fifteenth most popular magazine among students was *Playboy*, to which none of the libraries bother to subscribe. Incidentally, the number one choice of librarians was *Saturday Review*, followed by *Reader's Digest*. The students failed to mention *Saturday Review* and ranked the *Reader's Digest* a poor sixth after *Life*, and eleventh choice for libraries. A similar survey in 1937, revealed an overwhelming preference for *Esquire* among male students. But again, it then made none of the library lists.

Twenty years later through, *Esquire* was found in a small percentage of high schools, and the recent ALA *Periodicals for School Libraries* included it among its four hundred or so preferred titles—one would like to think this was due to its merit, although its indexing in *Reader's Guide* may just have had something to do with the choice. Needless to add, *Playboy* is not found between the entries, *Pigeon News* and *Plays*. Eldridge Cleaver has suggested the battleground of the future is not between races—it is the war between white kids and their parents. He might have added libraries to the enemy list.

I think it safe to assume. *Playboy* is probably not popular among any libraries, regardless of their size. Some, to be sure, have at long last recognized the literary importance of the magazine—a nice run around the moral left end of section policy—and have included it in the collection. Others, such as

Cornell where an eminently sane librarian, David Kaser, is in control, now try to make up for past mistakes. According to newspaper reports Kaser is seeking a complete run to fill in lacking and incomplete volumes. He notes that "earlier issues are almost unobtainable on the scholarly book market (especially in complete state, with the centerfold that researchers are known to find of particular interest)."[9] It might be added that an early selection mistake can be costly, as anyone knows who glances at the asking prices for reprints of defunct little magazines once considered objectionable on moral grounds by many librarians. And, of course, no one, even the New York Public Library (NYPL), is exempt from a mistake in judgment.

According to one dealer with a complete run of *The Village Voice*, the NYPL does not have early issues of this most famous of all early underground newspapers.

Too much, of course, can be made of a maverick such as *Playboy*. Personally, I am inclined to go along with the feelings, if not the methods, of five Grinnell College students who last February "threw off their clothing during a campus speech Feb. 5 by a representative of *Playboy* magazine to protest what they called the magazine's 'sensationalism of sex.' "[10] Still, *Playboy* is indicative of a general attitude by librarians towards magazine selection, the obverse of which is the case of *Evergreen Review*. During the past two or three years, and most recently in the *ALA Bulletin*,[11] it has become the *cause célèbre*, the walking papers, for a number of librarians. If one wonders where the librarians were some thirteen years ago when it first cranked up as a little magazine, one can only surmise that it takes ten or more years for the average library to discover a new, controversial title. At any rate, a number of librarians from Daniel Gore to the Los Angeles Public Library staff consider it of enough importance to include it in the collection—what is more, they are willing to fight for it.

Gore lost his job because he entered a subscription to the *Evergreen Review* for a small church-owned, West Texas college. He documented his expereiences in the *ALA Bulletin*, but more important are the reactions to his article. Several librarians disagreed with his stand because of their ambivalence between money and philosophy. One correspondent noted: "In articles of this nature there is never any indication that the money might better have been spent on other material."[12] Still, the heart of the argument was summed up by the writers who noted: "As a responsible librarian, he would be wise to recognize that some of his community might hold to another view; and the worst possible way to convert them to his own view would be to put on a petulant display of the pride and arrogancy of professionalism."[12]

The key words here are "some of his community." The correspondent, as in most cases of this type, takes it for granted that he is representative of not some, but nearly all, of the community. In magazine selection policies this is reflected in the ALA Standards, where the key statement for public libraries is that the library is to serve "most people most of the time."[13] The line between "some" and "most" is not lost in Brooklyn, where it is resolved—as it should be—by the policy statement: "As a community institution, the public library is dedicated to the concept of service to everyone."[14] Slowly coming around to the same notion of service, the Adult Services Division of ALA has drafted a new notion of "A Bill of Rights for Adults." Prefacing the yet-to-be-adopted policy statement, the Standards Development Committee says: "Society is complex and changing rapidly. To live and participate intelligently in today's world, every adult must have access to all available sources of information . . . . Each adult is an important, unique individual."[15] Now "each" and "every" replaces "some" and "most," and this, let me suggest, has a major implication.

Both by implication and logical extension, selection for all questions the moral underpinning of traditional selection. It opts for what some have called the new sensibility, situation ethics or the new morality.[16] Briefly, this is a view which refuses to accept the notion that generalizations can be made about what is aesthetically better or worse for all men. By admitting that magazines, for example, are no better or worse, only different, the librarian agrees that selection must be more a situational than a prescriptive matter. And if the library is truly going to serve "all" instead of "some," it has to take a long, hard, second look at some of its favored selection assumptions. I have mentioned that this may mean more of a consideration of what readers—particularly those who rarely or never enter a library—may want, rather than what they should want.

It also means that traditional criteria of evaluation must give way to more meaningful criteria, in this case to the twentieth century.

Present magazine selection criteria, if indeed they exist, are almost platitudes. In terms of so-called objective evaluation, the librarian fondly uses such phrases as: accuracy and objectivity of editorial content, format, publications of major learned societies, use in reference and research situations, local interest, points of view not represented in books, currency, supplementing the book collection—all are familiar, yet hollow words which summarize what every good librarian knows.

The problem, of course, is that the platitudes are too easily mouthed. A librarian may dismiss a distasteful point of view in a magazine by observing that its editor fails to be either accurate or objective. An otherwise mediocre, but well-read and much demanded magazine may be left off the subscription list because it is too much fun. As Berelson, Fiske, and countless other observers of the selection process have discovered, most librarians have mixed feelings towards selection.

It takes no perceptive genius to recognize that there is a subtle difference between confessions in *Modern Romances* and *Harper's Magazine,* that *Science Digest* falls somewhat short of the scholarly achievements of *Scientific American,* and that *True West* is not quite up to the *Journal of American History.* And even among the so-called quality magazines, it is not difficult to make a choice between one issued by the American Institute of Physics or any other scholarly organization and one issued by business-oriented publishers such as those who put out anything from *Popular Science* to *Popular Electronics.* The librarian is safe enough as long as he is speaking for the group supporting his choice.

Except for a few isolated surveys such as the one conducted by John Berry,[17] there is no evidence (other than personal impression and a few communications from students and teachers) that the degree of truly controversial magazines taken by the larger libraries, with the exception of the fifty largest libraries, is not severely limited. Public and academic libraries alike, fall far short at the extremes. Qualitatively they are their best in the noncontroversial, strictly educational items. The academic library may argue it does not serve everyman, but is this true? Will the present academic standards for collecting periodicals be enough when the words "open university" are no longer whispered but are a reality, and when everyman, regardless of his high school record, may at least have a chance to go to a university or college? Times are changing in colleges and universities, too. Look, for example, how well prepared most schools were for Black studies. Except for such obvious places as Howard University, Harvard, and Northwestern, how many schools of higher learning five or ten years ago equated everyman with more than the token Black? It would be interesting to know how many of the two hundred largest academic libraries had the annual *Index to Periodical Articles by and about Negroes* (Boston, G. K. Hall and Co.) or more or less substantial runs of the items it indexed. See how fast all are scrambling for back copies of everything from the respected *Journal of Negro History* to the pictorial, less than intellectually inclined, *Jet*.

And what demands are the young rebels going to make next on a library? To date they seem to flock to it to overturn catalog drawers, but the alternative, more dangerous threat is a voice in selection. And it will be a dissident voice. During the years of student unrest there has been a considerable amount of discussion as to what it all means. No one is quite sure, but something is terribly wrong. To many students it seems that education has become irrelevant, and it follows that the library has also become irrelevant.

It has been estimated that only about 10 percent of the campus population is trying to revolutionize the universities. An even smaller number are at work in high schools. Still, it takes no Toynbee to realize that it is the minority who often shape, indeed usually direct, our society. There was only one Chaucer, one Christ and four Beatles, but they literally revolutionized our literature, our moral attitudes and our life styles. When anyone begins a quantitative argument that the dissident press is unimportant, unimpressive and not representative, the danger inevitably grows that the critics will be victims of former President Lyndon Johnson's love of consensus. The ominous hint of just that happening is the phrase "generation gap"—a gap which, I believe, can be bridged in part by librarians abandoning the fallacious selection game that equates importance, if not always intrinsic quality, with research, education and morality.

Generally the dissident press is the voice of youth. It is the magazine or newspaper which not only fails to support the mid-cult view of the world, but attacks the view. It is the magazine to the left of suburbia's biases; it is the magazine via words and pictures which threatens the sexual tolerance of the split level bedroom; it is the magazine expounding political or religious views ahead of, or sometimes, behind the times. In this latter category might be added the publications of the conservative student group, Young Americans for Freedom. Their philosophy, as sounded in such papers as *The Renaissance* at Duke and *The Arena* at Stanford, is best summed up by a statement made to the *New York Times* by Pat Korten, editor of the *Badger-Herald* at the University of Wisconsin: "If the radicals take over a building we can have 300 people, just like that—some of the fraternity people, the football team, the ROTC group, the engineers. It could get rough."[18]

The format of little magazines usually appears in total disregard of the aesthetic expectations of the reader of *Reader's Digest, Life* or *Good Housekeeping*. A secondhand mimeograph machine will do as well as a million dollar webb press. The message, not the medium, is the editor's concern. Advertising is a minimal, usually nonexistent consideration. Frequently it is more dependent on the whims of the editor than on demands of the Post Office for publication dates. Finally, the audience is select. Every well-known journal of opinion such as *New Republic, Nation* and the *National Review* is short on circulation—about 400,000 total, or approximately one-thirteenth of readership of *Good Housekeeping* or *Playboy*. And while the magazines obviously ,do not have much direct influence on the public, the editors are quick to point out that the influence is meaningful because readers constitute opinion decision makers. Conversely, Robert Sherrill observes wryly that the reason the United States maintains a *Reader's Digest* mentality is that it has the largest circulation of any magazine in this country—some seventeen million. Its closest competitor is *TV Guide*.

Another major form of the dissident magazine is the so-called underground newspaper. Some fifty or more newspapers, claiming a combined circulation of close to one million, are issued from coast to coast on a more or less regular weekly or monthly basis. As one editor puts it, "Underground is a sloppy word and a lot of us are sorry we got stuck with it." He is right. It really is not that underground. If one accepts most editors' notion that the press is united in a belief in activism, it is a growing, potential force. And this is not only a political, but a cultural force. Writers and editors have broadened the editorial content to include topical comments on music, literature, art, theatre, film communication, economics, poetry and religion.

The underground newspaper differs from the little magazine in that it is purposefully designed to reach a large audience. The editors, and some of them are experts at persuasion, are attempting to mobilize young people. With such cries as "the underground press is the loving product of the best minds of my generation, running screaming through the Negro streets at dawn looking for an angry printing press," the canny editors have caught up with Madison Avenue. Like the purveyors of television advertisements aimed at children, the editors recognize that young people will soon comprise over 50 percent of our population. They are trying to capture their imaginations and to meet their needs. And to a degree, they are succeeding where *Boys' Life* and *Seventeen* are failing. The reason for their success is that they have seen through the monolithic mass media and the clichés which elders attempt to pass off to younger people as truisms.

Let it be noted that the revolution is coming to the high schools as well. There are a number of high school-based underground newspapers and magazines. None are concerned with the jocks or the mixer. All are politically involved with rights for the young. As a reporter in the *New York Times* put it, these revolutionaries who have to be home by 7:30 are asking more and more "What in hell am I doing here?"[19] Some of the answers will be found in their papers, e.g., the *New York High School Free Press* (208 W. 85th St., Apt. 2E) or the *Institutional Green* (Sean Daniel, 865 West End Avenue, New York, N. Y. 10025), to name but two. The answers are not quite what young adult librarians talk about.

Aside from youth, and those who think young, the little magazines have another patron—the *National Endowment for the Arts*. Established in 1966, it has offered grants of $250 to $1,000 to editors for use in the development of their magazines. Furthermore, it has financed the *American Literary Anthology,* an annual collection of articles, papers and poems for little, and not too little, magazines. Parenthetically, although the discussion here is almost entirely devoted to underground, activist little magazines and newspapers, the standard littles for a generation or more have been such well known literary magazines as *The Hudson Review, The Kenyon Review, The Sewanee Review,* and the like. The younger generation disqualifies them as members of the establishment, or worse, as members of the Decaying Liberal Movement. Age and success can often mean ostracism from the hard core little magazine circle.

Librarians and adults tend to treat the littles as abnormal temporary aberrations. Yet, many of their faithful readers think that these magazines are normal, that the *Reader's Guide* garden variety are incompatible with what they know America to be and what they consider the future to be. The March, 1969 *Wilson Library Bulletin* devotes itself to three articles on the underground press. A critic agreed with me that these papers are "really just reflections of a new type of younger generation." The uneasiness of America's youth is certainly there, along with articles proposing the legalization of drugs, criticisms of the political establishment, and a considerable amount of put-on regarding sexual mores. They are truly human, often sophomoric, even a trifle boring, but always a different voice than found in the mass media. I would suggest it is an important voice; one a librarian cannot and should not ignore.

But they do. For example, how many public (or for that matter university) libraries subscribe to even the basic underground newspapers—*East Village Other,* the *Berkeley Barb,* and the *Los Angeles Free Press?* How many have a file of such little poetry magazines as *Kayak, The Sixties,* or *Caterpillar?* How many take a few basic general little magazines such as *The Smith, Ambit,* or *December?*

In all fairness, though, a few have tried, and the results have been disasterous. Librarians cannot seem to win for losing. Just this year, John Forsman, head librarian of the Richmond Public Library in California, announced his resignation. Why? He had been under attack for his inclusion in the library of such publications as the *Berkeley Barb.* The story has been and will continue to be repeated wherever another minority (and I think it is a minority) gains control, i.e., the militant right wing. As I indicated earlier, I think what is operating in most libraries is not a willful neglect of today's rebellious youth, but rather an antiquated selection policy. The librarian who acts negatively is going to lose on all points—the thinking public will be lost, the right wing (and in some cases the left wing) will find reasons to attack. In the final analysis the only answer to an attack for service is a given amount of certainty on the part of the librarian that he is doing the right thing. All of which, admittedly, lends an air of danger and, hopefully, a little badly needed excitement to librarianship.

Another formidable aspect of the dissident magazine, at least for the ordering librarian, is finding them. A common argument against not buying this or that magazine is a lack of information. The library has reasonable expectations that the average periodical or scholarly journal will arrive in time to neatly enter into the computer or on a three by five inch card. Not so with the littles (or with the average little): 1) they may publish irregularly—Robert Bly's *The Sixties,* is only three or four issues away after an initial promise some years ago of a quarterly; 2) they may fold without proper notice—*The Chicago Choice,* a marvel of the graphic arts and poetry combined, began four or five years ago, issued four numbers, collapsed, then according to current rumor is about to begin again; and finally, 3) they come in odd sizes, formats, and are likely to switch in midstream, or just for-the-hell-of-it publish a number which will not fit in the regular binding. But these inconveniences aside, how does one learn about who is publishing what?

There are two, possible three excellent, rather trustworthy guides. The first, and by far the best, is Len Fulton's twin billing: *Directory of Little Magazines and Small Presses* which is issued annually and sells for $2.50 (5218 Scottwood Road, Paradise, California, 95969). Fulton also publishes a quarterly *Small World Press,* which updates information in the *Directory,* has rather good reviews of the publications—including prose and poetry issued by the little presses who may or may not publish a magazine or newspaper—and has perceptive articles on trends. Lately he has begun issuing an annual of this same magazine with a complete listing of books published by the little presses, a nice complementary item to *Books in Print.* An older directory is *Trace* (Villiers Publications, P.O. Box 1068, Hollywood, California 90028) which combines a little magazine of questionable quality with a directory. It is neither as complete nor as up-to-date as Fulton's efforts. The third approach is the old warhorse *Ulrich's International Periodicals Directory* (New York, R.R. Bowker). With the twelfth edition (1968), it finally recognized (albeit circumspectfully) the little magazine by including the listing under "Literature, General." If one knows the name of the publication, *Ulrich's* can be used, but as there are no descriptive notes the unwary librarian may think he is ordering a little magazine only to end up with a scholarly journal on the influence of tool sheds on Joyce's *Finnegan's Wake.* Also, there is *Magazines for Librarians* (New York, R.R. Bowker, 1969) which has annotated sections on dissident magazines, little magazines, underground newspapers, and poetry magazines. The library which subscribed to only a few of these would end up with a fairly representative collection.

In terms of in-depth annotations, Robert Muller's *From Radical Left to Extreme Right* (Ann Arbor, Campus Publishers, 1967) is by far the best current source for material on over 150 dissident magazines. Fortunately, he plans to update the work, and a new edition is planned for next year. The basic retrospective list is Walter Goldwater's *Radical Periodicals in America 1890-1950* (New Haven, Yale. 1st rev. ed., 1966).

A few selected lists have also been published in the library literature, e.g., Sanford Berman's "Where It's At" (*Library Journal*, Dec. 15, 1968) which includes notes on major left wing and peace publications. A counter is Henry P. Durkin's "Where It's also At" (*Library Journal*, May 1, 1969) which lists major conservative and right wing journals. Daniel Tatko's "The Underground Press and New Left Press" (*Wilson Library Bulletin*, March, 1969) annotates the major underground newspapers. In my column in *Library Journal* I attempt to give at least some attention to rebel magazines.

Given this much assistance, it is difficult to rationalize for lack of information the sparcity of the dissident press in a library.   And there are, to be sure, even other approaches. The best is to visit or to get in contact with a bookstore which stocks this kind of magazine. The Eight Street Bookstore in New York (the balcony section) has an excellent representative collection, as do many of the smaller stores in both the Village and the East Side. Jim Lowell of the Asphodel Bookstore in Cleveland, will gladly send volume 1, number 1 of new little magazines as they appear, and there is no charge for this service. The Underground Press Syndicate (UPS)—roughly equivalent to a magazine wholesaler and the A.P. and U.P. in one package—will send fifty underground newspapers to any library for a period of six months at a cost of $50. A sample packet of the dozen favorites may be obtained for a modest $4. And for nothing a library may obtain a list of UPS papers by writing Box 1613, Phoenix, Arizona 85001.

However, given a source is one thing, but finding materials in the magazines and papers is quite another. Admittedly, few of the titles mentioned here or in the guides are indexed. There are two indexes to little magazines. Over a number of years Alan Swallow issued *Index to Little Magazines*, which indexed thirty to fifty titles; however, the last edition of this came out nearly four years ago for the years 1964-1965. Relocated in Chicago, the firm plans to continue the work, but just when is a mystery. The second biennial volume of Stephen H. Goode's *Index to Commonwealth Little Magazines, 1966-67* was published by the Johnson Reprint Corporation in 1968, and covers forty-one titles. There is every indication the work will continue. Both in terms of time lapse—one to two or more years—and in terms of coverage, neither index is quite up to the more prosaic Wilson titles, and neither makes an effort to cover the left and right wing politically-oriented magazines.

There are now two efforts underway, or in the planning stage, to index politically radical magazines. The Radical Research Center is proposing a limited indexing of left of center periodicals while Sanford Berman, the well-known voice of the radical magazine supporters among librarians, is working out a complete, international index to both left and right wing periodicals. It seems symptomatic of present attitudes that neither is able to gain a few thousand dollars in financial support, although millions are spent on scientific and less controversial abstracting services.

In the final analysis, a separate index covering dissident and little magazines should be published on a regular basis. It is too much to expect more than a few of the more reputable ones, such as *New Republic* and *National Review* or *Poetry* and the *Kenyon Review,* to take up valuable space in a standard H. W. Wilson Company item.

So far I have considered, in a purposefully exaggerated form, some of the fallacies of current selection policies. But this world, and particularly the world of the library, is ruled by the sacred dollar. What, then, of the so-called practical considerations of opening a collection to suit everyman's needs. The pragmatist, the hard-headed administrator, will tell you that it is one thing to devise a selection policy for all and quite another to implement it with funds. Most of the financial blessings showered upon our 22,000 or so libraries—exclusive of schools—go to the fifty largest libraries which account for 30 percent of all current expenditures. The remaining 70 percent of the library dollar is spread so thin that often it is only sufficient to keep up with current practices, certainly not with any sweeping innovations. What it comes to, at least for the time being, is that 50 to 200 of the largest public and academic libraries are going to have to take the lead. Hopefully, through cooperative efforts and federal or state funds, the smaller libraries may follow.

There is never enough money, but is this because the larger libraries are more involved with collecting than selecting? Perhaps if a little more thought was given to the usefulness of a title rather than to saturating the library with everything good, bad or indifferent in a subject area, there would be funds for less esoteric, more readable items. But separating the chaff from the seed is no easy matter, and here the average librarian will raise the specter of the information explosion. Rather than defuse it via selection, he shudders and recites figures. Even a glance at an average-sized newsstand indicates there are more magazines around than find their way into libraries. Some estimate 50,000, others 200,000, with most of the dead weight being carried by technology and science. The first reaction of a librarian is to swear off serials work for administration. The second, as typified by many papers at this conference, is to attempt to control the game by automation, union lists, systems or true grit. None seems to be quite the right answer.

The only irrefutable answer is suggested by Nelson Algren. Upon concluding a review of one of Simone de Beauvoir's more intimate autobiographies, he plaintively asked: "Won't she ever shut up?" If only a small number of the world's editors, writers and publishers would "shut up" life would be considerably easier for us all; they, however, will not, as any issue of *New Serial Titles* woefully proclaims. Some of the commercial official-organizational publications, which have yet to hear of birth control, continue to breed at an alarming rate. This year, for example, ALA gave birth to at least two new publications, and state organizations continued to do their bit. What is more, some editors now speak of proliferation via tape and microform which may relieve the shelves, but will put an ever-increasing heavy burden on the checkers.

Given this gloomy situation, confronted with a never-ending stream of magazines and a makeship dike of space, money, staff and time, the average librarian is forced into some type of decision. It is obvious he cannot have all the magazines neatly filed and organized, so he must pick and choose. Well, "must" is not quite right. Long ago he learned there are rules which allow him to throw up a passable dike (passable, at least, in terms of his conscience and public expectations). The times may be "a changing," but he is sitting tight. He prefers a given number of ploys to explain his position.

The first is favored by large libraries. The whole point of a periodical collection is to delimit, to concentrate on a given subject area or areas, to collect everything available. Once the limits of the area are established, acquisitions is the primary problem. Traditional selection is non-existent. The librarian need make few or no value judgements. The librarian must know the basic current and retrospective bibliographies, be familiar with the subject in depth, and, hopefully, be able to draw upon the wisdom and advice of professionals in the given field. His primary concern is to net everything, casting and recasting month in and month out. His is a bibliographical nightmare, not a selection problem.

It is also a major bookkeeping problem. Each decision regarding a magazine tends to have a cumulative financial effect. Not only will the subscription usually run on the familiar "until forbidden" basis, but the subscription will constitute a first demand on the total materials budget until a cancellation is entered—a forbidding move for even the most hearty librarian. (It is so forbidding, in fact, that the University of Southern California advised librarians in 1964/65 that "unless a subscription is to be maintained, it should not be initiated." This has implications quite beyond the present paper.) And even if the magazine is a gift or an exchange, there is the added cost of binding, processing, shelving, microfilming, recording, etc., etc. And while it is not unusual to discard a book, the weeding of magazines is unusual, expensive and generally not done. In the pre-World War II years some 20 percent of the average academic library budget went for periodicals. It is now in excess of 30 percent or higher. The increase is due to many factors, and not the least of them is the cumulative factor of mounting one subscription upon another until saturation is attained.

While other more persuasive arguments are put forth for justifying an endless collection of material, one suspects the bookkeeping and all it involves is a subjective, strong force for continuing the status quo. The chorus favoring comprehensiveness is so great, as Margit Kraft observes, "that one feels like a heretic even to question it."[20] Yet she goes on to present a rather favorable argument for more heretics. Quoting several sources she notes, among other statistics, that in 1960, 65 percent of some 11,000 magazine titles in the John Crerar Library were never used in a twelve-month period; and from a total of 37,000 serial titles at the National Library of Medicine, 88 percent were not subject to a single loan during a period of one year. And of the 4,347 loaned, the heaviest use was confined to 161 titles. She then asks the type of questions all librarians should be asking:

If these libraries eliminated the periodicals for which there is no demand, would there be any loss to the advancement of knowledge? How long should unused periodicals be kept? ... Are we not the victims of a delusion by assuming that the sheer existence and collection of these periodicals for which there is no demand contribute in some way to scholarship?[20]

Were the answers irrefutable, the whole problem might be solved tomorrow by the librarian enforcing selection instead of collection. As it is, these are questions which cannot be answered emphatically "yes" or "no," for there are too many variables, too many unknown qualifiers. Still, if money is being used to build a dead collection, or, at best, a viable collection which is difficult to justify at the present use rate, one may reason that the demands of today's user cannot be denied because of our idea of the future. I would suggest that the large library which is not subscribing to magazines that students read either for enjoyment or for support of dissident views is banking too much on a future it may never see.

If selection is employed, money is then available. However, before pursuing what is to be done with this new-found wealth, let us for a moment examine the quantitative levels of magazine holdings among average-sized libraries. Quantitatively, a small library is fortunate to have 150 titles, but by adding 100 or so more, they are within the quantitative limits of the ALA Standards for most libraries—well within the limited adequacy of the collections of senior college and university libraries, where Clapp and Jordan set a modest 250 titles as a minimum requirement.[21] Add 250 or even a thousand more, and it would seem even larger libraries might function with relative efficiency for all but the dedicated scholar and the Ph.D. candidate. And add a larger library with unlimited titles, easily accessible via interlibrary loan, and the numbers game can be halted. In fact, this is precisely what is now being suggested (at least in part) via establishment of a centralized national lending library for serials.

Perhaps a second large national lending library might be considered, this one devoted not so much to back-up for the basic scholarly and scientific indexes and abstracting services, but to collect the thousands of little magazines, underground newspapers, dissident periodicals, and even short-lived expressions of opinions which may only make a broadside or one or two runs of a mimeographing machine. This will require a different type of library than the one so well known to the specialist.

If at least some of the students have been overlooked by the library, consider the forgotten American recently discovered, among other places, by Peter Schrag and Marshall Frady in the August 1969 issue of *Harper's*. He poses a similar, even more deadly threat to the public library, for as Schrag warns: "You'd better pay attention to the son of a bitch before he burns the country down," and the library along with it. In the word, special attention now must be paid to everyone—not simply to the researcher in the academic library or the middle-class white in the local neighborhood.

Another forgotten community member it seems to me, is the man or woman who may find little of value in *Playboy*, but supports such plays as

"Oh! Calcutta," or stands in line to see "I Am Curious (Yellow)." Aside from curiosity seekers, he or she represents the vanguard of the sexual revolution—a revolution which Gallup finds not likely to be blunted by the old morality. In a recent poll he delineated this potential library audience as the 66 percent of college students who think it is not wrong for men and women to have premarital sex relations, who by an almost equally large percentage find nothing wrong with pictures of nudes in magazines (even the *National Geographic*), and who, in the words of the 1957 Roth case, welcome "all ideas having even the slightest redeeming social importance—unorthodox ideas, controversial ideas, even ideas hateful to the prevailing climate of opinion."

Looking to the not too distant future we may approach the time when good, literate pornography will be a minor part of any library serving the needs of those who feel the need. If one accepts that sexual stimulation is not all that bad, one may go along with Kenneth Tynan. In his justification for pornography on the stage, he puts it this way: "Pornography is writing that seeks primarily, even exclusively, to bring about sexual stimulation. This can be done crudely or delicately. In the former case it would be bad literature; in the latter good."[22]

If the librarian should one day accept this notion, it might at least end the foolish gyrations of trying to justify everything from dear *Fanny Hill* to *Playboy* in terms of significant literature. It might, too, bring more than a few current nonreaders to the library. It might, in fact, open up a new window to the real, instead of the idealized world.

Throwing open a window in these troubled times requires confidence and not a little courage—it also assumes a detachment on the part of the librarian. For example, *American Opinion* supports right wing views which are quite beyond my notion of logic, taste or morality, the *Ladies' Home Journal* sends cold chills up my aesthetic back and the *Reader's Digest* seems as deplorable in its attitudes and objectives as the minds of the Americans who feed off it each week. Still, if one is to make a place in the library for everyman, and everyman's notion of what is good, bad or indifferent, it is necessary to assume the attitude of Nick von Hoffman, a reporter for the *Washington Post:* "The reporter can't walk into a situation in a towering rage. You don't have to agree with them, but when you disagree with them it's on the basis of what they say, not of the frightened things going on in the reporter's head. The reporter has to say: Am I going to react, or am I going to learn and observe and see."[23]

In terms of magazine selection there is no place for towering or even mild rage except against those who try to impose their "frightened things" on the library. The librarian must "learn and observe and see," not simply react.

In conclusion, all I ask is that librarians learn to do their thing reasonably well. If being a librarian in America is being a machine, I want nothing of it. If we are to be simply another pillar in the society we claim to mirror, I am checking out. And if one more student thinks that "if it isn't in the *Reader's Guide,* it may not have happened," I think we are lost. All I am suggesting is that there is a way out of what Jesse Kornbluth terms the "winter in our heads," and, hopefully, librarians will be there first with the mind defroster. It might not just be intellectually challenging, it might just be fun.

References

1. Bettelheim, Bruno. "Obsolete Youth," *Encounter,* Sept. 1969, p. 31.
2. U.S. National Advisory Commission on Libraries. *Library Services for the Nation's Needs: Toward Fulfillment of a National Policy; Report.* Washington, D.C., Dept. of Health, Education and Welfare, Office of Education, National Advisory Commission on Libraries, 1968.
3. Lasch, Christopher, and Genovese, Eugene. "The Education and the University We Need Now," *New York Review of Books,* 13:23, Oct. 9, 1969.
4. Orr, Robert W. "The Selection, Ordering and Handling of Serials." *In* Herbert Goldhor, ed., *Selection and Acquisition Procedures in Medium-Sized and Large Libraries* (Allerton Park Institute No. 9). Urbana, University of Illinois Graduate School of Library Science, 1962.
5. Bone, Larry Earl, ed. *Library School Teaching Methods: Courses in the Selection of Adult Materials.* Urbana, University of Illinois Graduate School of Library Science, 1969; Gaver, Mary, ed. *Readings in Building Library Collections.* Metuchen, N.J., Scarecrow Press, 1969; and Moon, Eric, ed. *Book Selection and Censorship in the Sixties.* New York, R.R. Bowker, 1967.
6. Machlup, Fritz. *The Production and Distribution of Knowledge in the United States.* Princeton, Princeton University Press, 1962, p. 209.
7. Public Library Association. Standards Committee. *Minimum Standards for Public Library Systems, 1966.* Chicago, ALA, 1967, p. 9.
8. Squire, James R., *et al.* "Student Reading and the High School Library," *School Libraries,* 16:15-16, Summer 1967.
9. "Wanted: Back Copies of Playboy," *Schenectady Gazette,* Oct. 9, 1969, p. 3.
10. "Indecent Exposure Charged to Five Grinnell Students," *New York Times,* Feb. 19, 1969, p. 43.
11. Gore, Daniel. "A Skirmish with the Censors," *ALA Bulletin,* 63:193-203, Feb, 1969; and "Commentary," *ALA Bulletin,* 63:553-56, May 1969.
12. "Commentary," *ALA Bulletin, ibid.,* pp. 554, 555.
13. Public Library Association. Standards Committee. *Minimum Standards . . . , op. cit.,* p. 9.
14. "Materials Selection Policy of the Brooklyn Public Library," *Library Journal,* 94:3026, Sept. 15, 1969.
15. "Library Services—A Bill of Rights for Adults." Chicago, ALA, 1969. (Processed.)
16. Oboler, Eli M. "The New Morality and the Old Librarian," *ALA Bulletin,* 62:1369-73, Dec. 1968.

17. Berry, John. "Demand for Dissent? Public Library Practice in the Selection of Dissident Periodicals," *Library Journal*, 89:3912-17, Oct. 15, 1964.

18. Weinraub, Bernard. "Unrest Spurs Growth of Conservative Student Groups," *New York Times*, Oct. 12, 1969, p. 70.

19. Pileggi, Nicholas. "Revolutionaries Who have to be Home by 7:30," *New York Times*, Section 6, March 16, 1969, p. 26.

20. Kraft, Margit. "An Argument for Selectivity in the Acquisition of Materials for Research Libraries," *Library Quarterly*, 37:293, July 1967.

21. Clapp, Verner W., and Jordan, Robert T. "Quanitative Criteria for Adequacy of Academic Library Collections," *College & Research Libraries*, 26:371-80, Sept. 1965.

22. Tynan, Kenneth. "Pornography? And Is That Bad?" *New York Times*, Section 2, June 15, 1969, p. 10.

23. Quoted in: Graham, Katherine. "Student Unrest and the Role of the Media," *University of Chicago Magazine*, 62:15, July/Aug. 1969.

Peter Gellatly
Serials Librarian
University of Washington Libraries
Seattle

THE SERIALS PERPLEX:
ACQUIRING SERIALS IN LARGE LIBRARIES

Are serials a drug on the market? We do not really know how many of them there are. William Katz suggests that the current rate of publishing "is increasing roughly three times as fast as the growth of the world's population," and he indicates the criticalness of the situation by stating that "while the world's population dies, the books linger on."[1] We are being told endlessly these days about how big a curse overpopulation is. As for the print explosion, one thing is certain—if Katz's figure is correct—we need never fear as we go shouldering one another off the earth's surface that we will be at a loss for something to read.

If we do not know how many serials are extant—people say that between 60 and 80 percent of the world's total publications are in the form of serials—we do have some idea as to how many periodicals there are. William Huff says that these number anywhere from 50,000 now, to a figure of 100,000 in 1979.[2] We know quite positively that magazines are being produced at a prodigious rate, and in my opinion we do not have to wait until 1979 to reach the 100,000 mark. We are already there.

Concerning the quality of what is being produced, it is good and bad at the same time. Some things are worth reading, and some are not. Recently Ashley Montagu said that he thought American magazines were flourishing in unprecedented fashion:

> What a looking-glass to the history and development of this country is the American magazine! Is there any country that has a more interesting and bedazzling variety of magazines than this? I strongly doubt it. For vigor and variety, I think it would be difficult to equal the performance of the American magazine.

29

America's intellectual vigor happily grows greater rather than less, and we
may expect this to be paralleled by an increase, rather than a decrease, in
the number and quality of its magazines.[3]

The question might be asked: How many serials does one need in order to
have an adequate collection? My own feeling is that the number should be
bigger than past history and finances are likely to permit. A library's
collection should not be merely representative, but full in the sense that it
provides for all of the reasonable needs of its library's customers.

BLANKET ORDERS

So much emphasis is being placed these days on blanket-order schemes
that it is scarcely a surprise to find librarians experimenting with methods of
obtaining serial publications in other than the one-item-per-order way.
Certainly the blanket idea appeals. Why not get everything automatically as it
appears, if this can be done without the fuss and bother that the separate
ordering of each item entails?

The University of Washington Libraries have blanket orders with a local
bookdealer for serial publications of the non-periodical type put out by
various American university presses, and while on the whole the experience
with these orders has been satisfactory, it has not been entirely trouble-free.
Of course, it would be too much to expect that all of the hitches and flaws of
the order-by-order arrangement are avoided by substituting for it the blanket
arrangement. Even the machine is not going to bring about this lovely state of
affairs. A non-linguist friend of mine suggests wryly that serials persons
should adopt as their slogan the expression *Schlamperei toujours.* He may be
right, if by this he means that our bumbling is indivisible and nonstop.

The blanket arrangement involves one inevitably in a number of
difficulties. For one thing, there is a certain amount of confusion at the time
the arrangement is first entered. Single orders already underway for items
included in the blanket order have to be cancelled, overlapping shipments
sorted out and conflicting billings squared away. At the same time, required
duplicate orders for items appearing in the blanket order have to be taken
care of in one way or another.

If the existence of old orders is awkward, so also is the uncertainty as
to what will be included in the new ones. The supplier says that he will of
course send everything in the publisher's catalog. Unfortunately, however, no
catalog is ever complete or completely accurate. Consequently, what an
over-all order brings—or omits—is generally a matter of uncertainty. For
instance, the University of Washington Libraries included monographic
publications of the Metropolitan Museum of Art in its over-all Harvard order.
As it turned out, the reason for their inclusion was not that they are issued
by Harvard, but merely that they are distributed by it. On the other hand, it
was found that expected items are sometimes omitted. It is a sad fact that
often new items are not sent until they are specifically requested.

Still, such difficulties can be expected to tidy themselves up with a
certain length of time. If this does not happen, then one must conclude that

the blanket arrangement brings with it no appreciable advantage, and even buying in the piecemeal, item-by-item way is as satisfactory. It is difficult to say whether the fuss and cost are greater in one instance that in the other. Since the University of Washington Libraries' experience with blanket orders has not been too pleasing, we do not find the blanket idea wholly irresistible. On the other hand, we are not certain that we have done enough experimenting with it to know how valuable it really is.

Bookdealers, however, greet the blanket-order idea with unanimous enthusiasm. Although many of them are not willing to accept blanket orders for serial publications, some do. As an inducement to would-be subscribers, Richard Abel, Inc. assumes responsibility for cancelling existing orders for items containined in the blanket order, and it also takes charge of returning duplicate shipments that arrive during the change-over period. Some firms have their own blanket-order programs. Stechert-Hafner, for instance, has at least four. These are identified by the initial acronyms: LACAP, BOPFA, FORFS and BOBNS. The acronyms expanded become: Latin-American Cooperative Acquisitions Program, Blanket Order Program for French Acquisitions, Foreign Fiction Service, and Blanket Order for "Book-News" Selections. The number of such programs available to libraries is becoming greater as time goes on. In most instances, however, serial items are considered to be outside the scope of the program.

A variation of the blanket arrangement can be seen in the operation of the Library of Congress's Public Law 480 Program. According to Public Law 480, some part of the money earned through the sale of surplus agricultural products abroad is set aside for the purchase and processing by the Library of Congress of books and periodicals put out in the countries concerned, and the later distribution of these publications to libraries at home. The areas from which publications are being obtained at present are the Indian subcontinent and certain parts of Central Europe and of the Middle East.

This program is unquestionably of use to libraries participating in it. Its usefulness extends in fact much beyond the enriching of local collections, as one of the conditions required by the program is that participants make the materials they receive available through interlibrary loan to anyone in this country who wants them. According to Mortimer Graves, the widest possible use of these materials is essential if the program is to prove fully effective.[4] Graves goes further; he asserts that librarians have a positive obligation to see that the materials are used properly:

> The richest and most powerful society in history, called to responsibility, if not leadership, in the spherical, scientific, social(ized), secular, dynamic, crowded, and contentious world promised us by the twenty-first century, must develop the facilities for knowing that world as completely as possible. Of these our libraries form not the least important element. Only with understanding can we escape disaster; without it fifty or more Koreas and Vietnams lie just around the corner.[5]

Librarians may find this assessment of the place of libraries in the coming century somewhat overzealous, but they are not likely to consider it entirely beside the point. A matter of more immediate concern, however, is how long the Public Law 480 Program can be expected to continue. There are suggestions that parts of it may have to be cut out, as Congress paves the way for national austerity; and if some parts go, others are sure to follow.

REPRINTS

The mass availability of reprints now offers help to persons who are attempting to fill in back runs of serials, or for that matter to buy old items that, for whatever reason, they do not hold at all. Within the last ten years or so, a good many reprint firms have come into existence. Some of the biggest of these are the Johnson Reprint Corporation, the AMS Reprint Service of New York, and the Gale Research Company of Detroit. There are, of course, many other such firms, some of which are themselves of fair size and importance.

Complaints of various sorts are made against the reprinters, but the fact that they reprint publications not available in other ways is a point not lightly dismissed. Among the complaints launched against them are that their prices are high and that they sometimes announce publication of an item too far in advance.

It is true that reprint prices sometimes seem extraordinarily high, but it is also true that these prices are not much out of line with prices paid for materials in print. An o.p. dealer complained not long ago to the *AB Bookman's Weekly* that he was having trouble in selling original editions of recently reprinted books, even though the prices he was asking were below those charged by the reprinters. He went on to say that he suspected acquisitions librarians were ordering items from reprint catalogs without first checking to see whether or not the items they were after could be had at less cost through the o.p. trade.[6] The editor's reply to this letter was to the effect that some reprints were indeed priced higher than they should be. And then, unable to resist a parting jab, he added "as to librarians . . . there's no point in getting wrought up about them as a class. They come in all sizes and styles, just as do dealers and collectors. Some are knowledgable, others couldn't care less about someone's else [sic] money."[6] No doubt every acquisitions person has given offense in the way described—not only of course to the dealer whose wares he has spurned, but to himself also by inadvertently foregoing the bargain that a little hunting might have brought him.

As for the too early advertising of reprints, the *AB Bookman's* editor has this to say:

> In the "early" days of "modern" antiquarian reprints—i.e., just after WWII—scarcity of O.P. books and periodicals, growth of old and new libraries, etc., all combined to produce some "quick-buck" reprinters. They would announce long lists of books "to be reprinted," "on press," "available soon," and the like. Reasons were many: to pre-empt titles and series, warn off other reprinters, obtain advance orders—and cash sometimes, with special pre-pub offers. Trouble was that such novice reprinters would fail to publish book(s) if there were insufficient advance orders, interest and cash, thus injuring genuine reprinter and purchaser who may have laid out money or allotted sum in budget. Fortunately, such practices are now at a

minimum. Even the few who had begun this way, and have still survived, have had to learn the hard way that confidence and trust are the twin beacons in the book fraternity. Thankfully, ours is not yet a huge field or a million-mass market, and it does not take too long to learn of the few firms that cannot be trusted.[7]

Behavior of the sort, it goes practically without saying, is anathema to librarians, who in ordering items long held-up in the publishing process find themselves saddled with at least two troublesome problems. First of all, they must reconcile their records (and maybe an irate customer or two) in the matter of the delayed receipt of the item. Also librarians do not like to allocate funds in one fiscal period for items that have no likelihood of arriving in that period, and they have good reason to slight such items. Their concern is not merely to keep the library bookkeeper happy, but, more importantly, to insure that allocated funds are not swept away in the general tidying-up that comes at the end of the fiscal period.

While abuses continue to exist in the reprint trade, their existence is much less obvious than it once was. Most firms specializing in reprints know that they have to behave in ways acceptable to their customers, and most are willing to comply insofar as they can with this requirement.

The number and variety of reprints available at the moment is sufficient to raise anyone's eyebrows. The fact is that most reprint publishers are on the *qui vive* for new titles to add to their list, and they welcome suggestions from anyone concerning such titles. In many cases, the publisher is willing to reprint an item even without a guarantee that sales will go beyond the break-even point. Where this point occurs is, of course, not always easy to predict. One may suppose, however, that an item with a possible sale of fifty or sixty copies is grist to the publisher's mill. The publisher's readiness to engage in what might seem a rather risky undertaking arises out of three conditions: the existence of a ready market for reprints; the cheapness and efficiency of photo-offset printing; and the conviction, which is invariably borne out in practice, that even sleepers held long enough turn a profit.

TAPE PUBLICATIONS

Tape publications were undoubtedly inevitable. There are magazines like *Wildlife Disease* that appear only on microfilm, and others like *Aspen* that are made up of bits and pieces put together in a special box or plastic bag. Certainly inventiveness in the field of magazine publishing is not lacking. And now comes *Computer Telejournal,* a magazine issued in what are called "electronic video-recording cartridges." These cartridges are read in videotape players designed to hook up to an ordinary television set.[8] A number of large, multi-magazine indexes have of course been available for some time on tape, as well as in hard copy—*Pandex,* for instance, and the *Science Citation Index*—but never until now has a magazine appeared in tape format, and in this format alone.

The precedent is one that could have a considerable impact upon the collecting activities of libraries. Despite McLuhan's second thoughts at a recent

New York Antiquarian Bookseller's Fair that the book is a communication medium that will endure, libraries are bound to find themselves before long in the business of collecting taped messages of one sort or another. The fact that few libraries are yet able to support a computer does present a problem, but one can take comfort in the thought that problems of this sort generally have a way of solving themselves in the end.[9]

The serials person's first encounter with the machine usually comes when he has decided to issue a computerized list of serials. We have all undergone this experience, and if we have emerged from it feeling a little bent (not to say stapled, spindled or mutilated), we are, nevertheless, convinced that the machine has a place in our future. As William Huff puts the matter: "'Automation' is no longer a trend, it has become a state of mind."[10] The fact is that now we not only tolerate the machine's presence—we actually welcome it. We may have qualms about giving the machine its way in all parts of our work. On the other hand, we are willing to turn a substantial part of our routine recordkeeping over to it without fuss.

Ray Bradbury and others predict that the time is close at hand when people will stop turning on the computer, and instead submit to being turned on by it. A systems analyst at the University of Wisconsin says that "people have consistently underestimated the speed of advancement in the computer field, and have consistently underestimated the extent of future developments."[11] It may be that we should be preparing now for technology's finest hour, an hour which may or may not coincide with that of our own decline.

As for tape publications, what is there to be said about them? The first thing one notices is that computers are being used now in the production of nearly all of the big, important indexes, and that some of the indexes themselves are available on magentic tape. An effort is being made by the Chemical Abstracts service, for instance, to produce all of its publications in machine-readable form as well as in conventional printed form. Similarly, the Institute for Scientific Information has plans for making the *Science Citation Index* and its other publications available in both ways, and the publishers of the *Engineering Index* expect before long to follow suit with their index.

The next thing one is likely to notice is that tape indexes are highly expensive. *Chemical Abstracts* in its printed form costs universities at this time about $1,000 a year (the price of this publication has been advancing by $200 to $300 a year for the past several years), and costs others even more. (The university price in 1970, incidentally, will be in the vicinity of $2,000.) Whether or not *Chemical Abstracts* will ever be offered in its entirety on tape is uncertain. At the moment various offshoots of it can be had in this form. *Basic Journal Abstracts* and *CA Condensates* are two of these. In each case, the price is $4,000 a year. In examining the cost of tape indexes, no matter where these originate, one is forced to conclude that he is going to have to find some means of supplementing his regular budget significantly if he is to participate to any extent in the advantages that the arrival of the tapes makes possible. Money problems are every librarian's bane, and these are clearly not going to become smaller as time goes on.

As has been suggested, the cost of tapes is not by any means the only cost that computer-age librarians will find themselves faced with. The cost of equipment, including that of machine ownership (or even rental), is still far beyond the means of most of us. An outlandish indication of the sort of budgetary difficulty facing us was presented in June of 1969 at the ALA Conference by a librarian from the Massachusetts Institute of Technology. This librarian cited the fact:

> that the amortized annual cost for space and equipment for his public card catalog was $3,000. To store the same number of cards and provide on-line access through a computer would cost $600,000 per year. Similarly, MIT can store a book for $.20 a year, which is the amortized cost of the land, building, and shelving. To "store" the text of that same book in "off-line" computer memory would cost $7.46 per year, excluding the cost of converting the text to machine-readable form.[12]

There is little doubt that the availability of publications on magnetic tape portends great changes in the life of most libraries, nor are its immediate effects lightly discounted. The availability alone of tape indexes permits in-depth searching of the literature of a subject that is far beyond the scope of most manual searches. It is possible, of course, to have any number of subject headings (or descriptors, as the new usage is) placed in the machine's memory rather than the few allowed in the manual search. The approach to one's subject is thus much broadened, and the effectiveness of the search is improved in corresponding fashion. Early experiments in machine-searching, in fact, sometimes produced results that were altogether too effective. It must have been disconcerting to a Medlars searcher, say, to find himself loaded down with twenty pages of references to a particular subject when one or two references alone would have filled the bill. Yet the search, properly conducted, provides both fullness and exclusivity, and it is these properties, along with the speed of the machine itself, that give tape indexes their unique importance.

CENTER FOR RESEARCH LIBRARIES PROPOSAL

If one needs a serial but does not want permanent possession of it, there is always the possibility of borrowing it. And the possibility becomes a necessity in cases in which the item is a dead one and not available for purchase anywhere. In such cases, the interlibrary loan mechanism is called into play, and with luck, the needed item is presented to the requestor, either in the original or in photocopy.

The interlibrary arrangement is important—no question of this—but it has its limitations. One big one is that the needed item cannot always be located, or, if located, it is not allowed away from its home library. The delay involved in the interlibrary process is also a matter of concern. Some delay is inevitable and expected; the amount occurring ordinarily is greater than most borrowers find easily acceptable. If quick interlibrary-loan service consists of completing a transaction within a week or ten days' time, it is clear that only inveterate users of the service will have the patience to accept gracefully the longer time lapse that generally occurs. Facsimile transmission offers hope that things will improve in the future, but, as David Heron and J. Richard Blanchard indicate, the prospects for large-scale use of facsimile transmission, while these exist, are not glowingly imminent. The fact that Heron and Blanchard made their remarks some time ago does not matter very much as the strictures these remarks contain are still valid.[13]

And now a riddle. When does one give pounds and pence and shillings away, and at the same time keep them (along with his heart presumably)? The answer is provided by the Center for Research Libraries. The Center has produced a plan whereby interlibrary borrowing can, all going well, be substituted for serial subscriptions. The plan, as outlined by Gordon Williams, is to turn the the Center into what he calls a "centralized national lending library for serials," a library which has serials as its stock-in-trade and other libraries as its customers.[14] The success of the plan, Williams says, is predicated upon the view that, depending upon frequency of use, there is a point at which it becomes cheaper for a library to borrow a serial than to acquire and maintain a subscription to it. To show how the plan works, Williams produced a series of mathematical models which made it possible to determine not only when a serial costs more than its use justifies, but also how much money can be saved by giving up possession of little-used serials in favor of access to the Center's copy of these serials.

In essence the alternative the Center offers to conventional methods of dealing with serials is itself conventional. Its application, however, is not. The Center proposes to relieve member libraries of the necessity of keeping serials on their shelves beyond the point at which this can be done with ease and economy, and it proposes further to make available to members through interlibrary loan any serials that they may need from time to time. One can scarcely say that there is anything new in the interlibrary-loan notion. What is new is the fact that the Center is about to engage in an interlibrary-loan operation on a scale that can only be described as vast. Another unusual feature of the plan—and one worth noting—is that while the Center is a non-profit corporation, the service it offers is not free. Actually, the Center now requires that libraries wishing to borrow from it obtain a Center membership, the fee for which is substantial, and that they must pay various incidental fees as they do their borrowing.

Even so, libraries can assume that what is offered is a fair bargain. Libraries may, in fact, voice the question: Is all of this too good to be true? Certainly misgivings about the Center's plan do crop up. A number are cited by the University of Wisconsin Library. This library suggests that the Center's mathematical models may not have been based upon a wide enough examination of library costs.[15] It points out also that the models fail to adequately compare the cost of access at a distance with that of local access, that they do not give enough weight to the value of browsing, and that they project savings which are more potential than realizable, as no guarantee exists that the Center will have any particular serial its members request.[16]

An objection of another sort has been registered by the director of the press at the University of Wisconsin. This objection concerns the fact that the borrowing or photocopying by libraries of the serials they need could work a hardship on publishers, particularly those which put out items of the more specialized sort.[17] Williams, in reply to the charge, says that there may be some danger in the plan to present publishing practices, but he thinks the danger is easily exaggerated.[18] He also suggests that it is necessary to find some means of overcoming today's information gap:

> I wasn't around at the time, but I can well imagine that the scribes set up a loud hullabaloo when the printing press began to undercut the market for handwritten books. Individual scribes undoubtedly suffered from this invention, yet I think it can hardly be doubted that the public benefitted from it. By decreasing the cost of copies it greatly improved the dissemination of information. As publication rates have steadily accelerated, and the number of people capable of using information, and needing to know, has enlarged to include most of the population, it is clear that individuals must rely on libraries since they cannot afford to buy for themselves all of the publications whose information they need to have access to. And, at the same time, the amount being published, and preserved from the past, is far more than every library can afford to acquire. In brief, we are in a situation still in which it is desirable to reduce the cost for the dissemination of information to the lowest practicable figure, in order that as much information as possible can be disseminated as widely as possible.[19]

If the Center's plan has objectionable features, the foregoing remarks make clear what some of these are. Still others can be added to the list. For example:

> That although ready access to materials is the Center's principal objective, no convincing proof is offered that improvement of access will be brought about by acceptance of the Center plan.
>
> That customer-reaction to the notion of service-at-a-distance has not been fully assessed.
>
> That the scheme implemented according to Center specifications would lock member libraries into an arrangement from which retreat, supposing this were desired, would be difficult, if not impossible.[19]

Setting aside all misgivings and objections, however, one cannot escape the thought that in accepting the Center's scheme, he may indeed be finding a way out of one of the most pressing dilemmas of the day: how to stretch resources sufficiently to give customers the kind of service they both need and have a right to expect.

It may be said, finally, that in accepting the Center's proposal, one proclaims his faith in the efficacy (and perhaps the perfectibility) of large-scale librarianship, since the proposal brought to fruition would establish a serials network of a scope and usefulness not before projected even by such bodies as ALA's Serials Committee and the Joint Committee on the Union List of Serials. Who knows? This may in fact be what libraries have been waiting for. In any event, librarians with a serials problem are advised to give the Center's proposal serious consideration.

STORING, DISCARDING AND SO ON

If acquiring serials is full of problems and pitfalls, getting rid of serials, once they are no longer wanted, can be difficult too. Librarians as a rule are not given to throwing things out. What usually happens is that once an item is acquired, it is acquired for all time.

From time to time, attempts are made by librarians who suspect the quality of their holdings to sift out items that no longer deserve a place in the collection, but such attempts nearly always bog down early due to a lack of time and money. About the most that can be done to keep one's collection in trim, it seems, is to take a good look at each new item as it arrives in order to determine whether or not it brings with it something that the collection needs.

A full-scale inventory of holdings is an undertaking not lightly entered into, and a full-scale review of the contents of one's collection is a project certain to give pause to anyone contemplating it. My own library examines each new item for relevancy and usefulness when it first arrives, and again at the end of the first subscription period. But the result produced by this effort is so equivocal—I doubt that one out of 1,000 items examined fails the test—that we will likely abandon ourselves before long to the hazards of rampant and unreviewed growth.

At first glance surveying one's collection as a means of getting rid of unwanted duplicate subscriptions is a prospect that appears to hold merit. It turns out, however, that in a large and decentralized system, such as that of the University of Washington, there is absolutely no way of getting rid of duplicate subscriptions short of removing from the system the units in which they are kept. Pleadings do no good, nor do threats, cajolings and headshakings. Twice in the ten years before the machine came to bless our efforts at the University of Washington, we drew up by hand a list of the duplicate subscriptions in our collection. In each instance, we spent long weeks in doing the job, and in each instance the result produced was negligible. The lists, of course, were splendid to look at, but somehow they failed to persuade anyone to cancel any of his own duplicate subscriptions, and even, for that matter, to stop ordering more of them.

A similar result was produced in a survey conducted some years ago at Berkeley. Helen Worden, in reply to a question concerning this survey, states that the survey was abandoned as a total loss:

> Berkeley's continuing survey of current serials was discontinued rather than completed some fifteen years ago and no study was done of the cost of the survey. The purpose of the survey was to reduce the incidence and control the speed of duplication of serials. It accomplished neither end.[20]

The Berkeley survey—"experiment" might be a more appropriate term, as the survey dealt with only selected parts of the collection—lasted for the better part of ten years, and it failed, according to George Piternick, because of "ineffectiveness, slowness and costliness." These three factors Piternick examines as follows:

Ineffectiveness. Of 2,196 titles submitted for consideration, only 32 (actually 31) or 1.5% were actually cancelled as a result of the review. Not only is this a very small percentage, but the average subscription price of the titles cancelled was only $5.44 per annum, far below the $8.17 mean value for Current Serials Fund titles in 1957/58. Thus the cheaper titles are those cancelled. This result is perhaps not too surprising—the relationship between low cost and insubstantiality is traditional—but the effectiveness of the review for bringing down the size of the Current Serials Fund is made even less apparent thereby.

Slowness. [When perpetuation of the continuous review was recommended, it was recommended also] that the frequency of the review cycle be made 7-10 years. Since the inception of the continuous review in May 1950, 2,196 titles have been considered, or about 244 titles per year. In that same period, more or less, the number of subscriptions carried [centrally] has increased from 6,688 to 11,064, a yearly increase of 625 titles. The cycle of review, therefore, instead of being 7-10 years, has become an infinite number of years. At present rates we'll never get through it even once.

Expensiveness. Preparation of the lists and their review are procedures consuming a great deal of time of library staff and of the academic personnel engaged in the review. In the preparation of lists new cards must be made, data obtained from the serials file, a subject codification of serial titles performed by professional staff, involving examination of back files, actual preparation of multilithed lists; submission to subject specialists and academic personnel involves record keeping, reminder notices, rechecking, etc. It would be almost impossible and not particularly relevant to find an actual cost in staff and academic time per title cancelled—my rough estimate would be over $200 per title cancelled. The argument may be made, of course, that this cost is in salaries already budgeted and hence not an added expense, but, at some stages at least, the Continuous Review is not entirely a "fill-in" operation, but interferes with other, more useful work.[21]

These were the principal factors then that led to the failure of the Berkeley survey. Piternick notes, however, that at least two others contributed to its failure—the difficulty of determining whether or not a serial was good enough to deserve a place in the collection, and the fact that the decisions made were sometimes so questionable that reversal was inevitable. Piternick recommended that the survey be discontinued, and this recommendation, as noted, was carried out.[22]

It becomes apparent as time goes on and library costs soar that the old notion of storing duplicate and unwanted materials against an unstated future need is not quite so prudent and useful a notion as it was once thought to be. The fact is that too much saving can actually be wasteful. One makes no gain in banking his money at 4 percent when the cost of living is increasing by 5 percent. The moral is that while thrift and foresight are admirable qualities, these can be used to one's disadvantage all too easily and too soon.

I am not suggesting that one should dispose of everything he has no immediate use for. It is a fact that items which one has no room for in his collection can have significance. Certainly one would not be inclined to throw out a duplicate run of so valuable a publication as *Jane's All the World's*

Aircraft. Garden-variety items are retained at peril, not of life and limb perhaps, but certainly of peace of mind and quiet efficiency of operation.

The case of the University of Washington Libraries—which may or may not be typical—throws cautionary light on the problem of storing unwanted and marginal materials. For years we saved everything, thinking that an eventual use would be found for each item put aside—even the most trifling and shabby. It was clear that we were not hoarding for the sake of hoarding, but on the other hand, it was not really clear that the only thing we had in mind as we moved materials into storage was the future good of our active collection. I have an unpleasant suspicion that we at Washington were actually using the storage device as a means of clearing our desks when no other means of doing this presented itself. In any case, our storage collection grew at such a pace that before long we found ourselves in possession of what some wag described as an acre and a half of duplicates.

And how much use did we get out of this collection of duplicates? Hardly any. One would suppose that a collection of such dimensions would yield treasure upon treasure. This, however, did not happen. The trouble was that vast files involve their keepers in vast labor, and this labor was invariably in an amount disproportionate to the good the files provide. We had our acre and a half of duplicates, and we worked hard to keep this collection in fit and usable order. Our work, however, turned out to be pointless. The number of items we were able to glean from the storage place for use in our regular collection was small to the point of disappearance. There were a few such items, but so few that even consulting the file—far from keeping it in order—was a waste of time.

What I am saying should not be construed as a polemic for the outright abandonment of the storage idea. There is some point certainly in being able to store things. Nearly everyone is tempted at one time or another to relegate to storage troublesome and bulky items that he both wants and does not want. And if he gives way in this case, he can take solace in the thought that in another he may stand firm.

Librarians of course have reason to worry about the uncontrolled growth of their collections, and an index to the size of the worry they feel appears in the fact that treatises on weeding keep coming out. Terms like "selective book-retirement," "seldom-used item," "obsolescence," "storage" and "discarding" dot our profession's literature. In considering such terms, incidentally, John H. Ottemiller makes the point that administrators would just as soon avoid their use, since they all have a negative connotation. He goes on to say, however, that they continue to be used simply because no satisfactory substitutes have been found for them.[23] Certainly the concepts these terms embody are concepts that librarians are frequently called upon to juggle. And as the amassing of materials continues (the rate at which this proceeds never fails to astonish), the terms are not likely to fall out of use.

The practice of storing useful but little-used parts of one's regular collection is not likely to be discontinued because stored materials cost less to care for than do materials kept in the main body of one's collection. The argument is clinched, moreover, by the thought that although immediate accessibility is denied in the case of stored materials, it is not needed very often anyway.

There is no doubt but that the idea is a useful one. Yet there are sizable objections to it. These are summarized neatly by Lee Ash in his book on the experiment carried out at Yale in the selective retirement of books. Ash states that at the beginning of the experiment it seemed reasonable to suppose that old completed serials and beginning runs of currently received ones could be relegated to storage without much trouble. He makes it clear, however, that this supposition soon went overboard:

> Faculty members were reluctant to transfer long serial sets to storage, particularly if there were no cumulative index to them. They said that faculty and students like to search through such material, and often from this come ideas for papers or dissertations or new angles on topics of great interest to their research. Those working on various editorial projects in the Library did not want anything to go to storage and especially not serials. The Reference Department staff objected to the transfer of any of the learned society serial publications to storage because of the heavy use they receive; further transfer of these was, therefore, suspended.[24]

Other objections were equally as telling. One of these concerns the fact that making additions to incomplete serials in storage is difficult to do. The matter as it affected the Yale experiment is described as follows:

> Since the Yale storage collection allows no space for additions, we could not put incomplete serials into it. Yet to weeders these were prime candidates for storage. We reviewed this problem from every angle but found no satisfactory answer. We agreed that, if not more than ten per cent of the volumes of a set were lacking, we would transfer the set to storage and put boxes on the shelves in place of the missing volumes so that there would be space for them if received. If more than fifty per cent of the set were lacking, we considered whether it should be discarded, whether it should be transferred to another library to fill its gaps, or whether we should try to fill in the gaps or replace the entire set by microfilm. But seldom were volumes to fill the lacks or a microfilm available. If a complete set for filming was located in some other library, usually the cost of a single copy was too high for its potential use in the University. Occasionally we decided to put an incomplete file in storage if nothing had been added to the set in years and it seemed unlikely to have additions in the future. In so doing, we took the risk of having to relocate the set or add a second call number if volumes were received later. The problem of incomplete serials in relation to compact storage has not been solved.[25]

Weeding problems are also of consequence. A library may decide that it will weed its collection, but in putting the decision into effect it will find, as the people at Yale did, that weeding can be as complex and time-consuming a procedure as any with which librarians must deal. According to Ash, the biggest weeding problem has to do with finding a sufficient number of qualified people to carry out the task effectively. A second is that as weeding progresses, it becomes an increasingly more difficult matter to unearth weedable items. And a third is that weeding can never proceed at a fast enough pace to make way for present growth in the collection. What Ash refers to as the "ever-normal-granary theory," the theory that the growth of an active collection can be controlled by putting in storage each year as many items as are added, is then overturned from the start.[26]

In spite of all of these difficulties, however, Yale adheres to the storage principle. It turns out, not unreasonably, that in cases in which a library's rate of accession surpasses the rate of growth of its physical plant, the library has little alternative but to accede to some form of storing.

PRICES

A truism to end all truisms is that the times are not what they were. What is certain, at any rate, is that we do not need a Keynes or a Kiesinger to tell us that deprivation and affluence have aspects in common. If the case were otherwise, librarians would surely not find, as they do at the moment, that all their affluence is insufficient to bring them the publications they need.

The good old days are definitely and irretrievably gone—and with them the possibility of finding a bargain that is a bargain. Far from this, prices are going up a a rate that is quantum, exponential and unspeakably horrible. It becomes more and more apparent that there is absolutely no way out of the price bind for anyone, let alone for the serials librarians.

What is happening is that the average library budget, which at best is seldom more than a threshold budget (i.e., one large enough to provide adequate, if mediocre, services) is being thumped and pounded and squeezed and mangled until every inch of it is contused and bleeding.

Bigness is constantly confused with virtue these days. And bigness, whether or not it is a virtue, has come upon the library scene with a vengeance. Rider was not far wrong in supposing that academic libraries double in size every sixteen years; the doubling process in fact now stuffs itself into a ten-year period. And an invincible corollary may now be offered to the Rider theorem. Stated bluntly this corollary holds that regardless of the rate of growth of the collection, the cost of building it up and maintaining it in an average way will more than double in ten years' time.

Proof is afforded by a glance at the latest array of price indexes for library materials.[27] William Huff and Norman Brown speak calmly of increases in the serials field that are considerably larger than one wishes to credit. If librarians neither whimper nor complain as things turn from bad to worse, their restraint is great, and serves as an example to those of us who are more inclined to find offense in the matter than they are.

I am not suggesting that Huff and Brown like what is happening. I know that they do not. They are as disturbed about it as any of us are, more than most in all likelihood. Yet one can hardly say that librarians in general are greatly agitated over rising prices. There has been a strange silence in our literature concerning the fact that prices are outrunning themselves. The indexes appear regularly with some accompanying comment on percentage gains (and losses?), but apart from this, one has much searching to do before he turns up anything else.

Is the price of serials all that bad then? The answer is "yes." In the past ten years' time, the indexes show that, true to the Rider corollary, the average price of American periodicals has about doubled, and that the average price of American serial services has made a similar bound into the blue.

If an increase of 100 percent spread over a period of ten years seems livable, its livableness becomes less obvious when one considers that the rate of increase is itself advancing at a considerable clip. Helen Welch Tuttle makes this point somewhat offhandedly in the *Library Journal*.[28] In talking about price increases, as these affect periodicals, she implies here and there that the rates are not static, but are in fact following a considerable inflationary bent themselves.

An English librarian, B. H. Baumfield suggested a short while back in a letter to the *Bookseller* that the air was full of what he termed "swingeing" increases in the price of books.[29] I am not sure that I can define properly the term "swingeing," but I am convinced that Baumfield knows what he means, and further that he is right.

Baumfield's letter, incidentally, served to bring to public view—in England, anyway—the immense rush among publishers and booksellers to bring their prices into proper perspective with the times. Since the appearance of the letter, a full-dress review of the price situation has been presented in the same publication. Notes and articles galore on the subject of rising prices have been printed, and (to use a familiar term) continuation of the series can be expected.

One item that came out some months ago is of particular importance. This is a statement drawn up by the British Publishers Association on prices and pricing methods. The statement begins: "No one denies that the prices of new books have tended to rise each year (it would be strange if they had not in a period of inflation and rising costs), but we suggest that the increase is smaller than is at first apparent."[30] It then proceeds to a discussion, using elaborate arithmatical examples, to show why this is so. The Association's argument is the same as one made elsewhere by Huff and Brown.[31] This argument states, in effect, that the intrusion of a few exceptionally expensive items into an otherwise unnotable group of items can inflate disproportionately the average price of the whole group. The Association concludes its statement with a list of conditions that tend to exacerbate the price bind: rising manufacturing costs, rising overheads, increasing competition and so on.

A few weeks after the appearance of this statement, the *Bookseller* issued a warning that libraries, which are more financially distressed now than ever before, would in all likelihood be putting forth efforts to eke out their budgets by raiding booksellers' profits.[32] This startling charge came about as a result of a librarian's suggestion that booksellers increase the discounts they allow libraries. The suggestion got nowhere, and in fact subjected its maker to considerable abuse at the hands of the booksellers present at that time.

Prices are getting out of hand, and librarians have reason to be unhappy over this. No one willingly accepts a price increase, but librarians have acquiesced silently in the imposition of one increase after another. Certainly we make little complaint about paying whenever we are asked to. Such apparent indifference to a matter that literally cries out for attention (it is after all a matter of the purse) is deplorable, and now it has brought us to the point at which our residual serials charge (that is, the amount we must pay in order to maintain our serials file in its present state, leaving aside the need for improving the file with new subscriptions) is climbing at the rate of about 15 percent a year.

Not to take too arcane a view of things, one might say that prices today bear little relation to value recieved, and further that the shrinking of the dollar will scarcely alleviate a situation that can only have damaging consequences for libraries.

LIBRARY-AGENT INTERFACE

In general an abundance of goodwill characterized the relationship that exists between libraries on the one hand and publishers and agents on the other. The somewhat acrimonious exchange, mentioned earlier, on the subject of library discounts can be pointed to as an instance in which the involvement of the moment generated heat, if little else. As a matter of fact, members of the booktrade are often helpful to libraries in ways that are both large and meaningful. A single example is enough to substantiate the observation. The blanket-order idea, which librarians are accepting with increasing enthusiasm, is not by any means our own invention, but an idea promulgated largely by publishers and booksellers.

An expression of the need for further exploring the library-agent relationship was made a short time ago by the ALA committee that put out the second edition of *International Subscription Agents*. This committee indicates that such problems as there are will be solved only after agents and librarians have subjected them to careful study.[33] It makes clear also that the quality of service a library receives depends to some degree upon how helpful the library is to the agent, and gives a few hints as to how libraries can be helpful:

> Purchase orders should include complete bibliographic detail and clearly state the requirements of the library. Subscription orders must be placed well in advance of the date they are to begin, and the agent must be told whether or not he is receiving a new order or a renewal being transferred to him from another agent. He must also know whether automatic renewal is expected.

> Cancellations, especially if substantial amounts of money are concerned, must be placed very early. Agents often pay publishers for renewal before they receive actual payment from libraries. Since this early renewal is part of the valuable service they offer and since it ensures receipt of material, a responsible library should understand the procedures involved. It is sometimes difficult, even impossible, for agents and libraries to get refunds for subscriptions already paid to the publishers. If the amount is small, it does not pay to try. Orders placed for second or third copies, etc., should clearly specify, by copy number, that such is the case in order to avoid time-consuming inquiries about the intent of the library.[34]

It is of interest to note in passing that agents do in fact pay for library subscriptions before they themselves receive payment from their library customers. This procedure, while necessary to the uninterrupted delivery of a subscription, can be awkward for the agent, particularly when payment of the agent's invoice is held up in the library. A conclusion not likely to attract opposition is that libraries owe it to themselves, and to their suppliers, to prevent undue delay in the matter of payment.

Another view is taken in this same matter by a Canadian librarian, who, in an open letter to the booktrade, says:

We appreciate that many of our suppliers have been considerably inconvenienced by our failure to settle outstanding accounts within the 30 day term which is customarily specified.

We have recently conducted a formal enquiry into the reasons for this, and we have discovered that one of the principle causes is the time required for shipments to reach us from dealers. For your information we list below the average number of days required for shipments to arrive in Edmonton.

Country of Origin	Shipping Time (from date of invoice to date of receipt in Edmonton)
Canada	9 days
U.S.	13 days
Great Britain	26 days
France	36 days
Holland	43 days
Germany	35 days
Switzerland	46 days
Sweden	26 days
South Africa	33 days
Italy	64 days
India	97 days
Roumania	62 days
Brazil	84 days

As we are unable, at present, to discover any way of circumventing the delays which result from shipment by surface mail, we should appreciate it if dealers would take this factor into account when submitting claim for payment against outstanding invoices.

Please accept our assurance that we are doing our utmost to ensure that all accounts are settled as speedily as possible, once the material is in our hands. For instance, the enquiry above-mentioned revealed that, on an average, invoices are processed and approved for payment by the Book Order Department within 8 days of receipt.[35]

The point is that the coin has two sides, that for every *quid* there has to be a *quo*.

Huff has invented a name for serials people. He calls them "serialists." It cannot be amiss then to call the work these people do "serialism." And as for serialism, how does it stand these days?

One answer is provided by Clara D. Brown, of Louisiana State College. Serials people know that the world is a hard place, that they will always be overworked and that nobody knows the trouble they have seen. Brown emphasizes this notion and feels that no change is likely to take place in the situation soon.[36] It is of interest that at the time Brown made her statement she was getting ready to retire. She had by then been a serials librarian for thirty years, and her sigh of relief at the thought of relinquishing all of the nonsense was positively earshattering.

Trouble is trouble, of course, and no one will deny that. Of more importance than a recital of the drawbacks of serials work, however, is awareness of the fact that its importance is growing steadily. The serials department of a library may indeed be, as Brown suggests, the tail that wags the dog.[37] Someone else has put the matter in another way. This person says that the activities of a serials department resemble those of the human stomach or brain in that they determine invisibly whether or not the functioning of the body they are part of can be bearable.[38]

One is free to say, at any rate, that serials librarianship has come into a robust middle life. It may be a little grizzled, a little stooped (after all, as Orwell maintains, we deserve to look the way we do by the time we are fifty or so), but it is struggling hard to put on a good show. And it may be succeeding.

References

1. Katz, William A. *Introduction to Reference Work* (McGraw-Hill Series in Library Education). Vol. 1. New York, McGraw-Hill, 1969, p. 36.

2. Huff, William H. "Periodicals," *Library Trends*, 15:405, Jan. 1967.

3. Montagu, Ashley. *The American Way of Life.* New York, Putnam, 1967, pp. 169, 171.

4. Graves, Mortimer. "Congress Helps American Libraries Discover the Spherical World," *ACLS Newsletter*, 19:6, Jan. 1968.

5. *Ibid.*, p. 7.

6. Hutchinson, Keith. *AB Bookman's Weekly*, 43:2506, June 30, 1969.

7. Malkin, Sol M. "The Specialists Reprint Trade," *AB Bookman's Yearbook*, pt. 1, 1969, p. 5.

8. "EDP Info. Magazine Gets TV Format," *Library Journal*, 94:2394, June 15, 1969.

9. "Editor's Corner," *AB Bookman's Weekly*, 43:2281, June 16, 1969.

10. Huff, William H. "Serial Observations—1967," *Library Resources & Technical Services*, 12:195, Spring 1968.

11. Wyllys, Ronald. "Automated Assistance in the Library: III," *U.W. Library News*, 12:21, March 1967.

12. Skipper, James E. "Rare Books, ARL, and ALA," *CU News*, 24:7, July 3, 1969.

13. Heron, David W., and Blanchard, J. Richard. "Seven League Boots for the Scholar? Problems and Prospects of Library Telefacsimile," *Library Journal,* 91:3601-05, Aug. 1966.

14. Willimas, Gordon, *et al. Library Cost Models: Owning versus Borrowing Serial Publications.* Washington, D.C., Office of Science Information Service, National Science Foundation, 1968.

15. Kaplan, Louis. "Owning versus Borrowing Serial Publications," *U.W. Library News,* 14:22, March 1969.

16. *Ibid.,* pp. 22-23.

17. "Owning versus Borrowing Serial Publications: An Objection and Reply," *U.W. Library News,* 14:14-15, April 1969.

18. *Ibid.,* p. 14.

19. *Ibid.,* pp. 15-16.

20. Worden, Helen M. Letter dated June 4, 1969.

21. Piternick, George. "Continuous Review of Current Serials Fund Titles." Berkeley, General Library, March 1959, pp. 2-3. (Unpublished.)

22. *Ibid.,* pp. 3-5.

23. Ottemiller, John H. "Forward." *In* Lee Ash, *Program; Report of a Three Year Project Directed by John H. Ottemiller, Associate University Librarian, under a Grant from the Council on the Library Resources, Inc.* Hamden, Conn., Archon Books, 1963, p. x.

24. *Ibid.,* p. 10.

25. *Ibid.,* pp. 10-11.

26. *Ibid.,* pp. 11-16.

27. "Price Indexes for 1969," *Library Journal,* 94:2571-73, July 1969.

28. Tuttle, Helen Welch. "Periodicals," *Library Journal,* 94:2571-72, July 1969.

29. In Letters to Editor, Baumfield, B.H. "Altered Prices," *Bookseller,* No. 3271, Aug. 31, 1968, p. 676.

30. A statement by the Publisher's Association. "The Price of Books," *Bookseller,* No. 3289, Jan. 4, 1969, p. 22.

31. Huff, William H. and Brown, Norman B. "Serial Services" in "Price Indexes for 1969," *Library Journal,* 94:2572-73, July 1969.

32. "Hard-Up Libraries 'Plan to Raid Booksellers' Profits," *Bookseller,* No. 3292, Jan. 25, 1969, pp. 246-48.

33. American Library Association. Resources and Technical Services Division. *International Subscription Agents.* 2d ed. Chicago, ALA, 1969, p. 2.

34. *Ibid.,* pp. 2-3.

35. Emery, D.C. "Open Letter to Our Suppliers," *AB Bookman's Weekly,* 43:2078, June 2-9, 1969.

36. Brown, Clara D. "57· Ways of Keeping a Serials Librarian Happy," *Stechert-Hafner Book News,* 23:81-84, Feb. 1969.

37. *Ibid.,* p. 84.

38. "Behind the Scenes, 1—Serials Department, Binding/Mending Division," *CU News,* 24:1, Feb. 27, 1969.

Kathryn Luther Henderson
Assistant Professor of Library Science
Graduate School of Library Science
University of Illinois, Urbana

SERIAL CATALOGING REVISITED—
A LONG SEARCH FOR A LITTLE THEORY
AND A LOT OF COOPERATION

THE CHARGE AND THE APPROACH

The charge to each person preparing a paper for this conference was that he approach current trends and problems and suggest possible solutions to the problems for the specific area of serials that he was to cover. This sounds deceptively simple in relation to serial cataloging, for indeed one can easily identify problems. But it quickly becomes evident that it is increasingly difficult to maintain a linear, "serial" approach to identifying such problems because while serial cataloging has problems of its own, it is always still involved with cataloging in general; with past, present, and future interpretations of the catalog; and with other bibliographical tools, both in and out of the local library. Therefore, while the catalog has its own functions to perform, it cannot escape still carrying on for the other tools should they fail to provide for local needs. And of course, today both problems and trends in all phases of librarianship are somewhat uncertainly noted because of the potential of automation in libraries.

The flood of materials of serial nature has created problems for both librarians and users of libraries. Surprisingly, the literature in regard to serial cataloging often seems to neglect the real problems of library *users*. And although this author has been both a serial cataloger and a serial user, the approach in this paper will be more nearly that of the user seeking to identify some reason for reconsideration of the past and present ways of dealing with serials which may be pertinent in the future.

48

This seems to call for looking at conditions which set the needs of catalogs; what the catalog is to do; the catalog's attempt to serve as an inventory and as a retrieval device; ways to enter serials in catalogs as reflected by catalog codes; and the role of cooperation and standardization as they affect serial cataloging.

CONDITIONS WHICH SET THE NEEDS FOR CATALOGS: or, Getting It If You Want It without Labor, without Difficulty, without Confusion

"A man should keep his little brain attic stocked with all the furniture that he is likely to use, and the rest he can put away in the lumberroom of his library, where he can get it if he wants it."[1] This statement is accredited to Sherlock Holmes and most of us admit that it was a good idea that the super sleuth had. But does it work as well for all sleuths of lesser orders? Apparently not, if one is to listen to the laments of Sylvestre Bonnard: "'And why' I asked myself, 'why should I have learned that this precious book exists if I am never to possess it—never even to see it? I would go to seek it in the burning heart of Africa or in the icy regions of the Pole if I knew it were there. But I do not know where it is.'"[2]

What Holmes is after and what Bonnard really wants is the information or content that one finds in the "books." Slamecka and Taube note that:

Information has been the subject of study of several disciplines; speaking broadly, philosophy, mathematics, linguistics, and engineering are all concerned with some of its aspects. The interest of philosophy is the truth, meaning and interpretation of information; mathematics is concerned with the "statistical" behavior of information as signals devoid of meaning; linguistics with its structural configuration; and engineering is interested in the spatial manipulation of physical symbols which represent information. Librarianship which handles physical materials in the engineering sense and their content in the logico-mathematical as well as the engineering and linguistic sense, must partake of the interests of all.[3]

Possessing the book in the modern library does seem to partake of the interests of all disciplines mentioned by Slamecka and Taube, for this possessing requires two primary kinds of access: 1) bibliographic access (i.e., knowing of the existence of the work which contains the information) and 2) physical access (i.e., having the physical embodiment of the work available for use). The first identifies the work as a bibliographical item and the second relates to the representation of that work in some graphic or readable form.

Our library catalogs, unlike some other indexing tools, have attempted to serve the needs of both kinds of access. In the last two decades this has proven to be no small job for a large library. The two often opposing access needs do not necessarily require the same talent or techniques or means to make them work. While the cataloging of any type of library material hits upon some of the problems relating to these dual attempts, it has hit serial cataloging with some of the most taxing of problems in recent times.

It is probably here, too, that the user and the librarian have the most common lack of agreement because while the user is concerned with a serial publication because of its content and information and often not because of its serial or physical nature, the librarian seems more occupied with its serial or physical nature. It is important to note that we as librarians have occupied our time with one aspect of access while users may have had quite another idea of the purpose of serial publications in our libraries. Perhaps in our attempt to meet one need, we may have slighted another.

Before the time of all the "explosions" which libraries have experienced in recent history, Verner W. Clapp noted that it was because of the development of techniques of classification, coding and subject headings that the librarians had appeared to have some authority in the matters of bibilography.[4] At that time, almost twenty years ago, Clapp felt that the tools of library organization had an enormous potential for the rationalization of all bibilographic work but the problem to be explored was how that potential might be realized. Our attempt today, as far as exploration into the ramification of serial cataloging is concerned, is in part to see if we have met that potential in our library catalogs in the last twenty years.

Rather obviously a library catalog is made to serve some need, a fact realized long ago by Gabriel Naudé (1600-1653), one of the first to make librarianship a career and to write on librarianship (*Advice on Establishing a Library*). Naudé indicated the need for a library to make some "order and arrangement" for the books it possessed, "for without it" he realized, "certainly, our inquiry would be to no purpose and our labor fruitless, since books are put there for no other reason than to be serviceable as need arises."[5] He further held that "to sustain the mind it is needful that the objects and things which it makes use of be so arranged that it may always and at pleasure distinguish some things from others, and discriminate among them as it will, without labor, without difficulty, and without confusion."[6]

The goal, then, of any type of bibliographical work in a library (including serial cataloging) seems to me to be summarized by combining some of the best elements of Holmes and Naudé into a phrase such as "Getting it *if* you want it without labor, without difficulty, and without confusion."

While we may concede that our *goal* remains the same as that stated in the past, we must also be constantly aware that a library catalog, like other tools, must respond to the bibliographic conditions and needs of its time. If we are to study the library catalog today, we have to consider what we expect it to do *today*, (even though it may not at present be able to actually perform all our expectations). This relates rather naturally to the needs of users *today*. It relates also to the characteristics of the *works* we will enter into our catalogs—as well as to how well other bibliographical tools are carrying out functions which the catalog may have at one time given up to them. (Other tools also exhibit changes—we sometimes forget that!)

WHAT THE CATALOG IS TO DO

What, then, is the catalog really to do? What the catalog is to do depends upon what the library is to do. This can cover a number of different activities and means to reach the ultimate goal. Recently, Seymour Lubetzky stated that although libraries may differ in many respects, each library has in common three basic functions: "The selection and acquisition of the materials required by the users, the preparation of catalogs of the materials acquired, and the provision of assistance in their use."[7] To perform each of these functions, Lubetzky maintains that an effective and reliable catalog is a necessity. The effectiveness of the catalog affects the process of acquisition because "an ineffective or unreliable catalog will take more time to search and may lead to costly duplication in purchasing and processing of materials already in the library."[7]

The very process of cataloging also depends on the condition of the catalog as it exists. "For the catalog, is not, or should not be merely an aggregation of freely produced entries of individual books and other items. . . but a systematically designed instrument in which all entries, as component parts, must be integrated. Thus the catalog, embodying previous cataloging decisions, is at once both the result as well as an important tool of cataloging, and an effective catalog is as essential to the process of cataloging as it is to the process of acquisition" continues Lubetzky.[8]

The third function, assistance in the use of the materials and the catalog, is affected in a more obvious manner by the effectiveness of the catalog. As Lubetzky says, "The assistance required normally involves the location of certain books, authors, or sources of information. These questions are similar in character to those arising in the processes of acquisition and cataloging, and the answers sought will similarly be affected by the condition of the catalog. The more effective the catalog—the more intelligible and responsive it is—the more frequently and readily will it yield the desired answers, either directly to the library's users or to the staff assisting them, thus saving doubly the time of the library's staff and users."[9]

We are glad to have this statement from Lubetzky for strangely enough what the catalog should do—its function—is not a prime topic in library literature. Library literature tends to record "how we did it" rather than "why we did it." Theodore S. Huang recently noted after reviewing the coverage of articles from 1948-1964 in the major sources of writing in relation to cataloging (i.e., the *Journal of Cataloging and Classification* and *Library Resources & Technical Services)* that "catalogers tend to write of particular experiences rather than in a general way."[10]

There are, however, a few encouraging notes that at least some people are taking a renewed interest in the function of the catalog. We have had the International Federation of Library Associations' Statement of Principles for the catalog which came from the International Conference on Cataloguing Principles held in Paris in October 1961.[11] While the Statement of Principles notes the functions for only the author-title catalog, these principles are aimed primarily toward the large research library and therefore, are very much related to all of us. They have achieved, in principle, the agreement of the major countries of the world. However, one might suspect that achieving international cooperation in theory, while it is no small accomplishment, may not be as difficult as convincing local librarians of the need for each library to participate in the accomplishing of the international goals. It is like brotherhood or love—easy to say when it relates to mankind but difficult to accomplish when your next door neighbor is involved.

In the study of information science in the past years, attention has been paid to what the catalog (or any index) should do. That the user is an important part of the system is recognized not only by P. J. Judge who says that "the user should be the most important element of the system, setting its goals, . . . influencing its mechanisms and limiting its possibilities,"[12] but by others as well. Edwin B. Parker indicates that the system should adapt to the receiver or user rather than the user to the system.[13] Philip Ennis notes a compelling need "for a renewed interest in the study of users" because of "the change in the ways knowledge is created and communicated."[14] These are but a few statements from the literature which bring to our attention once again the need to take a look at the library catalog to note just how we see it performing its function today.

There has also been a renewed interest in user studies. A potentially important catalog-user study has recently been conducted at Yale University. "There is a strong possibility or presumption" notes Ben-Ami Lipetz, "that the actions of a library user are shaped by the nature of the catalog facility that is available to him."[15] This statement alone may tell us much, but Lipetz, who is engaged in working with this study, tells us more. He states that "a library catalog is intended to make it relatively easy for a library user to identify and locate desired items in a collection. The catalog is a bridge between the information which a user brings to the library (in the form of written notes, or remembered clues) and the information or documents he hopes to carry away from the library."[16]

To test the ability of the catalog at Yale to perform this function, the researchers are investigating the nature of the clues, the differences in search patterns used to explore the catalog with the clues, the accuracy of the clues, etc. Lipetz hopes that at Yale they "will be able to use data from interviews and from the retrieved catalog cards, and from the works corresponding to these catalog cards, to seek means to improve the quality and efficiency of cataloging rules and catalog structure."[17] These are encouraging signs for the future—perhaps the results will inspire other large libraries to engage in studies of the same or related problems in their own institutions before beginning expensive operations to make computerized catalogs (or even manual ones!). Indeed, the invitation has already been issued by Lipetz: "It would be prudent to conduct studies similar to ours at a considerable number of large libraries of different kinds."[17] Some are probably already in existence but as Lipetz notes again, "I hope that they will not be long in coming. Since the computers are nearly upon us. With all the effort that has been going into research and development work on how to computerize catalogs, it would be nice to have more guidance on how to do it right."[17]

While "advice and guidance on how to do it right" in the past have been mostly available only on the local basis reporting of "how-we-did-it-and-there-fore-it-may-not-necessarily-be-how-you-should-do-it-but-we-will-tell-you-anyway basis," we have been able to conclude from the observations of what has been so recorded what the past functions of the library catalog seem to have been. Shera and Egan summarize it this way: "The functions that at one time or another have been delegated to the catalog may be divided into two major categories, those related to inventory and those related to retrieval, or location, of particular items within the collection."[18]

These seem to be our present functions, too, for if we take a careful look at the typical work operations assigned to a cataloger in almost any library situation, we would find that he performs work oriented around meeting inventory and retrieval functions. For is it not true that when a cataloger catalogs a publication (of any nature or type) that he performs these operations?

1. Chooses an entry to serve as the main entry.
2. Chooses added entries.
3. Constructs headings for main entry and added entries.
4. Provides a description of the physical item.
5. Determines the subject of the publication for subject cataloging.
6. Provides the necessary auxiliary entries such as references, information cards, etc.
7. Provides an inventory record of the item cataloged.
8. Prepares for the integration of all entries into an existing catalog.

Only the seventh item presumably relates exclusively to the inventory function while the rest purport to relate to retrieval functions, but a great deal of attention to inventory can be intermixed with the retrieval aspects as well.

No doubt, although the methods and means will surely change, inventory and retrieval will still be among the functions of the catalog in the future, for they are steps toward "getting it when you want it without labor, without difficulty, without confusion."

THE CATALOG'S ATTEMPT TO SERVE AS AN INVENTORY

Man's records began as precious possessions—property to be valued by an individual and held in pride for the next generation. Merely owning them implied knowing them, and if one knew the contents of his precious possessions, he had no need to provide an index to them.

Libraries began as book-oriented collections of single documents. There was little or no need to provide an index to the meager holdings of early libraries. But when the memory of a human begins to falter or when the size or complexity of any collection grows beyond human memory, then an index is created for convenience or necessity. If all one needs to do is to provide an index to rapidly call to mind the contents of his small collection, then a simple listing or inventory is all that is necessary, for there is little need in such situations to provide systematic indexes which show relationships.

Historically speaking, the inventory function by itself did not long serve. Soon grouping bibliographical belongings into areas—by type of bindings, by content, by subjects, etc., came into being, and the history of indexing in libraries since then is one of deciding whether the inventory function, or the second function, retrieval of an individual item or of the content of that item, is more of a necessity.

The "where they may be found" still implies some kind of inventory function and our shelflist and other means of recording holdings still pertain to the desire and need to keep some kind of *inventory*. But the functions of a library record-keeping system do not stop with the types of records that inventories can supply. They go beyond this to the ideas set forth by Pierce Butler in 1952: "Bibliography is the systematic process by which civilized man finds his way about in the world of books that he has created. A catalog is a bibliography of the books in a particular collection. Accordingly the practice of cataloging must conform to bibliographical principles. These stem from two major sources: the characteristics of the book and the characteristics of the reader."[19]

Just as the record system could not stop with the inventory function, so the self-contained book intended to be read through by the reader and absorbed as a whole unit could not suffice either.

And so we find, as D. E. Davinson points out that as early as 1700 B.C. an *Official Gazette* was published in Egypt. In 60 B.C. Julius Caesar posted a daily bulletin of government announcements in the Forum in Rome. *Ti-Pao*, a daily newspaper or court gazette, began to appear in Peking in 618 A.D. and continued until 1911. (Incidentally, it must have held some sort of world's record for existing without changing its name for it continued as *Ti-Pao* until 1664 when it became *King-Pao*.) Newsbooks in the sixteenth century and the *Journal des Scavans* published in Paris between 1665 and 1792 are among the other important early steps leading into present-day serial publications.[20]

While serial publications began as disseminators of daily news or government announcements (to satisfy the need for currency) they became political, social and literary reviews in the seventeenth and eighteenth centuries. But the greatest development of the serial came in the nineteenth and twentieth centuries as scientific production in all areas grew, as publication costs increased, as the need to have information more speedily came into being, and as scholarly societies multiplied and prospered as disseminators of their news and information. As Davinson notes: "From about 1880 specialised periodicals began to appear in increasing numbers, foreshadowing the flood which in the 1960's, far from showing signs of abating, is becoming larger each year."[21]

Today we have serials in boxes and on phonodiscs. Even multi-media kits are issued in serial form since series are serials. As our complex world becomes more corporate, it also attempts to serve the individual, and so we have serials made up for particular localities and regions. We even hear that some day we may have periodicals made up for individuals from computer profiles indicating individual needs.

As the individual unit (the book) or contribution became a part of the multiple or corporate unit of publishing and as a new type of physical publication brought into being new problems of recordkeeping involving both inventory and retrieval, libraries once more retreated to mainly the inventory function and left the retrieval of the individual item to agencies largely professional or commercial.

The retreat to the inventory has been a common pattern throughout library history for whenever new demands and new types of publications or new libraries develop, we always seem to return to inventory. The Middle Ages introduced us to large-scale inventory for the ideas of union lists came from that time although union lists were not fully realized until the twentieth century. During the twentieth century we have seen the proliferation of general and specialized union lists. The attention to union lists in this century has had an effect upon the local catalog as evidence by the advice of Andrew D. Osborn in his *Serial Publications*: "All the anticipated serial activity in the years that lie ahead implies that libraries must review their philosophy of collecting, processing, servicing, and preserving this perplexing, frustrating, at times elusive, but increasingly valuable type of publication. In the new philosophy the visible index and the union list should bulk large, and correspondingly cataloging should be de-emphasized."[22]

Since Osborn made that statement fifteen years ago, many changes have appeared in the world and on the library scene. Perhaps some of these things call for a reconsideration of the library catalog (or whatever we may call it in the future) in relation to its role for serials.

First, let us see what has happened to the "visible index and the union list" and how perhaps the very proliferation of such tools has made the library catalog appear a more desirable collecting device to make the bridge to the individual item when other tools are less than adequate or to provide only *inventory* to the serials and not to provide access to their contents. We are constantly told that we have to think of catalogs of the future not as carbon copies of those of the past, but as tools which go farther than those of today. This does not mean that we deny the need for an inventory of holdings either inside the local library or out of it for no library can exist without a knowledge of what it has and no library can exist today on just its own holdings. But in many ways, the proliferation of union lists has taken the time, space and money of the local library to provide inventory functions rather than retrieval functions. An idea of the number of union lists is given by William H. Huff as he reviewed the work in serials for the year 1964: "The *Union Lists of Serials; A Bibliography* compiled by Ruth S. Freitag was updated [in 1964]. Some idea of the serials explosion may be gained by comparing the edition published in 1943 which contained 387 entries with the 1964 edition which carries 1,218 citations and makes no claim for completeness."[23]

Important as the inventory function has been on the regional, national, and international level for serials, inventory still does not always result in "getting it . . . without some difficulty, labor and confusion." And as no library user wants to wait for an interlibrary loan to supply all his urgent research needs, local libraries have, in recent years, attempted to increase their serial holdings in various ways—from acquisition of the original to receiving the work in miniaturized, photocopied, or reprinted form.

With this growth of local serial collections have come administrative changes: library departments have been reorganized to handle the flood and library records have often been restructured around these organizational changes. The study of Dougherty, Wadsworth, and Axman found from a survey of sixty-nine libraries in 1964, that four typical patterns of library organization for serial work had developed: 1) serials grouped within acquisitions with the exception of cataloging which remains the responsibility of the catalog department, 2) serials unit independent of acquisitions but cataloging remains within the catalog department, 3) all functions related to serials work are centralized within one operating unit, and 4) decentralized serials work and its administration among more than one unit.[24]

For the year 1967, Huff also noted the growth of serial departments in the ten years previous and the evolving of central serial records and specially developed serials files along with the organization of "self contained" serial units.[25]

The characteristics of the "book" were, it seems, being given due consideration, but what about the characteristics of the "user" to whom serials had also presumably become more important? Indeed it has often been estimated that, at least in some types of libraries, 75 percent or more of the library use centers around serials. The user's interest is not in serials as serials but as carriers of the content (or information) which they embody. Apparently, the content was being given some consideration by indexing sources outside the local library for Huff comments on the greater in-depth indexing and abstracting necessary today.[26] And Davinson notes that "the abstracting journal, which has been the twentieth century attempt to systematise and organise the flood, now has more examples currently in production than there were individual periodicals 150 years ago."[27]

Foster Mohrhardt wrote that "Abstracts were originated to provide scholars with a convenient means for coping with increasing quantities of publications," but part of the problem for the user becomes apparent in the next part of Mohrhardt's sentence: "Now abstracts themselves have become so voluminous that specialized indexes often replace the use of abstracts by those who need up-to-date and speedy access to publication."[28]

Just because an index exists is no guarantee that it is helpful to all users. Writing about the problems of the medical libraries along this line, Pizer, Franz, and Brodman note that: "Published keys to the literature can hope to break down their subject fields only to the level of the most widespread needs; they cannot be expected to do demand subject searches on very specific topics for large numbers of requestors in remote areas. This specificity is the field of local libraries and information centers."[29] One can argue that the above writers speak of the medical library, which has its own specialized problems. This, of course, is true but one must also admit that medical literature has better bibliographical control than the literature of most other fields. So what must this say for the control of some of the other fields?

Many libraries continue to give only inventory control to monographic series. This is certainly one type of serial where a careful review of local policy needs to be made. Too often the availability of Library of Congress cards for the analytical parts of such series is probably the deciding factor here. Many potentially useful materials can remain hidden away on the shelves because of the lack of indexing of the individual item. Some of these series do not even have the rudimentary internal control which contents notes afford. Even if the series is eventually analyzed in some printed bibliography, the bibliographies are often late in appearing and the book may not be available until such time as its immediate use has long since passed.

Marian Harman noted as long ago as 1953, that "in theory, each monographic serial should be tested in order to determine whether it is to be analyzed or not . . . . A book which would be given 'normal' cataloging if it did not belong to a series should definitely be analyzed if it is published in a series."[30]

In a 1968 article, Jay E. Daily laments the increasing abandonment of the idea of analytics indicating that nothing on the subject even appears in *Library Literature* after 1963. He advocates the establishment of a cataloging center for analytics "which could analyze for everyone in several different ways. If it is wasteful to catalog a book more than once, the waste is multiplied when analytics are added by each library to the point that researchers would desire. The only possibility is to create the fund of analytics in some central information pool to which all cooperating libraries have immediate random access."[31]

While this kind of center does not seem within our immediate grasp, we cannot dismiss the idea from our minds nor can we wait to take care of the immediate problems, if these materials are shown to be needed by our users today. Naudé told us long ago that books are put in our libraries for no other reason than to be serviceable as need arises. A more recent writer indicates that "it is not sufficient to procure quantities of books; it is more important to make them accessible for the purpose of the users and thus to justify the expenses."[32] This latter author writes this as he explains a cooperative program by a number of German libraries to give control to the contents of periodicals, progress reports, surveys, collected works and Festschriften. This rather unsophisticated program makes use of catalog cards to distribute the information on the contents of such publications and the writer suggests that perhaps one day this program, growing out of local and national needs, may become international. At another time in my life, I would have thought the attempt for the catalog to give retrieval control to the *contents* of books and serials as an indication of naivety about using the total bibliographical network of the library. Now, I witness the changing times and become cognizant of the importance of considering the local situation *if no one else* is considering the needs of our users. This is especially so, if it is likely that our local users have individualized needs for which no general or special agency is likely to provide. The local tool in the age of networks promises to take on some new and important functions which may benefit not only its users but others as well.

Perhaps some day we will finally accept the cataloging done for monographs on shared and cooperative cataloging ventures; we will prove Robert D. Desmond wrong when he states that "serials cataloging will probably be the last bastion of rugged individualism,"[33] and then we can give attention to such needs as are not otherwise being met by centralized services.

One of the great functions of the catalog is that it gathers in one place the entries for the works contained in the library. It is a centralized, systematically arranged instrument made for the particular library. It does not ordinarily index items not in its collection as do other generalized indexes. The very proliferation of many indexes during the past has in a way but fragmented even more the search a user must make. No user knows of even a fraction of the specialized bibliographical services and "their very number and specialization are impediments in the sense that no library can acquire them all nor can an inquirer often make profitable use of them."[34] Even when indexing tools are available in large libraries, it has been impossible either to duplicate them because of space and financial considerations or to place all of them together in a common indexing section. And yet, in our world, this is a disservice to the user who, while he becomes more and more specialized, also looks to other disciplines to study interrelationships. Have we forgotten, then, in considering the functions of the library and its indexing services, the world in which we live? In this world "information pours upon us, instantaneously and continuously. As soon as information is acquired, it is very rapidly replaced by still newer information. Our electrically-configured world has forced us to move from the habit of data classification to the mode of pattern recognition. We can no longer build serially, block-by-block, step-by-step, because instant communication insures that all factors of the environment and of experience co-exist in a state of active interplay."[35]

I do not believe Marshall McLuhan was speaking of the same kind of serial building that we are but Gordon Williams was when he wrote:

> The sharper segregation of interests into narrower, and therefore more numerous, specialities has created more interfaces. This, plus the growing number of records, has made necessary more than guides to the location of records. It has made necessary guides to the information in the records that neither the library nor any other agency is yet satisfactorily providing....
> We must recognize and accept the fact that the information needs of everyone—humanist, scientist, and ordinary citizen—are now substantially different from what they were a hundred or more years ago, but that the techniques and organization used by the library to satisfy these needs are not substantially different from what they were then. More important, they are fundamentally inadequate to satisfy the present needs. If we are willing to accept the proposition that the demands for published information and for records that will enrich people intellectually and emotionally are to be satisfied by the library, then we must accept the proposition that every library is responsible for locating and making available to its patrons any published information they require, a proposition that has not been hitherto acknowledged."[36]

THE CATALOG'S ATTEMPT TO SERVE AS A RETRIEVAL DEVICE
FOR SERIAL PUBLICATIONS

We have already spoken of some of the aspects of retrieval for they have in a way been mixed in with what we called inventory. It is always difficult to point to the exact time where inventory, finding lists and retrieval functions of the catalog move from one and become another.

Shera and Egan indicate that "the conclusion from both experience and analysis seems inescapable that there are two basic functions of the catalog that are of outstanding importance: (1) accurate and speedy determination of whether or not an item known by author or title is in the collection, and, if so, of where it may be found; and (2) what materials the library contains upon a given subject and where they may be found."[37]

A good deal more attention has been paid in literature, and in libraries, too, as far as both monographs and serials are concerned, to the first role—locating author-title entries in the catalog. In certain kinds of libraries and catalogs these are the only point of access as far as serials are concerned. And so this paper will concentrate on those aspects, too.

In order that we may carry out the function of the author-title catalog, we put into a code certain agreed-upon standardized practices. A code helps us determine ways of accomplishing what we have set up as things that we want the catalog to do. A code is *not* a manual. It is *not* a how-to-do-it book, but it helps us carry out the purposes for the construction of a catalog which have been previously designated. It does not give ready-made answers because the problems presented by the materials themselves vary from book to book. But the code does set before us certain *common* situations which occur frequently and provides some means of making entries uniform for these situations. There is, of course, room for the use of judgement by the cataloger and there is nothing binding upon the library to follow a code; however, whenever cooperation among libraries is desired, standardization also becomes desirable.

In our codes as they have developed throughout the years, we seem to have been evolving toward two things: 1) the development of a theory of cataloging, and 2) the development of means to achieve cooperation or standardization.

Modern cataloging codes are assumed to have been born with Anthony Panizzi's 91 Rules for the compilation of the catalog issued in 1841 in *The Catalogue of Printed Books in the British Museum.* This code was developed during the time of a great controversy as to whether the catalog was to be an author or a classed catalog. Although Panizzi was on the side of the author catalog, the influence of the classified arrangement held over even into the rules Panizzi formed for certain kinds of publications including the ones with which we are most interested.

"All acts, memoirs, transactions, journals, minutes &c., of academies, institutes, associations, universities, or societies learned, scientific, or literary, by whatever name known or designated, as well as works by various hands, forming part of a series of volumes edited by any such society, to be catalogued under the general name 'Academies' and alphabetically entered, according to the English name of the country and town at which the sittings of the society are held"[38] in a prescribed order.

The rules continued: "The same rule and arrangement to be followed for 'Periodical Publications', which are to be cataloged under this general head, embracing reviews, magazines, newspapers, journals, gazettes, annuals, and all works of a similar nature, in whatever language and under whatever denomination they may be published. The several entries under the last subdivision to be made in alphabetical order according to the first substantive occuring in the title."[38] Similar headings were made for almanacs, calendars and ephemeras. These practices have persisted into recent British Museum printed catalogs, e.g., if one consulted under the name of the periodical *American Imago*, one would find a reference to Periodical Publications— *Boston, Massachusetts*.[39] The British Museum catalog, then "inventories" under the form heading Periodical Publications, subdivided by geographical subdivisions, all periodical (serial) publications published from that place. Our primary access point is under a form entry. The information it records for *America Imago* is as follows:[40]

> PERIODICAL PUBLICATION.— *Boston, Massachusetts*
> --The American Imago: A psychoanalytic journal for the arts and sciences, *etc. Boston, 1939— .8°.*
>
> *Wanting vol.* 1, *no.* 2-4; *vol.* 2, *no.* 1; *vol.* 3; *vol.* 4, *no.* 1.

Although some kinds of form headings still exist in modern cataloging codes (even the *Anglo-American Cataloging Rules*), other author catalogs have tended to play down the form heading in the way that Panizzi used it. Instead, catalogs have tended to relegate the points of access by form to subject entries and to form subdivisions of subject entries. Apparently, there *is* still a need to have points of access by form. In a study made in November 1963, at the Yale Medical Library, Brooks and Kilgour note that "location of a particular form of material (e.g. periodicals of biochemistry, textbooks of embryology) constitutes a definable group of subject searches."[41]

But has our preoccupation with separate serial records over the past several decades been in part an attempt to more adequately identify by form, since in many cases form in the subject entry is relegated to an indirect point of access through a subdivision? One knows, of course, the major reason for such serial records, but one also can perhaps sense an "unconscious" reason, too. Perhaps the use of fixed field coding in formats such as MARC will more quickly reveal, in the future, the *type* of publication and the several different interpretations of *form* in records. One particular problem with serial recording at present is the difference in definition accorded to the term "serials." If the inventory records for serials are separately located, the user is often confused because many serials are designated as such merely because of administrative decisions rather than because of a common definition of the term.

Panizzi's code introduces us to some theory in regard to the making of catalogs—a theory which in many cases is still with us for it influenced the next important code (Charles C. Jewett's *On the Construction of Catalogues of Libraries*). In many ways Jewett was able to implement the ideas of Panizzi better than even Panizzi had been able to because Jewett did not have the trustees of the British Museum to constrain him. Jewett's code was born from the desire for cooperation for he hoped that through cooperative efforts libraries could share the expense of printing book catalogs. He recognized that sharing implied some kind of standardization in the rules for entry—a fact which librarians even today have not always fully recognized. "Minute and stringent rules," Jewett writes, "become absolutely indispensable, when the catalogue of each library is, as upon the proposed plan, to form part of a general catalogue. *Uniformity* is, then imperative; but, among many laborers, can only be secured by the adherence of all to rules, embracing, as far as possible, all details of the work."[42] He stressed the need for principles to help solve the problems not directly discussed in his rules. One could only wish that some later code makers had reread Jewett on this point!

Ruth French Strout acknowledges other accomplishments of Jewett which we can interpret as being important to serial catalogs: "Jewett extended the principle of the corporate author further than Panizzi had and entered all corporate bodies directly under their names without the use of intervening form headings. He specifically established 'U.S.' as the author of public documents issued by particular departments, bureaus, or committees . . . . In the matter of form headings he departed from Panizzi completely and made no use of them at all for main entry. All these emendations proved to be significant and pertinent to the later development of cataloging in this country."[43]

Almost a quarter of a century passed from Jewett to the next set of important rules—those of Charles Anⴖⴖ.The factors shaping the arrangements of catalogs during that quarter of a century according to Jim Ranz were "the growing insistence for an approach to the subject content of books, the difficulty of maintaining up-to-date printed lists of rapidly growing collections, the development of the public card catalogue, the high costs of preparing and printing catalogues, and the inadequate funds available to libraries generally."[44]

There is almost a contemporary ring to the situations noted by Ranz, for one can certainly see some similarities between the last quarter of the nineteenth century and the last quarter of the twentieth. We are often being told today that it may be this quarter of the twentieth century which will see a change in the form of the catalog, too. Just as we have been restudying the purpose of the catalog so did Cutter include in his code the well known statement of "Objects" for the catalog and the statement of "Means" for accomplishing the objectives.[45] No other widely used Anglo-American code was to be based on stated objectives (except for descriptive cataloging in the narrow sense) until 1967. Cutter's code was to be the last code of any kind to this day to include subjects which may, in part, explain our present dissatisfaction with subject control for even the attempts of Cutter may have been less than satisfactory. Lubetzky notes that Cutter's attempt to incorporate rules for entry of description and subject cataloging was successful only to the point of making a record which "appeared as little more than a mere alphabetical interfiling of the author and title entries with the subject entries rather than involving any interrelation between them."[46]

Since the time of Cutter, as far as codes were concerned, catalogers were to occupy themselves with descriptive cataloging leaving it to the information scientists to eventually rediscover subjects "possibly," according to Phylis Richmond "because librarians have had such difficulty developing a logical system for author entry and the subject approach looks deceptively simple in comparison."[47]

Certainly some of this difficulty in developing a logical system for author entry came from the lack of a statement of principles in the 1908, 1941 and 1949 editions of the ALA rules.

With no principles, rules proliferated arising to meet new types of names and situations. The displeasure with the ALA rules from the 1908 edition through the 1949 edition is well known to all who have in any way kept abreast of the events in cataloging. At the request of the Board on Cataloging Policy and Research of the A.L.A. Division of Cataloging and Classification, Seymour Lebetzky, the consultant on bibliographic and cataloging policy at the Library of Congress prepared *Cataloging Rules and Principles; A Critique of the A.L.A. Rules for Entry and a Proposed Design for their Revision* in 1953.

Lubetzky's conclusions contain the seed for the objectives which were to eventually be embodied in the Statement of Principles of the International Conference on Cataloguing Principles, and, although never stated in the code itself, were to underlie the *Anglo-American Cataloging Rules,* 1967.

The Statement of Principles adopted at Paris in 1961, applied only to the choice and form of headings and entry words in catalogs of printed books in which entries under either authors or titles are combined in one alphabetical sequence. Although the principles were formed with special reference to catalogs enumerating the contents of large general libraries, they would be pertinent to other catalogs and hopefully to other kinds of bibliographical tools. The Statement indicated also the function of the catalog as point 2:

2. *Functions of the Catalogue*
2.1 The catalogue should be an efficient instrument for ascertaining whether the library contains a particular book specified by
   (a) its author and title, *or*
   (b) if the author is not named in the book, its title alone, *or*
   (c) if the author and title are inappropriate or insufficient for identification, a suitable substitute for the title; and
2.2 (a) which works by a particular author and
   (b) which editions of a particular work are in the library.[48]

And so while the long struggle for a theory or a set of principles may have reached some kind of a goal with these principles, one must ask if they can be carried out and if they will be recognized and used by libraries. Since they are not stated or reproduced in the code which is based upon them (except where the code departs from them), will they be known by the catalogers who use the code? Will they even have publications in their libraries which contain the statements? Will they make copies of the principles and insert them in the proper places in their codes as reminders of the principles which underlie the code even if they are not printed in the code? Only individual catalogers can answer these questions. The burden of the past which carried no principles will have a long-time effect on catalogs that exist and on catalogers who also still exist. Theory and cooperation have long suffered because of the lack of principles. A healthy sign for the future is the relative ease with which present generations of students accept and apply principles when they are clear cut and *meaningful*.

This might be a good time to take a brief over-all look at the *Anglo-American Cataloging Rules* (hereafter referred to as *AA*). There are a number of ways in which *AA* is a departure from earlier codes:[49] 1) While other American cataloging codes in this century have emphasized specific rules for various types of publications and various classes of persons and corporate bodies, the new rules are based upon the IFLA principles mentioned earlier. 2) The choice of entry and construction of heading have been treated as separate problems except when form subheadings are involved. 3) The choice of entry has been treated as a problem of determination of authorship responsibility and there are four general principles applicable here: a) entry should be under author or principal author when one can be determined, b) entry should be under editor when there is no author or principal author, c) entry should be under a compiler named on the title page in the case of collections of works by various authors, and d) entry should be under title in the case of other works whose authorship is diffuse, indeterminate, or unknown.[50] 4) Construction of heading has been treated as a problem of name with two subproblems: a) the choice of a particular name and a particular form of that name and b) the way in which the name should be presented as a catalog heading. 5) The rules for descriptive cataloging involving the description of the physical work have been included with rules for entry. These are based on principles previously stated in the 1949 *Rules for Descriptive Cataloging (RDC)*. The 1967 rules do not depart substantially from *RDC*. Inclusion of descriptive cataloging rules of this nature in a volume with rules for entry is a return to pre-1949 practice rather than a complete innovation. 6) The code also contains, as Part II, rules devoted to specific types of non-book materials in an attempt to provide uniformity of cataloging practice for this growing area of library resources. 7) Throughout the code, relevant general rules apply to any aspects of a specific problem that are not dealt with in a specific rule. The special section on descriptive cataloging for serials contains only such rules as are not met in the more general sections, and the rules in Part II are primarily those which are either additional to or different from those for book-like materials.

WAYS TO ENTER SERIALS IN CATALOGS

The continuing nature of serials gives them long periods of time in which to affect changes which somehow must be incorporated into the catalog record. In evolving toward theory and standardization to achieve cooperation in the cataloging of serial publications, this extended history of the publications has caused some difficulty. Also causing a problem sometimes is that a particular library may hold only a part of the run of a particular serial. These are characteristics of the "book" and these characteristics also lead us to the two basic problems in determining entries for serials: 1) What should be the *entry* of serials (a name or a title)? and 2) When they change their names, what should we do about the entry previously formed? We must add to this the problem of the characteristics of the "user" who usually approaches the serial from the point of view that it is the carrier of a particular *work* in which he is interested. His citation to that work is likely to be the name or title of the serial at the time the work was first issued in the serial.

There are further problems as to the source for obtaining the data elements necessary for forming the catalog entry. With books we find that there are title pages which, while sometimes not giving all the information needed or giving incorrect information, still are a basic source to rely upon. This may not be so true with serials, some of which have no title pages. If they do have title pages, they are not likely to appear at the time the publication is cataloged, especially if the publication is cataloged from the first issue. In addition there are often titles other than the title page titles by which a serial may be known or cited. Added to all of this has been the lack of guiding principles mentioned earlier for a code as a whole which has meant that various codes have tried different approaches toward satisfying the rules for choice and construction of entry for serials.

Cutter treated serial publications as one type of anonymous publication to be entered under title, but he could not resist the idea of different rules for different types of serial publications. The ALA rules also emphasized *type* of publication and in the 1949 rules a great deal of emphasis seemed placed upon the arbitrary characteristics of the presence or absence of distinctive titles.

Since *AA* tried to avoid special rules for special types of publications, we might have expected that serials in this code would have been entered under the general rules for entry. However, this was not the case and *AA* rule 6 deals with "serials."[51] We must admit, however, that there seem to be some legitimate reasons for this special rule, again partly because of the characteristics of the "book" and partly too, because of the difficulty of fitting serials into the pattern for authorship responsibility which underlies *AA* unless you understand *AA* clearly. An author is defined in *AA* as: "the person or corporate body chiefly responsible for the creation of the intellectual or artistic content of the work."[52] Michael Gorman is not alone is concluding that the definition of author "leaves some crucial problems unanswered" and "though the 1967 ... rules are firmly based on an author main entry heading, they lack an explicit adequate definition of an author."[53] Lubetzky also hints that there is a lack of a proper definition and formulates his own definition which he feels is a more practical definition of an author: "The person or corporate body *represented* as chiefly responsible for the *work*, i.e., the one in whose name the work is issued and who is purportedly responsible for it—whatever the character of the work or the medium containing it—except when one has erroneously, fictitiously, or dubiously been represented as the author of the work."[54]

A. Hugh Chaplin indicates that for serials (and other similar works) there are no strong consistent traditions among users or catalogers for locating these items in catalogs but rather a number of separate traditions which group themselves into two main streams emphasizing two opposing principles: title entry and author entry.[55]

His ideas seem corroborated by a story related by Derek J. de Solla Price who notes that "One of the most English anecdotes in scientific communication concerns a man who wrote a letter to *Nature* complaining about that Journal's policy. The reply was 'The Editor of *Nature* presents his compliments and fears he is being mistaken for its Author.'"[56]

Let us see how *AA* has codified the rules for entry of serials and for series added entries that are made for monographs in a series, whether the series is numbered or not:

> A. Serials not issued by a corporate body and not of personal authorship. Enter a serial that is not issued by or under the authority of a corporate body and is not of personal authorship under its title.[57]

This responds to the fourth general principle of *AA* for entry: "Entry should be under title in the case of other works whose authorship is diffuse, indeterminate, or unknown."[58] Another point that should be understood here is that a corporate body is defined by *AA* as "any organization or group of persons that is identified by a name and that acts or may act as an entity."[59] Commercial publishers typically do not bear the responsibility for the intellectual or artistic content of the works they publish and therefore are not considered as "corporate bodies" in the rules.

But the next section of the rule also seems to indicate that there are other situations where other types of corporate bodies do not function as authors in serial publications. And this section once again seems unable to avoid naming types of publications even though the intention had been to the contrary:

> B. Serials issued by a corporate body. 1. Enter a periodical, monographic serials, or serially published bibliography, index, directory, biographical dictionary, almanac, or yearbook issued by or under the authority of a corporate body, under its title with an added entry under the corporate body.[58]

Is there any reason for such a rule? Is this abandoning authorship? Is it a contrivance to enter under title without naming distinctive titles as the reason for like entry? "There is one reason, and only one reason," says Lubetzky, "why a serial, unlike a monograph, could not generally be entered under its corporate author or personal editor—and this is that, because it is 'intended to be continued indefinitely,' it is subject to change of authorship or editorship."[60] And so it is the "diffuseness" of the authorship as editorship which again guides us, rather than the type of publication; the types are named only to give direction to the cataloger who may not see the principle which is illustrated.

AA seemingly reverted here to the favorite sport of the earlier ALA code providing exceptions to the rules, for rule B has this exception: "If the title (exclusive of the subtitle) includes the name or the abbreviation of the name of the corporate body, or consists solely of a generic term that requires the name of the body for adequate identification of the serial, enter it under the body."[61] Lubetzky's explanation helps here:

> Again, looking at some annual reports of libraries, or other "house organs," issued under catchy titles, it will also be realized that a serial limited, largely

or exclusively, to the business or proceedings of a particular body is also not susceptible to a change of the issuing body, regardless of the character of the title. Both these conditions—a title including the initials or the full name of the issuing body, or a contents limited largely to the activities, business, or proceedings of the issuing body—are rational and practical reasons for entry of such serials under their issuing bodies as authors or compilers.[62]

And so now we have had diffuse authorship allowing entry under title as well as entry under corporate bodies as authors. *AA* adds a third dimension to choice of entry for serials:

C. Serials by a personal author. Enter a serial by a personal author under his name.[63]

This new rule seems to be quite consistent with *AA*'s authorship principles. Having considered what should be the entry element for serials, we now turn to the second problem in serial cataloging in regard to entry, i.e., what should we do when a serial changes names. Since the entry of serials can be under a name or under a title, the change in name can imply a change in the name of the author or in the title of the publication (and unfortunately, it is not uncommon to find that changes occur in both). There are essentially three ways to handle the problem of change of name in serials.

Cutter introduces us to two the methods, discussing them in rules 133 and 145 in his code. Rule 145 notes that "A periodical which changes its name is to be entered under each title." Each entry would then have the imprint that belongs to that title and a note "Preceded by" or "Continued as" or both, as required. "Or," rule 145 continued, "the periodical may be catalogued in full under the first title with a note of the changes."[64]

The third method for treating changes in title or issuing body for serials was to be introduced in the 1908 rules which called for entry under the latest form with brief entries under the earlier names referring to those which immediately precede and follow in a note introduced by the phrase "Preceded by" or "Continued as." The later ALA codes were to call for entry under the latest title with references from any earlier title or titles under which the periodical might have been issued. In 1964, the reference became an added entry to take full advantage of full bibliographic information at each point of access on the unit card.

The British, in their version of the 1908 rules, continued the tradition of entry under the earliest title with brief entries under later forms. Entry under earliest title was used by other bibliographical tools. The *British Union-Catalogue of Periodicals* continued to enter under earliest title until 1964 when "in the case of a change of title, a new entry is made for the change title."[65]

Because of World War II the British were not able to participate in the 1941 revision to the extent that they had in previous revisions and therefore not all British libraries adopted the ALA rules codified after the 1908 edition. In December 1965-January 1966, a survey of the practices and procedures of *Cataloging and Classification in British University Libraries* made by Joan

Friedman and Alan Jeffreys indicated that twenty-eight out of sixty-two libraries still followed the 1908 rules with seventeen following ALA (1949). In regard to serials, only thirteen libraries followed the practice of entry under latest title with eight still following the practice of entry under earliest title. Over half of the libraries followed the practice of entry under successive titles as practiced in the main volumes of the *World List of Scientific Periodicals*.[66]

The successive title method was to return to an American code after an absence of sixty-three years, for the method of treating changes in *AA* again advocates it. But not all libraries have come full circle to successive title cataloging because a footnote in the new code indicates that the Library of Congress will catalog each serial as a single bibliographical entity, regardless of change of title, issuing body, or name of issuing body, with the entry taken from the latest volume.[67] What it does not say in this footnote is that the librarians at the Catalog Code Revision Committee asked LC to continue this practice. I will comment on this later.

The *Anglo-American Cataloging Rules* continue rule 6 with part D—Change of title, author, or name of corporate body.

> 1. If the title of a serial changes, if the corporate body under which it is entered changes or undergoes a change of name, or if the person under whom it is entered ceases to be its author, make a separate entry for the issues appearing after the change. ... If the change in title is either of very short duration or of a very minor character, however, it is simply noted on the existing entry.
>
> 2. If the corporate body accorded an added entry for a serial changes or undergoes a change of name, make an added entry also under the new body or the name of the body.[68]

It may appear that cataloging under successive titles departs from the attempt of the Paris Principles to bring together the "works of an author." However, the Paris Principles themselves advocate successive title entry when they state: "When a *serial publication* is issued successively under different titles, a *main entry* should be made under each title for the series of issues bearing that title, with indication of at least the immediately preceding and succeeding titles."[69]

Lubetzky explains why the successive title entry can be preferred without violating the basic underlying principles of bringing together editions of works:

> a) a serial is, in its course of existence, susceptible to a change of scope and character which makes it in fact a different serial, and the new title may well signify that such a change has taken place, despite the continued numbering of the volumes;
> b) a serial does not have the organic unity of the monographic work, it is rather a source of various works, and both the one who cites and the one who looks for a serial is almost always concerned with the part identified by a particular title, not the history of the whole serial;
> c) this course is technically more suitable to the changing course of the serial.[70]

The pros and cons of this system have been adequately covered in previous publications, especially in those of F. Bernice Field in "Serial Entry" a working paper presented at the Institute on Cataloging Code Revision, Stanford University, July 9-12, 1958,[71] and by Paul S. Dunkin in a working paper prepared for the International Conference on Cataloguing Principles, October 1961.[72]   It does not therefore, seem necessary to cover this subject again except in summary form:

    1) Information needed for cataloging a serial is the same whichever system is used (see Figures 1-3).

    2) Realistically, one must admit that no method escapes some kind of recataloging or change in the record. Even entry under earliest title presumes that notes will indicate changes in names and that some reference or added entry will be necessary to direct the user.

    3) For earliest or latest title entry only one main entry will appear in the catalog as opposed to several main entries with successive title cataloging (see Figure 1). These multiple points of access have their effect upon added entries, too (see Figures 1, 2, and 5).

While the latest title is "neater" and requires fewer entries in the catalog, its very lack of duplication of entries, especially in the case of subject and secondary added entries, may preclude some user finding what he wants. This may be especially so when entry under title or corporate name is somewhat arbitrary and the user takes the added entry approach. It is also true that users do access the catalog for specific titles via subject entries and therefore, if the title had undergone a change from the title which the user brings as his clue or information, he will miss the subject entry if the main entry is other than the title he brings (see Figure 5). The duplication of entries, which to the economy-minded may save precious catalog space, may also create problems for the user—even to the point of keeping him from retrieving the item at all.

    4) With successive title cataloging, the cataloger catalogs only what he has. In the case of incomplete sets, he does not try to make an entry covering what he does not have. If there are extensive gaps in the holdings, the connections between titles may be lost (although there are always ways to explain this and some feel that it is really a more "honest" way than that used in cataloging under the latest title).

    5) It is probably the acquisitions librarian who suffers the most by successive title cataloging because he does not find the full bibliographical information at any one place that he enters the catalog. He does not need this full information for *every* serial in the collection, and so in a sense it is not as difficult for him to search other bibliographical tools as it is to make all the needed steps for every serial in the catalog.

    6) It is the user who benefits from successive title cataloging. He is more likely to bring to the catalog the title he has acquired from the citation which is likely to be the title at the time of publication (see Figure 5).

California quarterly of secondary education. v. 1-
Oct. 1925-
   Berkeley, Calif. *etc.*
     v. 24cm.
   *Quarterly, Oct. 1925-1934; monthly (except
June-Sept.) 1935-*
   Published by the California Society for the
Study of Secondary Education, 1925-27; *by the
California Society of Secondary Education, 1928-50;
by the California Association of Secondary School
Administrators, 1951-*
   *Title varies; Oct. 1934-Dẹc. 1960, California
journal of secondary education. -1961- Journal of
secondary education.*

   1. Education, Secondary—Periodicals. I. California
Society for the Study of Secondary Education. *II. California
Society of Secondary Education. III. California Association
of Secondary School Administrators.*

   Entries would also be needed for the later titles. Like
II and III these could be added entries, however, it is more
likely that they would be references since unit cards would need
to be completely duplicated and would not be available from a
centralized cataloging service. It is of course true that this will
have to be done for added entries II-III but there it is more
difficult to substitute reference as an appropriate entry form.

   Underlined portions of the above catalog entry, indicate
additions which would need to be made to the original catalog
entry as changes occur. The quarterly frequency statement would
not be mandatory but could be added for clarity.

FIGURE 1

CATALOGING UNDER EARLIEST TITLE

Journal of secondary education.
    v. 1-
    Oct. 1925-
    Burlingame, Calif. etc.
        v. 24 cm.

        Quarterly, Oct. 1925-1934; monthly
    (except June-Sept.) 1935-
        Published by the California Society
    for the Study of Secondary Education,
    1925-27; by the California Society of
    Secondary Education, 1928-50; by the
    California Association of Secondary
    School Administrators, 1951-
        Title varies; Oct. 1925-June 1934,
    California quarterly of secondary education.–
    Oct. 1934-Dec. 1960, California journal
    of secondary education.

        1. Education, Secondary–Periodicals.
    I. California Society for the Study of
    Secondary Education. II. California Society
    of Secondary Education. III. California
    Association of Secondary School Administrators.
    IV. Title: California quarterly of secondary
    education. V. Title: California journal of
    secondary education.

        Before 1964, the code called for reference
    instead of IV-V.

                        FIGURE 2
            CATALOGING UNDER LATEST TITLE

California quarterly of secondary education.
  v. 1-9; Oct. 1925-June 1934. Berkeley, Calif.
  9v. 25cm.

  Published by the California Society for the
Study of Secondary Education, 1925-27; by the
California Society of Secondary Education, 1928-34.
  Continued by California journal of secondary lucation.

  1. Education, Secondary—Periodicals. I. California
Society for the Study of Secondary Education.
  II. California Society of Secondary Education.

California journal of secondary education. v. 10-
  35; Oct. 1934-Dec. 1960. Berkeley, Calif.
  26v. monthly (except June-Sept.) 24cm.

  Continues California quarterly of secondary education.
  Published by the California Society of Secondary
Education, 1934-50; by the California Association
of Secondary School Administrators, 1951-60.
  Continued by the Journal of secondary education.

  1. Education, Secondary—Periodicals. I. California
Society of Secondary Education. II. California
Association of Secondary School Administrators.

Journal of secondary education. v. 36-
  Jan. 1961-
  Burlingame, Calif., California Association of
  Secondary School Administrators.
  v. 24cm. monthly (except June-Sept.)

  Continues California journal of secondary education.

  1. Education, Secondary—Periodicals. I. California
Association of Secondary School Administrators.

FIGURE 3

CATALOGING USING SUCCESSIVE TITLES

Work of the California curriculum commission. C.B.
Moore. Cal Q. Sec Ed 7:384-5 Je 32

Physical science for art students. T.B. Edwards.
Calif J Sec Ed 25:238-42 Ap 50

Diploma in education: what is it? G.S.C. Cheong
J Sec Ed 42:363-7 D 67

FIGURE 4

CITATIONS TO PERIODICAL FROM
EDUCATION INDEX SHOWING USE
OF TITLE OF PUBLICATION AT
TIME OF CITATION.

EDUCATION, SECONDARY–PERIODICALS.

American education

L'Athenee
1   3b
         3a
The Clearing house

Correspondez-Blatt

Educational forum

L'Enseignement secondare au Canada

Gymnasial-Zeitung

The High school journal

High school life

High school teacher

High school

Illinois Association of Secondary Principals.
   Bulletin

Independent school bulletin
2   3c
Kentucky high school quarterly

FIGURE 5

**SELECTED TITLES IN CATALOG UNDER SUBJECT HEADING
APPLICABLE ALSO TO PERIODICAL PUBLICATION
UNDER CONSIDERATION ILLUSTRATING WHERE
PERIODICAL ENTRY WOULD OCCUR USING
THE VARIOUS METHODS OF CATALOGING**

   1. Entry *California quarterly of secondary education* would appear at this point for Cataloging Under Earliest Title. No other entries under subject heading for this work with this cataloging
   2. Entry *Journal of secondary education* would appear at point for Cataloging Under Latest Title. No other entries under subject heading for this work with this cataloging
   3. Entry for each of the successive titles appear at the points indicated:
   a. *California quarterly of secondary education* b. *California journal of secondary education* c. *Journal of secondary education*

CORPORATE HEADINGS AND SERIAL PUBLICATIONS

Since serials and corporate bodies are often involved together, we must next turn our attention to corporate entries. Cutter acknowledged corporate authorship because he felt "Bodies of men are to be considered as authors of works published in their name or by their authority."[73] Cutter also acknowledged the problems that still are involved with corporate bodies: 1) what are their names, and 2) whether the name or some other word should constitute the heading. "Local names have always very strong claims to be headings," says Cutter, "but to enter the publications of all bodies of men under the places with which the bodies are connected is to push a convenient practice so far that it becomes inconvenient and leads to many rules entirely out of harmony with the rest of the catalog."[73]

As rules progressed through other codes, code makers were to forget the sage advice of Cutter on that point and to this day we are plagued by the entry of "names of bodies" under the "convenient practice" that had been pushed as far as to become inconvenient and lead to many rules entirely out of harmony with the rest of the catalog. It is another current problem in the cataloging of serials.

By the 1908 rules we find four kinds of corporate bodies capable of being considered as authors: government publications, societies, institutions (establishments), and miscellaneous bodies or organizations not provided for elsewhere. For all of the four kinds, specifications were names. The stage was set for problems persisting until today. The problems were further extended in the 1941 and 1949 rules and were the main impetus for the study of the rules by Lubetzky in 1953.

Efforts were made to clarify the corporate entry problem in code revision. That was when the objective was to make the best code possible without regard to economy. For some time, the efforts seemed as if they might pay off. After the unexpected ease with which the concept of corporate authorship was accepted at the IFLA Conference in Paris this seemed especially possible. For the first time in history, all the major countries in the world had come to accept corporate authorship. It is hard for Americans who have struggled with corporate authorship for over one hundred years to realize that only in the 1950s and 1960s did France, Germany and the Scandinavian countries come to accept that concept.

Acceptance of corporate authorship as a concept also meant, however, that for a corporate body to be chosen as an author, real authorship had to be present. The principles themselves stated that when a corporate body performed a function subsidiary to the function of author (such as editor), the entry should be an added entry rather than a main entry. The work of main entry then, according to the Paris Principles, was to take precedence when the work is by its nature necessarily the expression of the collective thought or activity of the corporate body (e.g., official reports, rules and regulations, manifestoes, programs and records of the results of collective work), even if signed by a person in the capacity of an officer or servant of the corporate body or when the wording of the title or title-page, taken in conjunction with the nature of the work, clearly implies that the corporate body is collectively responsible for the content of the work (e.g., serials whose titles consist of a generic term—Bulletins, Transactions, etc.—preceded or followed by the name of a corporate body, and which include some account of the activities of the body).

As much as American librarians might have wanted to support the Paris Principles in regard to corporate entries, the principles in this area were found to be among the most difficult to implement into *AA*. It was felt that some of these principles would cause hardships especially in large catalogs of research libraries which were likely to contain many corporate entries. Therefore, although the Catalog Code Revision Committee adopted the Paris Principles in 1962, they did so with some qualifications. Shortly thereafter, the Library of Congress made an extensive study of the theoretical merits of the Principles and of the extent of changes that would be necessary if the Principles were retrospectively applied. The Association of Research Libraries too, soon recommended that the Catalog Code Revision Committee reconsider certain provisions of the Principles. The American dream to have the very best code possible—one based on principles rather than arbitrary rules and one that could find international agreement—was therefore once again shattered by the large libraries and the desire for economy that sees only the accumulations of the past and present rather than a show of faith in the premise.

Two of the principles affected pertained to serial publications issued by a corporate body. The one we have referred to already—that main entry should be under the name of a corporate body when the wording of the title or title-page taken in conjunction with the nature of the work, clearly implies that the corporate body is collectively responsible for the content of the work. These included serials whose titles consisted of a generic term (Bulletin, Transactions, etc.) preceded or followed by the name of a corporate body, and which include some account of the activities of a body. The other rule held that among the works having their main entry under title were works known primarily or conventionally by title rather than by the name of the author.

The introduction to the Anglo-American Cataloging Code states the reason for the departure: "In its rules for serials (rule 6) the Committee held that the inclusion in the title of a serial of the name or part of the name of the issuing corporate body is too powerful a criterion to be nullified when, in unusual cases, no account of the activities of the body is included in the publication. It also held that 'known primarily or conventionally by title' is too vague a criterion."[74]

But the biggest departure to come from the Paris Principles was on the very point that had caused the most difficulty in application in the ALA codes—the problem of entry under place for corporate bodies. The Paris Principles (9.4) called for uniform entry under the name of a corporate body to be the name by which the body is most frequently identified in its publications. The Principles indicated exceptions to take care of variant names, names in several languages, conventional titles, etc., but generally a corporate body should be known by its name as presented in its publications.

The infamous rules 98 and 99 in the *AA* exempted local churches, etc., and certain other corporate bodies from entry under name and made an "exception for entry under place." A footnote told the unhappy reason for this exception: "These exceptions are required primarily by the economic circumstances obtaining in many American research libraries. The cost of adapting very large existing catalogs to the provisions of the general rules for corporate bodies without such exceptions is considered to be insupportable."[75]

The introduction perhaps more truthfully told the sad story of these decisions: "They have the effect of greatly reducing the impact of the Paris Principles on existing catalogs which are heavily infused with entries for corporate bodies under place names in accordance with all preceding cataloging rules."[76] They, of course, also had the impact of reducing the impact of the code on such libraries as may have wanted a better code and had been willing to pay the price for changing the arbitrary entry to one based on principles. Later on, the Library of Congress introduced superimposition so perhaps we could have avoided rules 98 and 99 after all. Superimposition means "that the rules for choice of entry will be applied only to works that are new to the Library and that the rules for headings will be applied only to persons and corporate bodies that are being established for the first time."[77]

In the days of international cooperation it must be noted, too, that even though we have a new Anglo-American code, there are basic departures between the "Anglos" and the "Americans." One such departure related to rules 98 and 99 which the British committee did not include in their rules, choosing instead to enter all corporate bodies under their names. "Any bodies with the same name," says Michael Gorman, "can be distinguished adequately by the addition of a geographic or other qualification . . . . This decision not to weaken the rules by arbitrary exceptions is a good one and will make the British text more effective, in dealing with corporate bodies, than the North American text."[78] I am inclined to agree with Gorman, and if large libraries are unhappy with this state of affairs brought about by 98 and 99, they must accept the burden of their own decisions on this matter. It was they who weakened the code.

It is rather obvious that the problems of corporate headings have not all been solved by the new code. Again, it seems that we are trying, because of our lack of codification of subject and form headings, to force into an author entry some of the parts of entry which belong elsewhere. As Gorman notes, the rules will not "clear up the foggy area in most cataloguers' minds, the area that leads to an inconsistent application of half-understood principles."[79] Again we have only evolved *toward* a theory and compromised it to standardization, but standardization of the past and our own existing catalogs rather than moving toward the cooperative opportunity that was ours.

ʼ BOOK-WORK AGAIN

The catalog is something of a luxury tool—it has multiple points of access and to some who do not define the catalog as a systematic tool, the preoccupation with the choice of a main entry or heading seems somewhat unnecessary in the days of unit cards and in the days of a computer that can make connections and links inside itself without the user ever knowing anything about its necessity for making the connections and links. The main entry was born in the days when unit cards were not used and when printed catalogs gave the full information only at one point of access (obvious again today in some book catalogs).

Some of our feeling about this in serial cataloging, no doubt, also springs from Cutter's philosophy on the matter. Cutter noted in regard to periodicals that "there are, however, some 'Journals' published by or 'under the auspices of' societies which are really periodicals, and should be so treated in entry, the society being not the author but the editor. Again, there are works which occupy a borderland between the two classes, in regard to which the puzzled cataloger should remember that it is not of much importance which way he decides, provided he is careful to make all necessary references."[80]

When we perpetuate this idea that the choice of main entry makes "little difference," we abandon one of the basic tenets in making systematic catalogs. The introduction to the *Anglo-American Cataloging Rules* explains the need for a main entry:

> Although the rules are oriented to multiple-entry catalogs, it has still been regarded as necessary to distinguish main entries from added entries. Since this distinction can be one of the most difficult operations in cataloging, it may be asked why it is necessary if all requisite entries are provided in the catalog and, when the unit-card system is used, the descriptive information on each entry is the same. The necessity persists because, for one thing, even in multiple-entry catalogs it sometimes happens that a work, other than the work being cataloged, must be identified by a single entry—e.g., a work about which the work in hand has been written or a work on which the work in hand has been based. Beyond this requirement in the multiple-entry catalog itself is the manifest general need, permeating all library, bibliographical and book-trade activities, for a standard mode of identifying bibliographical entries. Such standard identification is of great importance in single-entry bibliographies, book lists, order lists, bibliographical citations, and everyday communications referring to bibliographical entities. By prescribing what shall be the main entry, the rules respond to this necessity for a standard mode of identifying a work. They follow the principle, firmly established in modern cataloging and bibliography, that a work should be specified by its author and title or, if it lacks an author, by its title.[81]

In a review of the *Brasenose Conference on the Automation of Libraries,* Phylis Richmond comments on the confusion between the concept of main entry and the unit card which she saw evident in the conference *Proceedings:*

> The fact that the two have been combined in the card catalog apparently makes it difficult for people to conceive of them as separate entities. With the computer, as with card catalogs without the unit record approach, it is possible to use any entry and refer to a separate unit containing the total bibliographic detail. Theoretically it is possible to have the unit record in

any form, without main entry, but it is extremely difficult to achieve any degree of consistency in this manner. For computerized information retrieval, a slight change in entry from item to item by the same person can require much recycling by the user unless the input personnel, presumably catalogers, take pains to make either cross-references to some base form of entry or between variant forms of the same author or title. In this respect, entry under title has little advantage over personal or corporate author.[82]

While there are others who do not hold to this way of thinking, until they conclusively illustrate that we can in future catalogs locate *works* as well as *books*, we should, especially in large libraries, not give up this capability of the systematic catalogs.

While "book-work" may at first glance seem to apply more to monographic than to serial publications, I have already commented several times upon the need for attention to this distinction. We need to recognize that serials, too, are translated, appear under different titles even within the same "book," and are involved in a number of different ways requiring relational, assembling, and grouping functions. Serials also have other works written about them. A uniform entry often becomes the filing medium not only for the main entry but also for assembling functions under other entries.

Using the total bibliographic network of a library (or libraries) implies for sometime at least, the use of printed union lists. Such tools are likely to be single entry tools (or at best multiple entry tools only through references). The better we can achieve uniformity through a common main entry, the better is the user's chance of success with the tool.

COOPERATION—UNIFORMITY—STANDARDIZATION

Amost 120 years ago Jewett realized that if cooperation was to exist some codification leading to standardization had to come about. Other cataloging codes have also recognized this truth. Cooperation and standardization in cataloging rules since the turn of this century have depended upon the efforts of the American Library Association and the Library of Congress. The role of the Library of Congress has increased in importance throughout the period.

This increasing influence had its start in 1901, when the Library of Congress began to sell its cataloging services to other libraries. While Cutter's rules, too, had been the basis of the code used by LC, these rules by themselves did not long suffice and LC entered actively into the work of making the 1908 code by contributing the services of an LC staff member, J.C.M. Hanson, to be the code's editor. Hanson was not the last LC staff member to contribute this service to a national cataloging code. Seymour Lubetzky and C. Sumner Spalding will long be remembered for the talents they lent to the latest code. Both the 1908 code and the 1967 code indicate methods by which the library of Congress's policy influences that of other libraries.

From 1908-1930, the 1908 rules were interpreted and expanded by the Library of Congress. This was done without the participation of ALA.

During that period, two supplementary guides were issued which reflected the descriptive cataloging policy of the Library of Congress in relation to serials. Each was issued in several editions and formed something of a manual, rather than a code of rules to express the policies of the Library of Congress to other libraries. These were Mary W. MacNair's *Guide to the Cataloging of Periodicals*[83] and Harriet Wheeler Pierson's *Guide to the Cataloguing of the Serial Publications of Societies and Institutions.*[84] Later cataloging rules acknowledged the influence of these manuals.

After 1930, ALA and LC cooperated on code revisions for the influence of LC's decisions could no longer be ignored. Certainly we are today much more deeply involved with the necessity to consider LC's decisions than we ever have been before. And Lucile M. Morsch indicates that in the future we may have to accept LC's decisions for new and revised cataloging rules much as we did from 1908-1930.[85] As has become obvious, the role of the Library of Congress has become increasingly important in the area of cataloging including serial cataloging policies as well as in developing catalog codes and providing cataloging copy.

"Cooperative cataloging resulting in printed cards has always emphasized the analyzing of serial publications."[86] stated the 1944 *Cooperative Cataloging Manual.* The history of such aspects of cooperation had dated back to the 1880s with cooperative efforts initiated by the ALA Publishing Section. Beginning in 1900, the U.S. Department of Agriculture Library distributed its analytic cards for its departmental serial publication without charge to agricultural colleges and experiment stations.

Even after LC began to supply its cards to subscribing libraries, the Publishing Board (a change in name) continued publishing and distributing catalog cards for a considerable number of serials and sets; this continued until 1919. At that time, "H. W. Wilson offered to take over the indexing of these publications and incorporate it in the *Reader's Guide Supplement.*"[87]

As mentioned earlier, a *Cooperative Cataloging Manual* had become necessary by 1944, to achieve uniformity in certain details of cataloging practices in regard especially to entry.

When Title IIC of the Higher Education Act of 1965 produced shared cataloging as part of its plans (related only to monographs), it too de-emphasized the role of descriptive cataloging of the book itself by accepting that from the national bibliographies while still holding it necessary to establish headings (all direct points of access, in fact). However, although this is likely to eventually cause the end of most cooperative cataloging, we cannot de-emphasize the effect cooperative cataloging has had on rules.

Shared cataloging has, like many cooperative programs either aligned or non-aligned with the national programs, benefited monographic cataloging more than serial cataloging. Even some of our cooperative tools include only selected cataloging helps for serials. The post-1956 *National Union Catalog (NUC)* includes serials represented by LC printed cards but not those of other libraries. Serials first published in 1950 or later are listed in the *New Serial Titles (NST),* "to which bibliography the user is referred."[88]

Therefore, since the cooperative cataloging copy for serial publications for the nation seems to depend, for newer titles, upon LC, it has become imperative for LC to get this cataloging information to other libraries of the country as soon as possible. In the past, this has worked better for monographs than it has for serials because of LC's policy of waiting until a serial was bound rather than cataloging it from the first issue. In some cases this delayed cataloging for years. Not only did this impede the cataloging copy's reaching *NUC* but it also seems to have had an effect upon the form of entry in *New Serial Titles*. While the Descriptive Catalog Division prepared entries for *NUC* until May 1968, entries for *NST* were prepared either by the Serial Record Division or by contributing libraries. Although the Descriptive Cataloging Division had issued rules for supplying entries to *NST*, entries established earlier did not always correspond to those which were later established by the Descriptive Cataloging Division.[89]

In May 1968, the serials cataloging activities of LC were consolidated. The serials section of the Descriptive Cataloging Division was transferred to the Serial Record Division. In the processing department's *Cataloging Service Bulletin* Number 83, dated September 1968, it was announced that many English-language periodical-type serials were being cataloged from the first issue received rather than from the first bound volume.[90] (By the spring 1969 issue of *Library Resources & Technical Services* it was indicated that this had extended to "English, Germanic, Romance, Slavic, and Far Eastern Language periodical-type serials."[91] The September 1968 memo indicated that the practice would be extended to all English-language serials and eventually to all serials of this type as rapidly as possible. The conclusion made in the memo was obvious: "This should mean that catalog cards for periodicals will gradually become available in many cases years before they would have been available in the past."[92] In the cursory survey that I have recently been making of currently received proofslips, it has been gratifying to note the number of 1969 dates which now appear in the holdings statements of periodical catalog entries. This could not have been a reality without a realization by LC of the need to change its policy to help the other libraries of the nation. There should also be an appreciable effect in *NST* and result in the establishment of entries more consistent with cataloging practice in *NUC* and on LC printed cards.

It must be recalled at this point that the Catalog Code Revision Committee had requested that the Library of Congress continue cataloging under the latest title for serials which had changed title. This was done in the belief that there needed to be represented in one place, *NUC*, the complete history of a serial (or a complete a history as LC's holdings would allow). Even though the local library might itself use successive title cataloging, it was felt this full information under latest title would be a help to them. Since no other library's entries for newly cataloged serials are in *NUC*, only LC could perform this service. What the Committee does not seem to have realized is that it is quite likely this decision, because of availability of prepared cataloging copy and printed cards under the latest title, would perpetuate the practice as it has existed in the past and impede the change to successive title cataloging. So while the rules prefer successive title cataloging, the national cataloging service follows the policy of entry under latest title.

With the announcement in September 1968 of the new policy in regard to more immediate cataloging copy for serials, came another one bearing not quite such good tidings. It announced that the recataloging and reprinting of cards to reflect changes in serials will be discontinued except if LC is able to recatalog titles that have ceased publication. Such changes as occur would, however, continue to be announced in the "Changes in Serials" section of *New Serial Titles*. The Library of Congress would make interim entries for the serials with such changes in its own catalogs. However, since these entries would not include the bibliographical detail called for by the cataloging rules, they would not meet the LC's standard for publication and cards would not, therefore, be printed for sale.

The best laid plans of Catalog Code Revision Committee members have seemingly gone amiss as far as finding a "neat" entry in *NUC* is concerned. Although *NST* will reveal the changes as they occur, this may not be quite the same kind of data as might be found in a catalog entry and one's search must be structured between two tools instead of one. The interim entries seem in essence to amount to successive title cataloging but these entries will, of course, be reflected only in LC's card catalogs.

A letter from William J. Welsh, director of the processing department, dated September 5, 1969, further explains: "When entries are closed, when changes are relatively easy to determine and describe, or when, for other reasons, it seems wise or necessary to do so, the Library of Congress will, as in the past, print or reprint a card giving all of the changes undergone by a particular serial. The entries on those printed cards will be under the latest title."[93]

Hopefully from these several administrative changes at LC, we can expect more cataloging help in the future than we have had in the past for at least *new* titles of serials, but the problems of differences in entry for retrospective cataloging will undoubtedly persist. *The National Union Catalog, Pre-1956 Imprints* includes in its introduction an explanation of the problems it has encountered with serial entries.[94] Again some of these come because some libraries have followed successive title cataloging while others have not.

HOPES FOR "GETTING IT . . . " IN THE FUTURE

The September 5, 1969, letter from William J. Welsh mentioned earlier indicated that "the Library of Congress is planning to put serial information into the MARC data bank in the future."[93] *Serials; A MARC Format* was issued as a working document by the Library of Congress Information Systems Office in August 1969.[95] It should be understood that MARC II is a communications format and as such is a standard for *communication* of records on magnetic tape and not a standardization of bibliographical records for local files. The MARC format is based on the more general USA Standard for a Format for Bibliographic Information Interchange on Magnetic Tape.[96] There is no intent in either format for defining the content of individual records. Rather, these are attempts to define a generalized structure which can be used to transmit records on magnetic tape between systems. MARC does not, therefore, solve the problem ·of *standardization of records*. It has, of course, been the popular sport of the past decade to pass all local problems to the mythical "in-basket" of one's brain labeled "Waiting for solutions until the computer arrives." Many fears about the computer are unfounded; dreams of its potential do not "automatically" become realities without some sort of help from the human components. As Donald V. Black and Earl A. Farley have reminded us, "It is rather important for all of us who are interested in, and working at, library automation to recognize that a library, either now or of the future, is not made up of individual displays, computers, facts, librarians, books, etc., but a combination of these."[97] It's not too early to start preparing for the days that lie ahead when things *will* change. To paraphrase Charley Brown's Lucy, "Good heavens, I should hope so!" Certainly many of our problems today come from physical and external elements as from the linear mode by which we display our holdings in catalogs. C.D. Gull explains it this way: "Many cataloging decisions in the past have been based on the necessity of economy in the creation, operation and maintenance of large dictionary catalogs. The introduction of the computer into cataloging has reduced the need for this kind of economy and will permit greater attention to the needs of users of the catalogs and indexes by allowing an increase in the number of access points with increased depth of indexing."[98]

There we are—back once more to that user! No doubt in our changing world, he will require both uniformity and flexibility from the records of the future. In the past we have thought of uniformity and flexibility as being almost diametrically opposing goals—can we perhaps in the future live in "the best of two worlds?" Stanley D. Truelson, Jr., writes that needs for local adaptations are "not merely an illusion of perfectionist members of the library profession" but are "sometimes a genuine need, and means must exist to meet it."[99]

> What is required, therefore, is a feedback method whereby essential corrections to the standard record may be proposed by any user, reviewed by a coordinator of some kind, and acted upon when appropriate in order to give all users the benefit of the needed changes. In the national on-line computerized system which we may have in the future, such updating should be fairly painless. But, for the present, it is very difficult to erase the entry in published catalog or printed card and notify all who used the earlier version of the changes. This is one reason why advances in computer storage and distribution of cataloging data are important—indeed, essential—to the solution of the major problem of descriptive cataloging, our present inability to obtain and use a standard cataloging record which is satisfactory. The fact that computers may soon tackle this storage and distribution job, including updating where needed, is the bright ray of hope ahead in this field.[100]

In this paper we have been thinking about the attempt of serial cataloging to· provide means for "Getting it if you want it without labor, without difficulty, without confusion." Evolving toward the goal has required years of searching for theory and cooperation, neither of which has yet been fully attained although a number of codes and programs have aimed for that goal. Perhaps Michael Gorman has given us a reason why the goal has never been attained in the past. He indicated that the use made of the catalog, which is the most vital aspect of cataloging theory and practice, remains largely unexamined. "Until the aim of catalogue construction has been clearly stated on the basis of objective and accurate surveys of catalogue use, all cataloging theory will remain unscientific and open to doubt."[101] Perhaps studies now underway and those promised for the future will help us scientifically approach this problem. If so, then, perhaps we really will, by the end of the century, witness the library able to, as Frederick G. Kilgour suggests, "organize the information it contains of interest to a particular user for use by that particular user"[102] and at the same time serve as part of an international network. Then the goal of "Getting it if you want it" for all kinds of works will have become more of a reality than it is today.

There is little we can do about the past but to learn from it. The present calls for renewed efforts to work *toward* the goals of the future. The future promises to provide an interesting time for all of us if we seize upon the potentialities that lie ahead. "May you live in interesting times" is said to be an old Chinese curse. For us it may be a twentieth century privilege. The best of interesting times for "getting it if you want it without labor, without difficulty, without confusion" seems yet to be, but certainly most of those who may be privileged to bring it about may not be able to do so "without some labor, difficulty and confusion." Those responsible for these changes will not only live *in*, but participate *in* interesting times!

References

1. Quoted in: Vickery, B. J. *On Retrieval System Theory.* 2d ed. London, Butterworths, 1968, p. xi.

2. Quoted in: Shera, Jesse. "Bibliographic Organization," *Wilson Library Bulletin,* 40:703, April 1966.

3. Slamecka, Vladimir, and Taube, Mortimer. "Theoretical Principles of Information Organization in Librarianship." *In* Don R. Swanson, ed., *The Intellectual Foundations of Library Education; The Twenty-Ninth Annual Conference of the Graduate Library School, July 6-8, 1964* (University of Chicago Studies in Library Science). Chicago, University of Chicago Press, [1965], p. 67.

4. Clapp, Verner W. "The Role of Bibliographic Organization in Contemporary Civilization." *In* Jesse H. Shera and Margaret E. Egan, eds., *Bibliographic Organization; Papers Presented before the Fifteenth Annual Conference of the Graduate Library School, July 24-29, 1950* (University of Chicago Studies in Library Science). Chicago, University of Chicago Press, [1951], p. 20.

5. Naudé, Gabriel. *Advice on Establishing a Library.* Berkeley, University of California Press, 1950, p. 63.

6. *Ibid.,* p. 64.

7. Lubetzky, Seymour. *Principles of Cataloging; Final Report.* Los Angeles, Institute of Library Research, University of California, 1969, p. 2.

8. *Ibid.,* pp. 2-3.

9. *Ibid.,* p. 3.

10. Huang, Theodore S. "JCC/LRTS 1948-1964: One Man's View," *Library Resources & Technical Services,* 11:16, Winter 1967.

11. International Conference on Cataloguing Principles, Paris, 1961. *Report.* A. H. Chaplin and Dorothy Anderson, eds. London, International Federation of Library Associations, 1963, pp. 91-96.

12. Judge, P.J. "The User-System Interface Today: National and International Information Systems." *In* Symposium on Communication in Science: Documentation and Automation, London, 1966. *Communication in Science: Documentation and Automation.* Anthony de Reuck and Julie Knight, eds. London, Churchill, 1967, pp. 37-38.

13. Parker, Edwin B. "The User's Place in an Information System." *American Documentation,* 17:26, Jan. 1966.

14. Ennis, Philip H. "The Study of the Use and Users of Recorded Knowledge." *In* Don R. Swanson, ed., *op. cit.,* p. 26.

15. Lipetz, Ben-Ami. "A Quantitative Study of Catalog Use." *In* Dewey Carroll, ed., *Proceedings of the 1969 Clinic on Library Applications of Data Processing.* Urbana, University of Illinois Graduate School of Library Science, 1969, p. 47.

16. Lipetz, Ben-Ami, and Stangl, Peter. "User Clues in Initiating Searches in a Large Library Catalog." American Society for Information Science. *Proceedings,* 5:137, Oct. 20-24, 1968.

17. Lipetz, "A Quantitative Study of Catalog Use," *op. cit.,* p. 48.

18. Shera, Jesse H. and Egan, Margaret E. *The Classified Catalog; Basic Principles and Practices.* Chicago, ALA, 1956, p. 3.

19. Butler, Pierce. "The Bibliographical Function of the Library," *Journal of Cataloging and Classification,* 9:7, March 1953.

20. Davinson, D. E. *Periodicals; A Manual of Practice for Librarians* (A Grafton Book). London, A. Deutsch, [1964], p. 11.

21. *Ibid.,* p. 13.

22. Osborn, Andrew D. *Serial Publications, Their Place and Treatment in Libraries.* Chicago, ALA, 1955, p. 284.

23. Huff, William H. "A Summary of Some Serial Activities, 1942-1966," *Library Resources & Technical Services,* 11:316, Summer 1967.

24. Dougherty, Richard M., *et al. Policies and Programs Designed to Improve Cooperation and Coordination among Technical Service Operating Units* (University of Illinois Graduate School of Library Science Occasional Paper No. 86). Urbana, University of Illinois Graduate School of Library Science, 1967, p. 17.

25. Huff, *op. cit.,* p. 302.

26. *Ibid.,* p. 319.

27. Davinson, *op. cit.*, p. 13.

28. Mohrhardt, Foster E. "Introduction," *Library Trends*, 16:303, Jan. 1968.

29. Pizer, Irwin H., *et al.* "Mechanization of Library Procedures in the Medium-sized Medical Library: I. The Serial Record," *Medical Library Association Bulletin*, 51:315, July 1963.

30. Harman, Marian. "Policies for Analyzing Monograph Series; University Libraries," *Serial Slants*, 4:130, July 1953.

31. Daily, Jay E. "Analytics." *In* Allen Kent and Harold Lancour, eds., *Encyclopedia of Library and Information Science*. Vol. 1, New York, M. Dekker, 1968, p. 394.

32. Löhmann, Otto. "The Subject-cataloguing of the Contents of Periodicals as a Task of Comprehensive Libraries," *Libri*, 17:95, 1967.

33. Desmond, Robert D. "1968: A Summary Treatment of the Year in Serials," *Library Resources & Technical Services*, 13:389, Summer 1969.

34. Clapp, Verner W. *The Future of the Research Library* (Phineas L. Windsor Series in Librarianship, No. 8). Urbana, University of Illinois Press, 1964, p. 61.

35. McLuhan, Herbert Marshall and Fiore, Quentin. *The Medium is the Massage.* New York, Random House, 1967, p. 63.

36. Williams, Gordon. "The Librarian's Role in the Development of Library Book Collections." *In* Don R. Swanson, ed., *op. cit.*, pp. 89-90.

37. Shera and Egan, *op. cit.*, p. 9.

38. British Museum. *The Catalogue of Printed Books in the British Museum.* Vol. 1. London, Printed by order of the Trustees, 1841, p. ix.

39. British Museum. Dept. of Printed Books. *General Catalogue of Printed Books.* Ten-Year Supplement, 1956-1965 Vol. 1. London, Trustees of the British Museum, 1968, col. 908.

40. *Ibid.*, Vol. 35, col. 585.

41. Brooks, Benedict and Kilgour, Frederick G. "Catalog Subject Searches in the Yale Medical Library," *College & Research Libraries*, 25:487, Nov. 1964.

42. Jewett, Charles C. *On the Construction of Catalogues of Libraries, and of a General Catalogue; And Their Publication by Means of Separate, Stereotyped Titles.* 2d ed. Washington, D.C., Smithsonian Institution, 1852, p. 14.

43. Strout, Ruth French. "The Development of the Catalog and Cataloging Codes." *In* Ruth French Strout, ed., *Toward a Better Cataloging Code; Papers Presented before the Twenty-First Annual Conference of the Graduate Library School of the University of Chicago, June 13-15, 1956* (University of Chicago Studies in Library Science). Chicago, University of Chicago, Graduate Library School, Library Conference, [1957], p. 21.

44. Ranz, Jim. *The Printed Book Catalogue in American Libraries: 1723-1900* (ACRL Monograph No. 26). Chicago, ALA, 1964, p. 55.

45. Cutter, Charles A. *Rules for a Dictionary Catalog.* 4th ed. Washington, D.C., U.S.G.P.O., 1904; republished by the Library Association, London, 1948, p. 12.

46. Lubetzky, *op. cit.*, p. 98.

47. Richmond, Phylis A. "Reviews [of Susan Artandi's *An Introduction to Computers in Information Science*]," *Library Resources & Technical Services,* 13:303, Spring 1969.

48. International Conference on Cataloguing Principles, Paris, 1961. *Report, op. cit.*, pp. 91-92.

49. *Anglo-American Cataloging Rules.* Prepared by the American Library Association, the Library of Congress, the Library Association, and the Canadian Library Association. C. Sumner Spalding, ed. Chicago, ALA, 1967, p. 5.

50. *Ibid.*, pp. 9-10.

51. *Ibid.*, pp. 20-23.

52. *Ibid.*, p. 9, fn. 2.

53. Gorman, Michael. *A Study of the Rules for Entry and Heading in the Anglo-American Cataloguing Rules, 1967 (British Text).* London, Library Association, 1968, p. 6.

54. Lubetzky, *op. cit.*, p. 29.

55. Chaplin, A. Hugh. *Trandition and Principle in Library Cataloguing* (Bertha Bassam Lecture in Librarianship, No. 1, 1966). Toronto, University of Toronto School of Library Science, 1968, p. 17.

56. Price, Derek J. de Solla. "Communication in Science: The Ends—Philosophy and Forecast." *In* de Reuck and Knights, eds., *Communication in Science: Documentation and Automation, op. cit.*, p. 199.

57. *Anglo-American Cataloging Rules, op. cit.*, p. 20.

58. *Ibid.*, p. 10.

59. *Ibid.*, p. 11, fn. 4.

60. Lubetzky, *op. cit.*, p. 41.

61. *Anglo-American Cataloging Rules, op. cit.*, pp. 20-21.

62. Lubetzky, *op. cit.*, p. 42.

63. *Anglo-American Cataloging Rules, op. cit.*, p. 22.

64. Cutter, *op. cit.*, p. 62.

65. *British Union-Catalogue of Periodicals; New Periodical Titles.* London, Butterworths, 1964, p. 1.

66. Friedman, Joan and Jeffreys, Alan. *Cataloguing and Classification in British University Libraries: A Survey of Practices and Procedures.* Sheffield, Postgraduate School of Librarianship, Sheffield University, 1967, pp. 20-21.

67. *Anglo-American Cataloging Rules, op. cit.*, p. 22, fn. 12.

68. *Ibid.*, pp. 22-23.

69. International Conference on Cataloguing Principles, Paris, 1961. *Report, op. cit.*, p. 96.

70. Lubetzky, *op. cit.*, p. 43.

71. Field, F. Bernice. "Serial Entry." *In* Institute on Cataloging Code Revision, Stanford University, 1958. *Working Papers.* Stanford, Calif., 1958. III-1-26.

72. Dunkin, Paul S. "Problems in the Cataloging of Serial Publications." *In* International Conference on Cataloguing Principles, Paris, 1961. *Report, op. cit.*, pp. 191-98.

73. Cutter, *op. cit.*, p. 41.

74. *Anglo-American Cataloging Rules, op. cit.*, p. 3.

75. *Ibid.*, p. 141, fn. 26.

76. *Ibid.*, pp. 3-4.

77. U.S. Library of Congress. Processing Dept. *Cataloging Service Bulletin*, no. 79, Jan. 1967, p. 1.

78. Gorman, *op. cit.*, p. 18.

79. *Ibid.*, p. 14.

80. Cutter, *op. cit.*, pp. 59-60.

81. *Anglo-American Cataloging Rules, op. cit.*, p. 2.

82. Richmond, Phylis A. "Reviews [of *the Brasenose Conference on the Automation of Libraries.* London, Mansell, 1967]," *Library Resources & Technical Services*, 13:147, Winter 1969.

83. U.S. Library of Congress, Catalog Division. *Guide to the Cataloging of Periodicals.* Prepared by Mary Wilson MacNair. 3d ed. Washington, D.C., U.S.G.P.O., 1941.

84. U.S. Library of Congress. Catalog Division. *Guide to the Cataloguing of the Serial Publications of Societies and Institutions.* Harriet Wheeler Pierson, compiler and ed. 2d ed. Washington, D.C., U.S.G.P.O., 1938.

85. Morsch, Lucile M. "An Incubus and a Hindrance," *Library Resources & Technical Services.* 11:409-14, Fall 1967.

86. U.S. Library of Congress. Descriptive Cataloging Division. *Cooperative Cataloging Manual, for the Use of Contributing Libraries.* Washington, D.C., U.S.G.P.O., 1944, p. 10.

87. *Ibid.*, p. 6.

88. *The National Union Catalog; A Cumulative Author List Representing Library of Congress Printed Cards and Titles Reported by Other American Libraries. 1968.* Vol. 1, Washington, D.C., Library of Congress, 1969, p. vi.

89. Kuhlman, A.F. "The Consumer Survey of New Serial Titles," *Library Resources & Technical Services*, 11:138-44, Spring 1967.

90. U.S. Library of Congress. Processing Dept. *Cataloging Service Bulletin*, no. 83, Sept. 1968, p. 3.

91. Welsh, William J. "The Processing Department of the Library of Congress in 1968." *Library Resources & Technical Services*, 13:185, Spring 1969.

92. U.S. Library of Congress. Processing Dept. *Cataloging Service Bulletin, op. cit.*, p. 3.

93. Letter from William J. Welsh, Director, Processing Dept., Library of Congress, dated Sept. 5, 1969.

94. Dewton, Johannes L. "Introduction to the National Union Catalog, Pre-1956 Imprints." In *The National Union Catalog, Pre-1956 Imprints; A Cumulative Author List Representing Library of Congress Printed Cards and Titles Reported by Other American Libraries.* Vol. 1, London, Mansell, 1968, p. xiv.

95. U.S. Library of Congress. Information Systems Office. *Serials; A MARC Format; Working Document.* Washington, D.C., Library of Congress, 1969.

96. "USA Standard for a Format for Bibliographic Information Interchange on Magnetic Tape," *Journal of Library Automation,* 2:53-65, June 1969.

97. Black, Donald V. and Farley, Earl A. "Library Automation." *In* Carlos A. Cuadra, ed., *Annual Review of Information Science and Technology.* Vol. 1. New York, Interscience Publishers, 1967, p. 297.

98. Gull, C. D. "Convergence toward Common Standards in Machine-Readable Cataloging," *Medical Library Association Bulletin.* 57:34, Jan. 1969.

99. Truelson, Stanley D., Jr. "The Need to Standardize Descriptive Cataloging," *Medical Library Association Bulletin,* 57:24, Jan. 1969.

100. *Ibid.,* pp. 24-25.

101. Gorman, *op. cit.,* pp. 66-67.

102. Kilgour, Frederick G. "Computerization: The Advent of Humanization in the College Library," *Library Trends,* 18:33, July 1969.

Additional References

A.L.A. Catalog Rules, Author and Title Entries. Prepared by the Catalog Code Revision Committee of the American Library Association with the Collaboration of a Committee of the [British] Library Association. Preliminary American 2d ed. Chicago, ALA, 1941.

American Library Association. Division of Cataloging and Classification. *A.L.A. Cataloging Rules for Author and Title Entries.* 2d ed. Clara Beetle, ed. Chicago, ALA, 1949.

Catalog Rules: Author and Title Entries. Compiled by Committees of the American Library Association and the [British] Library Association. American ed. Boston, ALA, Publishing Board, 1908.

Cataloging Rules of the American Library Association and the Library of Congress. (Additions and changes, 1949-58). Washington, D.C., Library of Congress, 1959.

Coward, R. E. "The United Kingdom MARC Record Service." *In* Seminar on the Organization and Handling of Bibliographic Records by Computer, Newcastle-Upon-Tyne, 1967. *Organization and Handling of Bibliographic Records by Computer.* Nigel S. M. Cox and Michael W. Grose, eds. Hamden, Conn. Archon Books, 1967, pp. 105-17.

Curran, Ann T. and Avram, Henriette D. *The Identification of Data Elements in Bibliographic Records.* Final Report of the Special Project of Data Elements for the Subcommittee on Machine Input Records (SC-2) of the Sectional Committee on Library Work and Documentation (Z-39) of the United States of America Standards Institute, 1967.

Dunkin, Paul S. *Cataloging U.S.A.* Chicago, ALA, 1969.

Institute on Cataloging Code Revision, Stanford University, 1958. *Working Papers.* Stanford, Calif., 1958.

Jolliffe, J. W., *et al.* "Why Libraries Differ–and Need They?" *In* Seminar on the Organization and Handling of Bibliographic Records by Computer, Newcastle-Upon-Tyne, 1967. *Organization and Handling . . . , op. cit.,* pp. 62-68.

Kuncaitis, Yadwiga. *Union Catalogs and Bibliographic Centers; A State-of-the-Art Review.* Prepared for the State Library of Ohio. Columbus, State Library of Ohio, 1968.

Lubetzky, Seymour. *Cataloging Rules and Principles; A Critique of the A.L.A. Rules for Entry and a Proposed Design for their Revision.* Prepared for the Board on Cataloging Policy and Research of A.L.A. Division of Cataloging and Classification. Washington, D.C., Library of Congress, Processing Department, 1953.

Piercy, Esther J. "Policies for Analyzing Monograph Series; Public Libraries," *Serial Slants,* 4:135-40, July 1953.

Quartz, Beatrice M. "Policies for Analyzing Monograph Series; College Libraries," *Serial Slants,* 4:124-28, July 1953.

U.S. Library of Congress. Descriptive Cataloging Division. *Rules for Descriptive Cataloging in the Library of Congress.* Washington, D.C., U.S.G.P.O., Library of Congress, 1949.

James Orr
Hertzberg-New Method, Inc.
Jacksonville, Illinois

LIBRARY BINDING

In analyzing and evaluating binding methods today, as well as projecting and forcasting for the future, let us first focus our attention on some of the significant changes and developments taking place in the industry. Within the last decade, mechanization and technological advancements have made impressive gains in updating library binding. All indications are that this is just the beginning, and that we are moving into an era of accelerated automation and development.

Prior to this time, of course, steady progress was realized in binding technology, but it was in far more moderate degrees than what is being experienced now. The sewing machine formerly constituted one of the main mechanized functions, and could probably be considered the most sophisticated operation in the over-all binding process. Other essential but less complex machinery consisted of stamping and type setting equipment, cutting machines, semi-automatic rounding and backing equipment and book presses. These devices usually encompassed the full spectrum in a modern library binding operation.

The reason mechanization was relatively slow in being introduced to the binding industry can be attributed mainly to the many detailed and intricate operations that are necessary in the normal binding process. There are unique differences between library binding and job or edition binding where giant runs of new issues of the same size and format are handled. In binding books, periodicals, newspapers, monographs and pamphlets, the binder seldom sees two sizes alike; instead he sees a conglomeration of different sizes, shapes and formats. By and large in binding for the library we are working with individual titles and the condition of the volumes received can vary anywhere from extremely good to extremely poor; usually however, volumes sent for binding

90

and restoration are sent because they are in poor condition. Every volume must be checked page by page in the collation process to insure completeness, and torn and frayed pages must be mended with great care and precision. Close inspection must be made in checking for adequate margins, as well as condition and texture of paper. This will determine how the volume is sewed and if it can be trimmed. If there is an adequate margin on the binding edge, and the paper is durable and in reasonably good condition, the volume will be oversewed. If the volume has a narrow margin and the signatures are intact, tape or through sewing will apply. Through sewing allows a very flat opening, and for this reason many art and music books are sewed this way. Volumes consisting of single sheets can be sewed in this manner, but it is necessary to make folds or signatures first.

Another way to sew volumes with single sheets is by hand oversewing. Also, in preliminary binding preparation full page spreads, maps, graphs and irregular size insertions must be set out and hinged. Adequate stubbing and fill-outs are inserted to compensate for irregularities in the thickness and format. Extremely brittle or dried out pages are laminated.

Special and specific individual library instructions must be followed on all orders. Periodicals have far more detailed instructions than books. For example, in just the one operation of handling ads and covers, there are a number of variations. Some libraries want ads and covers bound in, others want them removed. Some libraries request the front cover only be bound in each issue, or that the front cover only be bound in the first issue, or the last cover only be bound in the last issue. In handling supplements the library might want them bound in place, bound in back; or bound separately. Then too, periodicals must be bound in conformance with the library's established patterns so that the newly-bound volume will match the bound sets already on the library shelves. For this reason it is imperative to keep very detailed and specific records on binding color, trim size, collation arrangement, lettering and lettering alignment for every periodical title that each individual library binds.

The aforementioned operations and instructions are just some of the normal everyday procedures that a library binder performs; from this can easily be seen that binding does not have the most ideal conditions for applying automation and mechanization. However, with the proliferation of serial publications and printed material of all kinds, it was inevitable that changes would and must take place in library binding. Change it did, and new machines specifically engineered and designed for binding for libraries are making their debut at an unprecedented rate.

Now there are machines which uniformly and evenly grind off the old back or spine of the book or periodical. The depth of the grind can be carefully regulated and controlled so that only the bare minimum margin is removed. Machines are now available that will fold and press endsheets and cut off excess sewing thread all in one operation. New rounding and backing machines round and back a book all in one operation, virtually eliminating some of the older antiquated hand methods and semi-automatic machines that were much in use in recent years.

The success and achievement of most of this new equipment results from the fact that it can readily adjust to all sizes without any special adjustments or handling. Stamping machines are available that work on much the same principal as the typewriter, thus eliminating some costly type set-up and stamping time. In our plant we have adapted intertype and lineotype machines to automatically set type from a punched tape. Not only is this faster, but it also provides greater accuracy. We also have automatic machines that apply backlining very securely to all sizes of volumes in a precision operation. The old hand method of pasting a book into its case is giving way to new machines that can do this at the rate of eight books per minute. Putting books in press between boards is being replaced by new automatic presses which can handle any size volume without adjusting for size and which require only seconds compared to the hours needed the old way.

In the not too distant future a completely new sewing machine which was developed by the library technology project, and promises to be one of the big innovations of our time, will make its appearance. It will use less margin in sewing, and allow very flexible free opening. The sewing pattern is cleat-like in design, and provides considerable over-all strength and durability.

Also, in the offing is a book sizing computer which by means of a sensing device will instantly read the length, width and thickness of the volume to be bound. This data will be shown in lighted figures on the machine itself, and in addition will provide a printout on tape to accompany the volume through the binding process. Board, end papers, and cover stock can be selected in as little as three seconds, about twenty times faster than previously possible.

In addition to the above innovations, we must not lose sight of the new adhesives, polyvinal resins and polyesters that are making a major contribution in providing great strength, durability, and speeding up handling and processing. Adhesives hold the key to many new developments. From our own experience where we have actually bound millions of paperback books with adhesive, and backed each volume with a two-year or fifty circulation guarantee, the results have proved extremely gratifying. Polyester film has unlimited possibilities, its capabilities and full potential seem indeed promising. New book cloths, buckram and cover material are also being introduced.

In the light of new and improved machines, methods and materials, we felt greater achievements were now possible. Having had long experience in serving many of the large university and college libraries throughout the country, we found ourselves performing basic binding operations with many minor variations. We also found that these minor variations are a large contributing factor to higher cost for both the library and binder. In view of this we set out to see what could be done to modernize and streamline our methods. The bulk of our work for universities and colleges is with serials. In analyzing the variations that we encountered in binding serials, we found three categories: collation, lettering and lettering alignment.

We decided to establish one standard way to provide uniformity in lettering, lettering alignment and collation that would be acceptable to all libraries. We named this program H.N.M. Standard Binding. The basic fundamentals are as follows: first, a lettering alignment scale was designed, and lettering positions were assigned and correlated to the height of the volume. By doing this consistently, unformity could be assured in lettering the title, volume, month, year, and all other pertinent information that must appear on the spine of the periodical. For simplified instructions and record keeping, each position on the lettering increment scale is identified with a number. The periodical title is assigned a master code number, usually consisting of four digits. Concise binding recordkeeping and preparation are now possible by the use of this simple numerical system of identification.

The bindery furnishes the library with a standard 3 by 5 inch card for every periodical title that is bound. The card contains the master title number, typewritten periodical title, and the number noting the stamping location and position for each title word. With this data, there is no longer a need for sample volumes, patterns, rub-offs, or sample backs. The library simply fills out the binding ticket by writing in the master title code number, thus eliminating the need for filling out detailed binding tickets. The libraries have the complete binding records with all of the necessary binding data and information in their possession at all times. Libraries have also found that processing time is greatly reduced, and new binding personnel can be trained considerably faster and with greater efficiency than previously.

All standardly bound journals are lettered in white, which provides clear sharp legibility and is compatible with other colors. There is a standard collation arrangement, and all ads and covers are bound in. Our standard binding is also compatible with the computer; the data and information on our standard cards can be transmitted to the computer. Binding sequence can be identified, and preprinted binding tickets can be produced when journals are scheduled for binding.

When we first introduced standard binding, it was presented to only one or two libraries at a time so that changes could be made if any problems occurred. A few problems did develop that caused a few changes, but all in all the program functioned very well and was enthusiastically received by the libraries using it. Our standard binding was made available to everyone.

Up to now I have discussed only the advantages offered through standardization. Of course there have been disadvantages that have occurred, mainly a break in the traditional binding pattern when the initial switch-over takes place. Also, some libraries contend that binding volumes complete, ads and covers in, make the volume too thick. Actually the initial break in pattern styles is usually minor in appearance; the library still selects the binding color which makes the pattern change less noticeable than might be anticipated. In regard to the added thickness created by leaving ads and covers in, most journals contain only a small portion of full-page ads that can be removed. In many cases ads may be considered pertinent to the text since they do represent a history of the times.

In the past and in many cases today, a binder might find himself binding one periodical ten different ways for ten different libraries. One library might request insignificant minor differences because they are traditional with that library. Other libraries simply feel they must hold to an established pattern and style because it is important to the aesthetics of the library. Binders of course are always anxious to respond and meet the customers demands, and have been concerned that suggested changes or alterations could have adverse effects on their business. In our experience we have found the opposite to be true.

In conjunction with the new technological improvements at our disposal, binders now have greater freedom in developing and exploiting new types of binding. This has come about through the new performance standards. The new standards allow binders to use the most suitable materials available. They are now free to experiment, and are not held tightly to specifications for material. In other words it is not how the volume is held together, but rather how well it holds together. In this way if a new and more durable method of binding is developed, it should be possible to use the method immediately. The development of these standards had been a joint effort of the American Library Association and the Special Libraries Association. The standards undoubtedly can and will be improved and augmented in the years ahead. Through joint efforts of cooperation on the part of both libraries and binders, significant new improvements should be the end result.

William T Henderson
Binding Librarian
University of Illinois, Urbana

BINDING—A LIBRARIAN'S VIEW

There are two valid reasons for binding serials: preservation and convenience. Other reasons may be given or may be apparent at times, such as the prestige derived from a complete bound run of a particular title, or inertia which allows continued binding of unneeded materials rather than weeding out copies and titles no longer within the scope of a collection. In most of the larger libraries there probably are examples of binding for both of these reasons, and others also; but, for the most part, the majority of our serials are working stock, not show stock, and they must earn their care and space. Most of what is bound is done so in order to preserve it for future use and to make it more convenient for present use.

By preservation I really mean two things; and, although I was taught that one should not use a word in its own definition, I really must use the word preservation again in defining it here. We must simultaneously preserve materials on two levels or fronts. On the one hand I mean preservation in the sense of keeping or saving from harm, but in its second and more specific meaning, I would like to link preservation to the word permanent as it is used by the paper chemists and book conservators. Permanent paper is paper which is so chemically constituted that it will retain the major part of its original strength and other attributes over a long period of time—300 years or more. Papers with this capability are made of well-purified cellulose fibers held in a solution which is nearly neutral or slightly alkaline, which tests very near a pH of 7 on the chemists' scale for measuring acidity or alkalinity. Paper of this kind will last a long time, especially when it contains small amounts of a mild alkaline compound which will buffer acid compounds deriving from the atmosphere, ink or other sources. Materials printed on such papers must be bound to take advantage of this.

But it is not enough to make paper which can last for 300 or more years. Permanent paper is not necessarily capable of withstanding mechanical action any more than non-permanent paper. We can wear out any paper unless it is protected from unneeded and heedless wear and this gets us back to the regular meaning of preservation. One of the differences between permanent and non-permanent paper is that after a period of time permanent paper can still take normal use or withstand normal folding and manipulation while non-permanent paper can take normal wear and tear for only a comparatively short time, after which it becomes weak and brittle. This is why we have so much unbindable, and potentially unbindable, material on our shelves. The chief cause of the problem is the use of chemicals in the manufacture of the paper which either are acidic or become acidic in time and thus break down the cellulose fibers causing weakness and eventual decomposition. Because of this link between the chemical and physical qualities, papers expected to survive for long periods of time usually are described by a compounding of the adjectives permanent and durable, so that they are described as permanent/durable with one of these terms on either side of the diagonal.

Binding in order to preserve materials for use in the distant future must recognize this combination and purposely aim at protecting both the chemical and physical qualities of paper. This is why I wish to link the ideas of preservation and permanence, for we must bind in such a way that we do not undo what the papermaker did in making paper permanent. We must not introduce materials from which acid can migrate into non-acid paper and weaken it. Binding must be a true preservation practice.

In much the same way, I would like to link the protection side of binding to the idea of durability in paper. Binding must do those things which foster the continuing physical strength of paper. This is the traditional role of a binding. The binding is there to absorb or buffer the physical beating which books take as they are read, shelved, dropped, hauled on back seats or floors of cars and on the carriers of motorcycles, caught in sprinkles of rain, used as props for doors and windows and all the other things, normal and otherwise, which may and do occur to the volumes in our collections.

In terms of binding then, preservation has two interrelated levels. Binding must preserve the chemical qualities of paper which make it permanent and it must protect it from all kinds of wear and tear from the outside in order that the paper of the contents can serve its purpose as the carrier of the printed word.

Since I have been involved in binding, I have become an ever more enthusiastic proponent of the doctrine that binding is the first line in the adequate protection and preservation of our collections. This is both because of what I have learned about paper permanence and durability from the publications of William J. Barrow and others who have been teaching us and leading us in this direction, and also because of what I have seen.

In the binding division, in addition to the current unbound serials and new paperback books which stream in by the thousands, we see a smaller but constant stream of older, used, and worn volumes which are sent for rebinding. We find among these, of course, many which were printed on paper which has not proved to be permanent. These we have to cope with, to salvage, to handle as best we can. We even give up on some of them. But there are others which come to us for rebinding which were printed on paper which has proved to be at least somewhat permanent in that it still is strong enough to be able to take normal use. The most outstanding of these, I think—the ones which show best what binding can do in a difficult situation—are those which come from the University of Illinois Chemistry Library. Atmospheric pollution, especially that traceable to sulphur compounds, has long been considered a major cause of deterioration of bindings and paper, and Noyes Chemistry Laboratory which has housed the Chemistry Library and major elements of the Chemistry and Chemical Engineering Departments has for many years contained one of the most polluted atmospheres, at least as measured by the human nose and eyes. My own experience with its foul smell and nose and eye burning capacity goes back twenty-two years to the days when I sat in its auditorium for lectures in freshman chemistry courses. Out of this library, which was air-conditioned only about five years ago, come some serials which were bound many years ago in which the contents are still sound, but which need rebinding now primarily because the outer cover has worn out. Careful examination shows a little more evidence of chemical penetration and discoloration, apparently from the atmosphere, along the upper edges of pages than is found on the fore edges and tails: but this is generally not especially serious. The binding margins and sewing, a very critical area for us, show none of this. Page by page examination of the contents shows, on a few pages, some spattering of chemicals which apparently happened as pieces were in use in a laboratory. The greatest wear is evident in the cases which are typically faded and worn to shreds along the backs with very apparent evidence of heavy handling by hands typically covered by perspiration and traces of accumulated chemicals. The buckram, or its remains, in the hinge area is frequently about as strong as a badly worn, but favorite old shirt, which gives way on a sticky, humid day. These bindings have served their purpose, and served it quite well. The volumes they protected so well are easily rebound for us on the old sewing and returned to use.

In contrast are those older materials which have not been so protected. They come from many places—backfiles of serials put together by used book dealers, incomplete volumes left on the shelf for years in the hope of their being completed, duplicates dredged up from another library's basement or attic, or a similar private repository. Some have kept well and are easily bound. Others are bindable if special mending and sewing are used. Others are not bindable.

If protection and preservation alone could be our aim, binding might carry with it less emotional impact than it does, since then the problems of uniformity of color and lettering might be less important than they are. If binding had only to provide the proper environment for the paper of the contents and prevent the mechanical damage inherent in any use of library materials, then ideally materials would be tested routinely and deacidification and buffering of the paper in those needing it could be done on an inexpensive and mass production basis so that their chemical balance and permanence would be assured. We could then build bindings of a nature suitable to enhance their long usefulness. Such a binding could be plain, sturdy, of a standard design and color, identical from piece to piece and title to title except for size, which would have to be adjusted to each volume.

Since the binder must provide for cover color and lettering, he can, and must, relate his knowledge of paper chemistry to binding practices in order to improve on what he is doing. I want to try to do this now with the *Standard for Library Binding*[1] of the Library Binding Institute (LBI) because this is the basic standard behind much of the binding done for American libraries, the so-called class A library binding. There is a great deal to be said for binding under this standard. As it has evolved over the years, it has provided libraries with a basic document on which to base binding programs and it also has provided a point of departure in formulating varying specifications which have been useful in particular situations, and it, of course, provides a basis for bindings which are standard in many respects even though they are not necessarily uniform, especially in appearance. Bindings fabricated according to its provisions are strong, durable and capable of taking a great deal of wear and tear.

This standard has been criticized both constructively and destructively from time to time on a number of counts. Most of the constructive criticism is summed up quite well in the little publication entitled *Development of Performance Standards for Library Binding, Phase I*[2] issued by the Library Technology Project in 1961. Other good critiques appear in the journal literature (see Additional References).

One aspect of it, not discussed to my knowledge to any degree anywhere in the literature, is the consideration of the relationship of the pH of paper and other binding components to the ability of bindings to perform as desired and needed. The edition published in 1958 contained provisions relating to the pH of two of three classes of acceptable cover fabrics. These fabrics were pyroxylin-impregnated buckram and pyroxylin-coated drill, which is a lighter weight fabric than buckram. The statement regarding pH was the same for each fabric and reads as follows: "The pH value, as determined by standard methods, shall be not less than 6.5 and not more than 7.5, but in the case of 'acid dyes' it shall be not less than 6.0."[3]

The edition issued in 1963 reduced the number of fabrics permitted for use to one, pyroxylin-impregnated buckram, and included the same statement regarding pH which was in the earlier edition.[4] However, in copies of the 1963 edition of the standard—which was revised in 1965—the section describing cover materials is quite different in content from its counterpart in the unrevised 1963 edition, and includes no mention of pH or of acceptable degrees of acidity or basicity for binding cloth.

This means the disappearance of the only pH requirement which we have had on an industry- or library-wide basis. Its occurrence at this time is a cause for alarm, for the last decade has been a time of growing awareness and knowledge of the importance of pH and paper permanence. The person best known and most responsible for this was William J. Barrow. He did not discover acid paper or its cure or its prevention, but he did confirm the work of others. Furthermore, he was successful with the aid of the Council on

Library Resources, in explaining it to the library world. We have been treated to a succession of definitive reports from his laboratory, reports which have been both widely distributed and widely discussed in the profession.

I do not know why this apparently backward step in the evolution of library bindings was made, but it has extended even further than the changes in the LBI Standard. In March 1967, the University of Illinois Library at Urbana-Champaign received from the National Bureau of Standards copies of a proposed revision of the commercial standard for book cloths, including buckrams and impregnated fabrics, with a form letter inviting our comments upon the revision and a blank form for recording our reaction.[5] We compared the revised standard with our then current specifications and noted a variety of differences–including the absence of any pH requirement. In a note included on our response sheet we questioned this omission and pointed out the importance of the pH factor. From Mamie Hardy, Technical Standards Coordinator, Product Standards Section, Office of Engineering Standards Services of the Bureau of Standards, came a reply.[6] She described the deletion in the 1965 version of the 1963 edition and indicated that she had taken up the matter of pH with a representative of the general services administration who had indicated to her that, while pH was of importance with paper, it was not important with binding fabrics.

Our present specifications contain nothing about pH. However, we have been discussing with the binder the possibility of instituting the use of acid-free end papers in our bindings. Our interest in this was renewed at the 1969 Conference of the Graduate Library School of the University of Chicago which dealt with the permanence and durability of library materials, and the portents are that we shall indeed have permanent/durable end papers in the near future.

A consideration of binding standards is not complete today without inclusion of the "Provisional Minimum Performance Standards for Binding Used in Libraries"[7] introduced in 1966 by the Library Technology Project. This standard is still new and neither binders nor librarians have much experience in using it. By design it is intended not to limit its users to particular materials or techniques, but to leave them free to design bindings to perform in a particular way or to fulfill particular needs. This standard puts us in a position of having to decide what we want a binding to do.

If our concern with permanence and durability, preservation and protection, acid versus alkaline papers, strengths and weaknesses of binding standards and the decisions to be made in formulating binding specifications seem to have carried us out of the library into the laboratories of chemists and physicists, I can only warn that these next paragraphs will not necessarily return us to the familiar.

If we take seriously the American library's traditional policy of attempting to serve the needs of library users, to render practical services first and worry about other matters later, then we have but one answer to the question, "For whose convenience do we bind serials, or any printed material in a library?" If we take the usual answer to this question seriously and assume that the reader's convenience is paramount, then the best way of serving him, in so far as most serial material is concerned, would be to have each article in our holdings available separately from all the others. Such a single article approach would preclude the unhappy situation which arises when a bound volume is out to a patron and is badly needed by another for a different part of the contents. It would also prevent the absence of the whole volume for binding at the very time its contents are probably most useful and most sought after. There is nothing really very new or novel in the idea of issuing separate articles. Were it new, we would probably call them mini-monographs in this mini-minded time in history; but they have long been known as pamphlets. It is my understanding of the history of publishing that the difficulties in economically disseminating such separate short writings resolved themselves in the magazine format. The rise of science and technology with their need for the timely short article to report new observations and developments undoubtedly helped hasten the growth of serials together with the complex of auxiliaries for their use—i.e., indexing services, abstracts, union lists, etc.—which are familiar to us and which we accept as a part of the working apparatus as much as we do serials. It is perhaps ironic that many of these aids to serial use are also serials.

Further, librarians, aided and abetted by the publishers of serials who issue title pages, contents sheets, and indexes which give their magazines much of the appearance of books, have bound them up so they look even more like books. The use of titles, subtitles, series designations, volume numbers, dates, parts, pages, and other bits of information on the spines add to this illusion even though they are there as aids to the user hunting the issue containing the article or articles he is interested in finding. This is an oversimplified sketch of the way we arrived where we are today, saying and thinking that we are serving the needs of our patrons. But is it not more nearly true that we bind for two groups of users? There are the patrons, whose interest is in finding the information they need. They do not care for the most part, about the completeness of the library's file of a title, or its condition, so long as they find what they need.

Then there are library staff. They use serials too; and, although there are exceptions, most of their use is aimed at making materials available to other users. These are the people who are responsible for and who care for the collections.

Binding has been and continues to be one of the chief techniques a library staff uses to keep serials together in a logical and usable order as well as the chief technique used to keep them intact and to protect them from damage. We have learned, some of us to our sorrow, that it is sometimes best to deprive users temporarily of materials while they are away for binding in order to assure that they will be available over a longer period.

From the point of view of most librarians, the single article approach is not very practical. Most libraries and most library staffs are inundated with materials as it is, and the thought of trying to manage collections in the form of countless separate articles with all the record keeping, all the problems of organizing, filing and shelving which would accrue have simply been too much to contemplate. These factors have worked against our taking magazines apart just as they brought magazines into being in the first place.

Now that I have played the advocate for both sides of this question, you may have guessed that my sympathy is divided. We have not given the reader what he really wants; and, until the copying machine came along, it was not possible to do so in any practical way. We now have some of the best of both worlds. With the machines at hand in many libraries, and with affluent readers willing to pour their nickles and dimes into the coin boxes, many are obtaining their own copies of articles, chapters, and even whole publications; and libraries still have the comparative security of their bound volumes. The machines have brought with them their own type of wear and tear on the volumes from which copying is done. I take this as additional evidence that we need greater variety and flexibility in our binding specifications in order to obtain volumes which actually do meet our needs.

What one may think of the convenience aspect of serial binding may depend upon whether or not one is in the role of library patron or in the role of librarian. The convenience of the reader is probably best served by what was termed the single article approach. This, however, is not and has not been a very practical approach for library staffs, whose personnel are responsible for maintaining collections in usable condition. There is continual tension in this area, which the copying machine may be resolving to the advantage of both sides.

These two reasons, or sets of conditions, are the focus of the work of serials binding. Where are we going? What are the new developments in the field? What can we look forward to in the future? These and other questions related to them are our next consideration.

We should see two things occurring with regard to binding specifications. First, we shall begin to include in our local adaptation of the LBI Standard provisions aimed at assuring the permanence of the materials used in bindings. As it now stands, this standard assures the use of materials which initially are durable, and it will not be especially difficult to include provisions for bringing the pH of some of the components, notably end papers, boards and inlay paper within the recommended pH range because acid free, permanent papers and paper products are on the market. This availability will increase. Glues which fall within the recommended pH range should not be too difficult to specify either. But back lining cloth, thread, and binding fabrics, including buckram, may present more difficulty. This points to the need for a program of research, testing and publication aimed at developing or identifying products of known permanence and durability. To date much of the work of this type has been oriented to other library needs and has produced paper and paper products including catalog card stock, acid free kraft paper for use in envelopes for archival storage and similar stock for use in archival file folders, as well as permanent/durable paper for printing. Some work was done on polyvinyl acetate glues by Barrow and was published in *Permanence/Durability and the Book-IV; Polyvinyl Acetate (PVA) Adhesives for Use in Library Bookbinding.*[8] I have not found in the literature work in this area relating to binding cloths, back lining cloths, and thread.

The second thing we should note in the near future are the pioneering use of Library Technology Project performance standards. A number of avenues are open to those of us who wish to experiment in our binding programs. One of these is the use of this standard to serve as the basis for binding serial materials which we presently tend to over-bind in the sense that the probable use of the materials is not going to be great enough to demand the heavy buckram and boards normally used in class A bindings. Some of this material is such that it should be available for moderate or light use for many years; and it seems that this is a good place to start devising lighter and possibly less expensive bindings which at the same time measure up to high standards of permanence and durability.

The open and nonrestrictive nature of the performance standard should make it quite easy to use as basis for bindings of a variety of kinds suited to materials and to libraries with widely varying needs. But the anticipated use levels and anticipated time the materials are to be retained must be clearly understood and stated so that materials with the proper qualities may be selected and used and so that librarians observing them in use will know their capabilities.

Another avenue open under the performance standard is the use of alternate methods of fastening pages together. By this I mean the use of new sewing and gluing techniques. The new Smythe-Cheat sewing machine promises sewn volumes using less margin and giving greater flexibility in opening than does machine oversewing. Likewise, the use of adhesives in perfect or glued bindings which have worked well for a number of years in the binding of paper-backed books, offers much promise. It has not been used extensively in binding serials because the weight of serial volumes and the extensive use of coated papers in them have been too much for the glues available; however, the development of glues which penetrate deeply into paper fibers and at the same time retain their plasticity for many years give promise of overcoming these limitations. The greater ease of opening provided by more flexible sewing and gluing should improve the performance of bindings on copying machines.

That the problem of deterioration of paper is now widely recognized bodes well for the future in the area of paper. We shall see an increase in the use of permanent and durable papers by publishers. Its use to date, however, in periodical publishing has lagged behind that in monograph publishing. This is an area where we can work, both individually and as a profession, to encourage publishers.

Nor is the outlook all bad insofar as the volumes on our shelves are concerned. True, we still have our holdings on papers of unknown quality, too much of which is poor rather than otherwise. However there was much hope evident in the Chicago meeting in the report by Richard Smith of his efforts to develop a practical and economical method for the deacidification of bound materials. A successful basic technique exists. The need now is for the development of equipment to implement Smith's processes on a commercial basis. I can conceive of the emergence within a few years of commercial deacidification services, possibly in conjunction with central processing centers, large jobbers, large library binders, or some combination of these. This would permit both the deacidification of doubtful materials at the time they are received into a library system and also would permit us to screen our collections and work on those parts for which deacidification can assure longer usefulness.

In connection with existing paper stocks, convenient and simple ways of testing paper for the presence of acid and acid causing materials have been developed. These are reported in *Permanence-Durability of the Book-VI; Spot Testing for Unstable Modern Book and Record Papers*[9] issued in 1969 by the W. J. Barrow Research Laboratory. The tests described can be performed readily in a library workroom, office or stack area and require the removal of approximately four square inches of paper from the materials to be tested. There are four tests designed to indicate the presence of groundwood, indicate pH, indicate the presence of alum and indicate the presence of alum-rosin size.

We may in the future see developments which will involve materials and techniques quite different from those presently in use. I anticipate such developments because the greater part of present binding costs are labor charges, and the most logical way to keep binding charges from increasing too rapidly is to decrease the amount of labor required in the fabrication of bindings. The glued bindings now being used on separates are a development along this line, and the performance standard leaves the way open for binders and librarians to experiment with both new methods and new materials.

I will not be surprised if there is not a basic change in the binding case. The construction of cases using boards, buckram and paper applied one to the other, largely by hand, is traditional and expensive. In this era of rapid technological development we may see the introduction of some sort of one piece case which folds around the contents and is attached to them to provide external protection.

These are a few of the things which are under development or which may happen. The ever increasing output of published materials, some hints in the literature of greater ease of access to serials, and increasing numbers of persons interested in using library collections all point to continued heavy use of the materials and to the continuing need for their being kept and maintained in usable and accessible condition.

Running through the literature on binding is a theme with a number of variations, the central idea of which is standardization. This can be traced back many years, at least to the publication by ALA in 1915 of a little handbook entitled *Binding for Libraries*.[10] The LBI Standard is one of the chief products of this movement. I do not want to recount the developments in binding standards, but I do want to indicate how standardization has influenced the binding program of the library of the University of Illinois in Urbana-Champaign, especially in recent years. Our special involvement begins with a speech made by Ernst Hertzberg before the Serials Section of ALA.[11] In this paper, Hertzberg lays the groundwork for all the standardizing in which his firm has taken a lead in the last two decades. He pointed out four areas in the binding process in which standardization would be to the advantage of both libraries and binders. The advantage accruing to libraries would be in lower binding costs and to binders in simplified work procedures.

The four areas were trim size, lettering, collating and color. All had to do primarily with appearance and all were areas where the patterns were almost as numerous as the libraries in a binder's account book. This was the beginning of standardization for Hertzberg. In 1955, at the mid-winter meeting of ALA, Hertzberg's firm asked several of their customers to attend a meeting at which the criterion binding plan was introduced. In this plan, volumes were to be bound as indicated by the binder. Materials and workmanship were in accordance with class A standards; but additional standard procedures adopted included the binding in of all covers and advertisements, prescribed binding color and lettering, and a standard trim size. There were included specific ways of treating indexes, title pages, contents sheets, and supplements, and there was provision for hand sewing when needed. At the beginning the program included fifty titles, but within a year it had grown to seven hundred. At one point the program included approximately one thousand titles, and by 1966 it had dropped back to about five hundred, at which point it remains. This was a proving ground for standardization of features not covered by the LBI Standard.

By 1963 Hertzberg was ready to begin using their broader and more inclusive Standard Lettering Plan within the bindery. This is a program which applies to virtually all serial titles in much the same way Criterion applies to its special list. Fewer features are prescribed by the bindery than in the earlier program, but it does include the binding in of all ads and covers, includes a more or less consistent internal arrangement, a predetermined pattern for stamping lettering, and a uniform trim size. The entry or title, together with codes indicating the type size and placement of stamping on spines, the trim size, and a plate number are embossed on steel addressograph plates. The plate numbers are unique and are used to arrange the plates in sequence alphabetically.

Initially it was planned to sell sets of plates to libraries using the system; however, their expense, weight, the necessity of a machine to use them, and problems in distribution and storage all combined in the eventual provision of card files of impressions of the plates. By late 1965, sets of approximately seventeen thousand cards were ready for distribution to interested customers. The University of Illinois Library (Urbana) decided to adopt the program for the following reasons:

1) it would save time and increase our productivity,
2) it would give us greater consistency in the stamping on finished volumes,
3) in the event of a change of binders we would not be dependent upon rub offs, but on the card file, and
4) it could be incorporated into machine-readable records without difficulty.

We decided that the most practical way for us to use the system, which we early dubbed SLP for Standard Lettering Plan, was to incorporate the binder's card file into our file of binding records which are also maintained on 3 x 5 inch cards filed in shelflist sequence. The problem was getting the alphabetical file of SLP cards matched up with our file in Dewey number order. This involved a rather grand search for call numbers using the library's

Periodical Holdings List, the central serial record, and the main card catalog. We also determined that it would be a useful thing to have a file of the SLP cards remain in alphabetical order to serve as an alphabetical index of the system within the binding division. We stretched the time of searching, typing call numbers, rearranging and filing cards into our binding records over a period of several months, but actually did most of the work in six or eight weeks. During this time we also redesigned our binding ticket to make it suitable for use with the coded plates, and at the end of May 1966, we initiated the new system.

After the first two weeks, the system was working quite well; and after the initial four weeks, I could not have forced the staff back to the old way had I wanted to try. We have now been using the scheme for about three and one half years. On July 1, 1969, we ceased using Criterion and now have all our serials on the Standard Plan. It works well in the ways we thought it would, and it has provided some added bonuses. Not only have we increased productivity, cut errors traceable to our typing, achieved greater consistency in the finished product, and reduced revision time to practically nothing; but also we have found that we can train new staff to use the new system much more rapidly and much more effectively than the old system. Formerly a new binding clerk's training period seemed to take up to six months. Eight weeks now seems to be enough, and a number of clerks have learned enough of the system in much less time to work effectively and efficiently.

References

1. Library Binding Institute. *Standard for Library Binding.* 4th rev. ed. Boston, Library Binding Institute, 1963.
2. *Development of Performance Standards for Library Binding, Phase I* (LTP Publications, No. 2). Chicago, Library Technology Project, ALA, 1961.
3. Library Binding Institute. *Standard for Library Binding.* Boston, Library Binding Institute, 1958, pp. 7-8.
4. Library Binding Institute. *Standard for Library Binding.* 4th rev. ed., *op. cit.* p. 37.
5. "Recommended Revision of CS57-40, Fabrics for Book Covers. TS-113." Feb. 27, 1967. (Processed.)
6. Letter from Mamie Hardy, Technical Standards Coordinator, Project Standards Section, National Bureau of Standards, dated April 11, 1967.
7. American Library Association. Library Technology Project. *Development of Performance Standards for Binding Use in Libraries. Phase II; Report on a Study Conducted by Library Technology Project* (LTP Publications, No. 10). Chicago, Library Technology Project, ALA, 1966, pp. 1-10.
8. W. J. Barrow Research Laboratory. *Permanence/Durability of the Book—IV; Polyvinyl Acetate (PVA) Adhesives for Use in Library Bookbinding.* Richmond, Va., W. J. Barrow Research Laboratory, 1965.

9. W. J. Barrow Research Laboratory. *Permanence/Durability of the Book–VI; Spot Testing for Unstable Modern Book and Record Papers.* Richmond, Va., W. J. Barrow Research Laboratory, 1969.

10. American Library Association. Committee on Bookbinding. *Binding for Libraries* (Library Handbook No. 5). 2d rev. ed. Chicago, ALA Publishing Board, 1915.

11. Hertzberg, Ernst. "The Bindery Industry," *Serial Slants,* 1:10-19, July 1950.

Additional References

American Library Association, Library Technology Project. *Development of Performance Standards for Library Binding, Phase I; Reports of the Survey Team. April 1961* (LTP Publications No. 2). Chicago, Library Technology Project, ALA, 1961.

Bunn, R. M. "Binding of Periodicals in the National Lending Library," *Journal of Documentation,* 18:20-24, March 1962.

Cutter, Charles. "Restoration of Paper Documents and Manuscripts," *College & Research Libraries,* 28:387-97, Nov. 1967.

Grove, Lee E. "Predictability of Permanence in Perfect Library Bindings," *College & Research Libraries,* 22:341-44, Sept. 1961.

Hertzberg-New Method, Inc. *HNM Criterion; List of Titles Available in the New Criterion Standard Binding.* Jacksonville, Illinois, Hertzberg-New Method, Inc., Dec. 1955.

Hertzberg-New Method, Inc. "Presentation of the New Criterion Standardized Periodical Bindings." Edgewater Beach Hotel, Chicago, Illinois, Feb. 1, 1955. (Mimeographed.)

Library Binding Institute. *Library Binding Handbook.* Boston, Library Binding Institute, 1963.

Melcher, Daniel and Shatzkin, Leonard. "Proposed Standards for Library Bindings: What is Strong Enough?" *Publishers' Weekly,* 192:18-20, Dec. 11, 1967.

Osborn, Andrew D. *Serial Publications, Their Place and Treatment in Libraries.* Chicago, ALA, 1955.

Peele, David A. "Bind or Film; Factors in the Decision," *Library Resources & Technical Services,* 8:168-71, Spring 1964.

Roberts, Matt T. "Oversewing and the Problem of Book Preservation in the Research Library," *College & Research Libraries,* 28:17-24, Jan. 1967.

Schick, Frank L. "Bookbinding Problems and Promises: Steps toward a Re-evaluation of Standards," *Library Resources & Technical Services,* 4:131-38, Spring 1960.

Tauber, Maurice F. and associates. *Technical Services in Libraries: Acquisitions, Cataloging, Classification, Binding, Photographic Reproduction, and Circulations Operations* (Columbia University. Studies in Library Service, No. 7). New York, Columbia University Press, 1954.

U. S. National Bureau of Standards. Product Standards Section. *Recommended Revision of CS57-40, Fabrics for Book Covers. T.S.-223.* Feb. 1967. (Processed.)

Virginia State Library. *The Manufacture and Testing of Durable Book Papers, Based upon the Investigations of W. J. Barrow* (Virginia State Library Publications, No. 13). Edited by Randolph W. Church. Richmond, Virginia State Library, 1960.

W. J. Barrow Research Laboratory. *Permanence/Durability of the Book–V; Strength and Other Characteristics of Book Papers 1800-1899.* Richmond, W. J. Barrow Research Laboratory, 1967.

Williams, Gordon R. "The Librarian's Role in the Development of Library Book Collections." *In* Chicago. University of Chicago Graduate Library School. *The Intellectual Foundations of Library Education.* Don R. Swanson, ed. Chicago, University of Chicago Press, 1965, pp. 86-98.

Samuel Lazerow
Chief, Serial Record Division
Library of Congress
Washington, D.C.

SERIAL RECORDS: A MECHANISM FOR CONTROL

Consideration of serials has, to some extent, been pushed aside, allegedly temporarily, as we have struggled for solutions to many other complex library problems. The sheer volume of serial holdings in large research libraries and the enormous resources required to gain control over them have caused administrators to face what sometimes must seem like an intolerable dilemma. They see the need for relieving a deteriorating situation, but they are understandably reluctant to pour funds into what many of them view as a bottomless pit.

At the same time the astronomic rise in the quantity of serial literature in recent years cannot be ignored. Today the reputation of a research library depends on its total holdings, and serials represent a very sizable portion of a research collection. Some major libraries estimate that as much as three-fourths of their holdings are serials, and it has been indicated that in science and technology alone more than 50,000 serials are published currently.[1]

It has always seemed something of a paradox to me that concentrated attention to problems of serials controls has been so long delayed at a time in our history when the scientists who are so dependent on them are more and more active. Librarians have been quick to institute acquisitions arrangements that would insure collection of the scientific and technical publications for which the scientists have clamored. Yet one of the greatest disenchantments of the scientific researcher for a very long time has been the lack of adequate control over serial publications. He has not been timid either about expressing his unhappiness as he has repeatedly asked why librarians have not been more concerned about providing easier access to journals and their contents. Serials, therefore, are very much with us and the problems of their control are not going to vanish.

The principal focus of my remarks concerns the essential matter of a recording mechanism for serial literature—the need for this instrument that enables the librarian to tell the user whether a serial publication is in the collections, whether a particular issue has been received, and where it is located. The serial record is the tool that enables the librarian to add or delete titles, watch for missing issues, prepare holding lists, determine when unbound serials should go to the bindery, respond to requests about serials, follow subscription expirations, institute claims, arrange for exchanges, and insure that issues of the title keep coming.[2]

Librarians have called serial records many things—not all of them complimentary and some not repeatable. A serial record can be defined very simply as a recording device for posting the receipt of incoming serial publications. A serial has been defined by the Library of Congress as "a publication issued in successive parts bearing numerical or chronological designations and intended to be continued indefinitely. Serials include periodicals, newspapers, annuals (reports, yearbooks, etc.), the journals, memoirs, proceedings, transactions, etc., of societies, and numbered monographic series."[3] The National Agricultural Library interprets serials "to include any title issued in parts which is incomplete in the library collection, thus periodicals, annuals, biennials, and even incomplete works-in-parts are considered serials."[4] I am inclined to agree with Osborn's practical definition of a serial as "any item which lends itself to serial treatment in a library."[5]

There are divergent opinions today about the organization of serials activities in a library. In large organizations the serial functions may be grouped together in one department. It has been argued that this type of organization eliminates duplication of recording, simplifies routines, reduces possibilities for error, accelerates production, reduces communication problems, and eliminates departmental bias. On the negative side there are the factors of expense, space requirements, and the overlapping of purely serials functions with non-serial library activities.

In the three U.S. national libraries—and I have been associated with each one—considerable attention has been given at various times to the location issue. On these occasions administrators have had to consider such questions as these: What are the pitfalls to be encountered and to be avoided with respect to centralization? What procedures should be instituted to prevent duplication of posting in the central serial record and the custodial unit? Is the serial record primarily an acquisitions activity or is it a cataloging operation? Is it something in between these? What are the relationships of the record to other activities of the library?

In the national libraries centralization has been the choice. The National Agricultural Library (NAL) has placed the serial recording function with the catalog and records activity; the National Library of Medicine (NLM) placed serial controls in the acquisitions area of its technical services division. The Library of Congress adopted a comprehensive approach in the early 1940s when it established its central serial record as a section of the then accessions division. Archibald MacLeish described this innovation in his 1942 *Annual Report:* "Perhaps the organizational change of greatest long-range effect is the establishment of the Serial Record."[6] In centralizing serials he was responding to one of the central recommendations of a group of advisers known as the "Librarian's Committee," which had been asked to survey operations and recommend improvements. Establishment of a central control over serial literature was a major recommendation of the committee and one of the first to be implemented by the Library.

Since that time the Library has shifted its serial record from divisional to sectional and back to divisional status. Similarly, NAL and NLM today operate their records as independent units. We have all found that staffing and personnel requirements are more easily met in a centralized activity.

While there may be conflicting opinions about location, there is more likely to be agreement on the functions of a serial record. Basically they are:

1. to record serial issues as they are received in the library (preceded, to be sure, by the receiving and sorting routine, a sizeable and complex activity in a large library);

2. to forward or route issues from the central register to various other parts of the library;

3. to provide a serials information service to other library units and to clientele of the library;

4. to prepare the temporary and/or permanent cataloging records for serials; and

5. to place claims with the publisher for missing issues and to take other action necessary to assure completeness of the file.

In my division at the Library of Congress there is a sixth operation—the editing and publishing of *New Serial Titles*, but I shall not discuss this complex activity in this paper. Each of these areas is vital in the control and management of the flow of serials through the library and in the servicing of the literature.

When the Library of Congress began to develop its comprehensive serial record, the functions which this tool was intended to provide were described in the Librarian's *Annual Report* to the Congress for the fiscal year 1942:

> When completed, this record will contain an entry for every serial publication received in the Library, exclusive of the newspapers . . . and all non-serial continuations issued in parts, such as in fascicles or loose-leaf form. The information for each title will include a record of current issues received, a complete record of the holdings, source of publication, the location within the Library of current issues received, information regarding volumes bound, the call number of classified holdings, essential historical notes, such as changes in title or publisher, and billing information.[7]

There have been long and involved discussions and several reorganizations in the years since LC's Serial Record began, but by the late 1940s the Serial Record was firmly established in the Library of Congress as an important part of our bibliographical apparatus.

The development of the record was steady, although there were inconsistencies and gaps and frustrations over the years due to a shortage of dollars and manpower. The lesson of experience has taught that no matter how solid the advance planning, the responsibility can be met only if adequate resources are available.

In the Library of Congress our serial record program is organized roughly around the basic functions already enumerated. Preliminary to the accessioning, of course, is the receiving-sorting activity—an operation that sometimes reaches unmanageable proportions in a large institution. The national libraries have found it expedient to have a variety of ways of grouping material—by language, title, size; color is another possibility.

The basic function of recording incoming serials involves the checking of the title, the noting of changes in titles, as well as the complicated business of tracing successive changes in title in order to make a workable accessioning record. The inconstancy of serials publications constitutes one of the principal problems faced by the staff of any serial record operation. Serials resemble people, and they mirror their activities, sometimes positive, sometimes negative; like people, serials are born, they marry, they multiply, they separate, and they die. The staff must deal with these many varieties of behavior in the daily recording of incoming issues.

This most important work of recording involves much more than the mere posting of receipts into the file. There are the basic steps of searching incoming serials against a record of previous decisions and ascertaining whether the library kept the particular serial, in how many copies, what cataloging treatment was given, how the copies were assigned, etc. The real work is to establish what the serial is and where it goes. Obviously, the serial record must be organized to facilitate in every way possible the primary function of registering issues.

The accessioning function brings up the question of the form of entry to be used—should the serial record entry be a quick and dirty entry for purposes of rapid posting, or should it conform to the cataloging rules practiced by the particular library? A serious discussion is taking place today on this question, with many libraries endorsing the concept of listing the serial in the way in which it will usually be requested.

Format is another matter that must be determined here. It is important to choose a format that will guarantee an optimum posting situation as well as provide a workable claiming mechanism. Routing, cataloging, and retention decisions must be clearly displayed in the record and, if the file is divided by date, provision should be made for easy transfer of holdings information.

This raises the question of file division. Should the serial record list holdings from the first issuance of the title up to the present time or should the record be divided into two parts—a current file and a non-current file? I believe the latter arrangement is preferable. The vast majority of incoming items are current; reference consultations in large files are costly, and it is therefore, important to keep the record uncluttered with old entries not relevant to the piece in hand.

Routing is also a basic function because all service divisions are dependent upon it. There exists in most libraries the need to send journal materials to places other than the custodial unit, as in the case of journals needed for circulation among staff and among resident scientists. This requires the development of a control system over journals in transit, the institution of a simple routing system (pre-prepared slips, perhaps located in the visible file), the indoctrination of personnel in the importance of proper routing, and the prompt return of the literature to the collections. Unless individual serials can be transmitted expeditiously from one location to another, additional copies of a title may have to be acquired, and this of course adds to the cost. It is, therefore, clearly in the interest of the acquisitions librarian as well as the serials reference librarian to cooperate in the solving of routing problems.

One of the principal reasons for the existence of the serial record is the need to have available data with which one can respond to questions about the availability of specific serial issues. These inquiries come in increasing numbers by letter, by telephone, and in person. This past year in the Library of Congress our reference service accelerated to the point where we were required to install additional telephone equipment and special jacks to accommodate it.

The availability of a current, well-maintained serial record in a large research library is invaluable to users of the collections. It eliminates visits to the shelves; it avoids the necessity of searching through unwanted items to find what is desired; and it provides the patron, the cataloger, or the reference librarian with immediate access to information about materials that may be vital to ongoing research investigations.

There has been mention of the growing dependence of the scholar on journal literature. The reference function of the serial record serves this important need. After all, research is valid only if its results are publicly verifiable, and such verification is not possible unless there is convenient and prompt access to the published document. The serial record, through its reference service, assures this accessibility.

The cataloging function is handled in different ways in different institutions. For years the Library of Congress followed the practice of preparing temporary cataloging records in the serial record division, with permanent descriptive cataloging being the assigned function of the descriptive cataloging division.

After several studies and some debate we concluded that there were economies and efficiencies to be realized by combining the two operations, and in 1968, the serials section of the descriptive cataloging division was absorbed administratively into the serial record division. The merger has proved to be wise. Serial record searchers, serial record catalogers, and printed card catalogers (formerly in descriptive cataloging division) have been organized into working teams (by language) so that incoming material can be moved from one person to another with a minimum of duplication of effort. Information is transmitted by the searchers to the catalogers, who then decide upon appropriate entries with a minimum of further searching. A typist assigned to each cataloging team prepares the necessary records. In this way the visible file entry and cross references, the report to *New Serial Titles*, and the information for the printed catalog card are handled in one operation. This group approach has enabled us to move slowly in the direction of preparing printed cards from the first issue of a publication received. We hope that this arrangement will eventually take clerical work away from the catalogers and that our searchers will profit from the supervision of the catalogers in the team structure. Moreover, the close working relationships developed between the different levels of catalogers have permitted more individual training and instruction, and this has accelerated production.

In serial processing much emphasis must be placed not only on efficient checking techniques but also on development of a sound program for claiming replacement copies and issues not supplied. Since librarians have much contact with serial publications, they are quick to realize how important it is for a reseach library today to have complete runs of serials. Incomplete serial sets constitute one of the most serious problems the librarian can face. The number of titles which the *Union List of Serials* indicates as being generally complete in large libraries is pitifully small; the number of full sets in almost any given area is inadequate for research needs.

These gaps in holdings cause many problems—inadequate service, binding delays, and increased cataloging costs. If all serials arrived on schedule there would be no need to develop and maintain a follow-up and claiming activity. But because of the many reasons for non-receipt of current serials, there must be some system for insuring the receipt of all issues due and available before they become out-of-print.

My personal philosophy of the serial record function has always included the belief that one of the essential purposes of a serial record is to facilitate the claiming of missing issues. Indeed the necessity for claiming can be viewed as a major reason for establishing and maintaining a serial record. There are some who maintain that claiming can be done from examination of the shelves and the charge file, but in actual practice this is not practical. It is far more satisfactory to use the checking record as the basis for claims to publishers for specific issues of a current subscription or for claims to dealers for items to fill in gaps in the collections.

Some of the most critical problems concern the dwindling stock of old numbers in the face of growing demand. Exchange of duplicates among libraries has helped to ease this situation to some degree. The *Union List* assists acquisition of older issues by pointing out gaps so that libraries can try to fill them.

The claiming system must be as automatic as possible, ideally with claims entered on the basis of each day's checking, supplemented by periodic and systematic scanning of the full record. Claiming should be carried out as a by-product of the daily posting—this is known as "skipped issue claiming." Of course this method does not take care of the situation in which titles have ceased coming altogether.

It would therefore appear essential to arrange for review of the entire serial file at regular intervals to find overdue items. This however, is costly and time-consuming; in a large record, such as that of one of the national libraries, it would require a full-time claiming crew to assure this thorough review on a regular basis. As a consequence, the claiming function in a large serial record is sometimes on a catch-as-catch-can basis.

There are a number of methods for setting up claiming systems—the use of a variety of colored cards to designate frequencies of publications (all of the cards for each color can then be scanned for delinquent issues at specified times in relation to the frequency); attachment of colored signals to the exposed edge of the checking cards, with each color representing either a frequency of publication or signaling the specific time for searching. Tallman has described in some detail the various ways in which colored signals and other devices can be employed in the claiming procedure.[8]

In large and complex serial records, the conventional practice of writing claims becomes time-consuming and burdensome. My experience with manual files has indicated that use of a camera of the photoclerk family is a far better claiming device. Instead of typing the name and address of the journal and the title and issues desired on a form postal card, it is possible by the photographic system to superimpose the number of the missing issue upon the title and address section of the entry card with a mask bearing a standard message to the dealer. The resulting photoprint then becomes a claim notice that can be slipped into a window envelope and mailed. This photographic procedure raises the production rate (it is possible to do about 120 photoprints an hour) at a fraction of the man-hour cost of the manual method, and the camera, of course, makes no mistakes.

In summary, libraries have a responsibility to see that gaps are filled. In order to assure the completeness and current receipt of all issues, a systematic review of serial record entries should be made at regular intervals, according to some acceptable system. Special forms can expedite the searching and claiming of delinquent issues. Claim post cards or photography can be dispatched quickly and will bring a high percentage of missing items. The result will be more complete and accurate records of serial holdings.

Since serial checking and the other activities involved in serial processing represent a mass operation in large libraries, it is obvious that the choice of equipment must be based on the need to eliminate wasteful effort. In the three national libraries three major types of serial equipment house the national serial records:

1. The blind or vertical file. NAL employs this method which involves the filing of 3 x 5 inch catalog cards in catalog trays. This method has the disadvantage of not allowing the user to view a number of entries simultaneously; he must riffle through a number of cards to locate the item desired. It must be explained, however, that NAL has relied on this method primarily because it set as an objective the photograhic renewal of its record at least every three years.

2. The pure visible file. The Library of Congress follows this method—a method that permits the serial record to do triple duty as a reference tool, a binding record, and an inventory of serial holdings. This equipment is an improvement over the vertical file. It offers an eye-finding system that is quicker for the user than the traditional catalog card file.

3. The vertical-visible file. NLM has adopted this method and, as the name indicates, it combines features of the other two types. This tub-like equipment, which has arrived on the market within the last ten years, offers conveniences in use over the other two types. It is, however, the most costly, and therefore libraries with the pure visible file cannot easily shift to the newer apparatus. Preference for the vertical-visible file is understandable. Entries here are more easily visible, more quickly retrieved, more conveniently extracted and replaced, and more readily expanded.

In recent years there has been interest in the rotary files and in the use of marginal punched cards, but the visible index continues to have the important advantage of being able to accommodate overriding slips. This eliminates the need for frequent retyping of checking records as they become full. In some libraries the rotary files are used to complement the visible files, and Osborn makes the practical suggestion that visible indexes might be used for high-frequency serials and motorized rotary files for low-frequency serials.[5]

Like everything else, recording serial data is going to be affected by automation. There is not time here to go into any detail even about punched card possibilities. Magnetic recording drums with random access have already made some of our current equipment look antiquated, and technical advancements in the decade ahead will certainly bring new equipment ideas that will merit experimentation if the prices are not prohibitive and if cooperative serials programs can be extended.

PROBLEMS

The continuing information explosion, the necessity of constantly changing entries, and the uneven receipt of some titles are among the major problems faced by the serial record administrator. Since libraries of even moderate size face a constant arrearage problem, it is easy to understand the difficulties which large institutions encounter when they attempt to avoid backlogs of unrecorded serials.

To cope with an arrearage that appeared likely to grow to unmanageable size because of staff shortages and rapid staff turnover in the face of rising serial receipts, the Library of Congress mounted a special drive to eliminate its arrearage of unrecorded serials. A combination of techniques was employed: sorting procedures were simplified; special categories were designated to assure rapid separation of masses of incoming pieces; alphabetizing breakdowns were made as easy as possible; production goals were established; and progress reports at set intervals were required. Daily analyses of work records identified progress and pitfalls. An evening shift comprised mostly of university students expedited production. On June 30, 1969, we were able to report "no arrearage" for the third consecutive year—a million and a half serial pieces received and a million and a half pieces processed. Nevertheless, arrearages are a constant dread and staff shortages in vital areas a continuing and threatening problem.

The need for regular, systematic claiming has already been mentioned. Again, any delay in establishing a firm program here is contributing to future problems, not only in the serial record itself but in all aspects of service. The longer we wait to claim, the less success we will have in assuring completeness of our serial holdings.

Organizational and administrative problems often confront the librarian. Lack of space, deteriorating, outmoded, or inadequate equipment, duplication of records, overlapping of functions and responsibilities, lack of established guidelines, failure to understand the full mission of the serial record, and, of course the necessary considerations of money and manpower—all these are factors that can contribute to keeping a serial record in what has sometimes been described as a state of magnificent disrepair.

It is necessary also to include among the problems the question that continues to be asked by administrators as they deal with monumental library needs and limited resources—is there really a need for a serial record?

The idea has been advanced from time to time that it is not necessary to have a written record of the serials coming into a library, that if one wishes to discover what is in the library, it is necessary only to go to the shelves or to consult the charge information. Such a practice, it is alleged, saves one step in the process, both from the point of view of labor and time, and expedites access by a patron to the actual materials. This might have some validity in a perfect world where the publisher never loses an address plate; where the post office never loses or sends off to Calcutta an issue of a journal destined for a library; where the perfect ordering process automatically renews, without fail, every serial title that the research library is supposed to receive; or where subscription agents are infallible in placing subscriptions. However, all of us know that this perfect world does not exist, and it would therefore seem necessary to maintain a checking record in order to compensate for customary failings in people and in organizations. This would seem to argue that the major function of a serial record is the claiming function, and I am inclined to believe that this is true.

There are also those who argue that the proper time to record a library's serials holdings is when the volume is completed and gathered for binding; at that time, it is reasoned, the collator can detect any missing items and the item can then be claimed or otherwise acquired to complete the binding. This thinking, however, assumes another aspect of our mythical perfect world where publishers keep issues in stock indefinitely, always available to libraries to complete their holdings. We know this is not the situation, that publishers' overruns are very meager and that stock is exhausted very quickly.

Moreover, the absence of a written record on receipt of a serial issue can complicate service in numerous and embarrassing ways. Suppose in the Library of Congress, for example, there were no current record of incoming titles or issues. When the White House or a member of Congress telephoned seeking an issue of an unusual foreign journal, the absence of a serial recording device would make it necessary for the telephone attendant to search the shelves to ascertain whether the journal was there; if not, the charge record would have to be checked, and if there were an arrearage of unshelved items, this would have to be examined. Even if all of these investigation could be made immediately and the answer was still negative, the validity of the response would be uncertain, especially if the issue in question were the most recent.

The card catalog was once considered to be the place for detailed statements of serial holdings. Today this is considered awkward and expensive, at least for live titles, and it is generally recognized that holdings statements belong in a separate file.

The complexity of serials handling resulting from the expanding number of journals, accompanied by the continuing inflationary costs of maintaining quality controls, has led administrators to look for simpler methods that could assure lower costs. Some have gone so far as to advocate the abandonment of all serial controls prior to full cataloging.

While I recognize, of course, that life in the real world requires some kind of economic accommodation, I am convinced that we must explore avenues of possible savings. There are greater advantages to be gained, for example, from more experimentation with simplified cataloging, wider acceptance of standards, and various shortcuts in sorting and checking processes. If we are to give convincing evidence of leadership in this area, we must be innovative, but total abandonment of conventional controls is not an innovation I would recommend.

Because of the staggering statistics of large serial records and the apprehension that serials librarians inevitably feel as they search for the magic formula to guarantee currency in serial records despite the heavy volume and limited staff and funds, we would be well advised to keep in mind the possible remedies that automation can offer. As Hammer has pointed out in an earlier article, it is unfortunate that "the enormity of a library tends to hinder the development of a machine system,"[10] and this fact slows the entrance of the largest libraries into the computer field. The LC serial record, with its 300,000 entries, is a case in point.

Still, positive steps are being taken by the three national libraries. Phase I of the National Serials Data Project has been completed with the Library of Congress as executive agent. Under this program the Library of Congress developed a draft format for recording serial bibliographic data in digital form. This format has been issued by the Library of Congress as *Serials: A MARC Format.*[11]

The pilot project now being launched by the Association of Research Libraries, under a grant of funds from the National Agricultural Library, represents the next step of the cooperative effort of the three national libraries to build a national data base of serials information. Our objective here is to produce a union list of the live scientific and technical serials held by the three national libraries and to provide data about the characteristics of serials and the effectiveness of various techniques for handling serial information. Policy guidance is being given by the U. S. National Libraries Task Force on Automation and Other Cooperative Services, with support from the Council on Library Resources. The experience to be gained with live science serials promises to be of value to serials librarians as they work toward eventual expansion of a national data base to encompass serials in other disciplines.

Serial networks have been under discussion for over a decade. As Osborn commented in 1955, "The greatest development which can be anticipated in public service is of course the introduction of television facsimile reproduction machines. The day will surely come when the libraries of the country are linked up in a vast network of these machines ... when library networks are established serials will represent their principal commodity ... [and] cooperative programs of collecting, listing, and servicing [serials] will have to be developed on a large scale."[12]

Perhaps one of the most significant benefits to come from the computer age will be the heightened importance of cooperation in our most costly library activities. Certainly serials stand as a major example here. In the manual serial record we have a prime candidate for computer application. The obstacles to machine processing are also present, however. Old records are distorted by years of varying practices by many hands; incomplete or inaccurate entries have not been changed because there was never enough manpower to devote time to the past; editorial cost estimates are fantastically high; the prospect of operating dual systems for a temporary period after automation is not attractive to library administrators; any savings to be gained from automation appear to be hypothetical rather than real, at least in the foreseeable future.

This editing cost problem and its interference with progress in serials automation is sufficiently critical to justify a serious search for compromises that might offer some promise of a solution. Clearly, we cannot afford to accept a policy of despair and allow our serial records to continue to deteriorate further because of lack of funds to put them in some degree of uniformity and editorial excellence. An imperfect solution, of course, is to put the record data as presently listed in machine-readable form. Proponents of this policy argue that it will cost less to edit the tape from the imperfect machine run than to edit the entries before inputting them. The danger here is that one may overlook the high cost of inputting irregular, inconsistent, erroneous, even useless data that will have to be deleted eventually, and the inevitable duplication of costs in reprogramming and correcting the earlier errors. It would seem more logical to look for some cooperative approach that could assure the proper preparation of entries in one master record. All research libraries could then benefit from the product of the edited record when automated techniques are applied. It must be emphasized, however, that this utopian situation cannot be realized without a broad sharing of costs and responsibilities.

It is because of some of these complexities that we hesitate. Yet the technology is here; many professions are using it. They are doing more work and doing it more quickly; it seems clearly in the interest of sound serials controls to move ahead with a cooperative serials systems effort as quickly as collective resources will permit.

At the same time the manual serial record, the basis for any automated system, must be regarded as a vital target for studies in work simplification, organizational improvements, and functional coordination. It may be costly to change our thinking and our processes, but not nearly as costly in the end as will be apathy or delay.

Serials and serial records are not about to go out of style. What is required today in this serials era is the assignment of a high priority to collective attacks on these controversies and obstacles. One of the hopeful signs is the growing interest of such groups as COSATI, the Council on Library Resources, Inc., the Association of Research Libraries, international bodies such as UNESCO, and the national libraries of the United States. With the endorsement of these groups, librarians will be compelled to press for dynamic serials approaches that will be attuned to today's needs and tomorrow's clientele.

References

1. Downs, Robert B. "Research in Problems of Resources," *Library Trends*, 6:147-59, Oct. 1957.

2. Becker, Joseph. "Automating the Serial Record," *ALA Bulletin*, 58:557-60, June 1964.

3. *Anglo-American Cataloging Rules*. Prepared by the ALA, the Library of Congress, the Library Association, and the Canadian Library Association. Chicago, ALA, 1967, p. 346.

4. Schachtman, Bella E. "Current Serial Records; An Experiment," *College & Research Libraries*, 14:240, July 1953.

5. Osborn, Andrew D. *Serial Publications, Their Place and Treatment in Libraries*. Chicago, ALA, 1955, p. 17.

6. U.S. Library of Congress. *Annual Report of the Librarian of Congress for the Fiscal Year Ending June 30, 1942.* Washington, D.C., Library of Congress, 1943, p. 28.

7. *Ibid.*, pp. 138-39.

8. Tallman, Johanna E. "A Survey of Methods of Claiming Serials," *Serial Slants*, 7:76-85, April 1956.

9. Osborn, Andrew D. "Evaluation of Serial Equipment for Library Purposes," *Serial Slants*, 6:118-22, July 1955.

10. Hammer, Donald P. "Reflections on the Development of an Automated Serials System," *Library Resources & Technical Services*, 9:225, Spring 1965.

11. U.S. Library of Congress. Information Systems Office. *Serials: A MARC Format.* Washington, D.C., Library of Congress, 1969.

12. Osborn, "Evaluation of Serial Equipment for Library Purposes," *op. cit.*, p. 122.

Donald P. Hammer
Head, Libraries System Development
Purdue University Libraries
Lafayette, Indiana

SERIAL PUBLICATIONS IN LARGE LIBRARIES: MACHINE APPLICATIONS

While many areas of library operations can be improved or even radically transformed by automation, the one area that probably stands to gain most, and needs the most help, is serials. It has been well known for ages that the irregularity and inconsistencies of serials can unhinge any librarian, but a new revelation of the automation age is the unhinged computer programmer. It is unfortunate that the irrationality of publishers of serials requires the best efforts of the librarian, the programmer, and the computer to bring some semblance of order to the publishers' bibliographical world. Since we cannot, however, unscramble the publishers, we will have to sacrifice librarians and programmers.

There is not much that the librarian can do about erratically published journals, arbitrarily combined issues, whimsically numbered issues, or capricious title changes. Unfortunately, the computer cannot do much about these things either, but it can keep track of them and maintain order with a little less chaos than the humans have done. Perhaps someday all of the publishers will automate their processes, and then the millennium will have arrived—at least for computer manufacturers. In the meantime, librarians and computer programmers working and communing in the joys of togetherness can do much to develop and to maintain a serials world slightly short of the millennium.

It, too, however, will be chaotic, for in addition to the contributions of serials to the confusion, the computer will add its own. When serials and computers are thrown together the maxim can only be, "If anything can go wrong, it will!" The computer and its operator can contribute to the disorder just as well as the publisher. The computer that refuses to read tape 2, but

120

will happily read tape 1 all over again, the operator who puts the paper in the printer backwards, and the operator who disregards console messages are all examples. All of these contribute to a normal serials atmosphere—a sort of organized chaos. We must conclude, therefore, that the computer will bring us *automated* organized chaos.

In spite of all the problems, however, the computer has long since proven itself to be an instrument of vast potential for library service, and through concentrated effort that potential can be unlocked. Some librarians and some computer people have already expended much effort in the development of automated serials systems, but to date, as fine as many of the efforts are, they, like the computers they use, are only in the horse and buggy stage of automation. What the future holds no one can be sure, but without a doubt much greater sophistication in input methods and in mass data storage will be among the first improvements necessary before the automation of serials can be considered a problem solved.

Very few libraries have developed a major serials automation program and most of those that presently operate machine systems are small libraries. A few important reseach libraries, perhaps half a dozen, have made significant advances in serials automation. The vast majority of libraries are waiting for someone else to solve the problems. While this is understandable, it is not very constructive. The problems of serials, automated or otherwise, require the total effort of the library world and not just that of a few brave and steadfast souls who are strongly motivated toward research. This reluctance to become involved has resulted in very spotty automated serials developments across the country.

Since most publishers cannot or will not make an effort to correct the bibliographical wrongs of their colleagues, perhaps the united efforts of librarians can persuade the recalcitrant and indifferent publishers to accept at least the national standards for periodical format (USASI Z39.1-1967)[1] and the internationally used identifying code, CODEN.[2]

In the meantime, those librarians interested in improving their serials procedures and services will have to continue struggling on their own. Many of them have attempted to alleviate some of the problems through the production of serials book catalogs. These have extended from lists of an individual library's holdings to state-wide union catalogs. Most of the state-wide catalogs have been limited to certain types of libraries, such as academic, medical, etc. A few state union catalogs are exactly that and include all types of libraries. Few, if any, of the book catalogs have actually supplanted previously existing card catalogs. This then means that these libraries are supporting duplicate systems of serials data display and, at least economically, defeating the purpose of the book catalog.

The production of book catalogs ranges in complexity from keypunch-and-print through computer-compiled holdings statements. In quantity of data, they extend from simple title-finding lists to comprehensive catalogs of historical data presented in the tradition of the *Union List of Serials*.

Some libraries have attempted to solve their serials problems in the accounting area. These libraries have set up subscription systems that maintain the budget, produce historical subscription records, and print out renewal lists on demand. Other libraries have courageously squared off with the major dragon and devised check-in systems. These range from simple systems (keypunch a card when an issue arrives) to check-in by cathode ray tube (CRT) consoles (see Figure 1).

Automated serials systems include four main functions: acquisitions and fiscal, check-in, display, and public service. In manual systems, display is considered either as an aspect of check-in or as a public service depending on the library concerned, but in automated systems, display is greatly emphasized because of the special production efforts necessary to create the display device—at the present time, usually a book catalog. Public services will not be discussed; however, this area would include such activities as automatic indexing, selective dissemination of information (SDI), abstracting, KWIC and KWOC indexes, circulation, etc. For our purposes, then, we will be concerned with three of the four main functions: acquisitions and fiscal, check-in, and display.

Figure 1. Cathode Ray Tube Console

When a large library decides to develop an automated serials system, it is essential that the administration understands that it is about to embark on a major expenditure of library resources, both financial and personnel. Hopefully, the administration realizes that the project will be a long-term one—extending over at least several years—and provision should be made accordingly. If the administration is not willing to allot sufficient funds for the methodical and well-organized development of a system, it should not become involved in systems development at all. At most it should choose to mechanize a facet of serials operations that it is willing to finance, and then be satisfied with that. If the administration honestly intends to automate serials operations, the library's needs should be determined and then supported to the fullest extent. Anything less in the end will net failure and embarrassment.

The development of an automated serials system requires extensive planning by trained personnel concerned with that alone. It requires a team of full time, experienced computer programmers supervised by a systems analyst, and, if the library does not have its own equipment, it requires the active interest and support of those who control the machines. In contrast to those fundamental and rather obvious requirements, some library administrations have attempted serials systems development by using their regular serials staff to plan the system and by hiring student programmers to carry out the programming function. Since "slave labor" has been used for both functions, the administrator ends up with a comparatively inexpensive failure.

It seems obvious that the development of a highly technical and intricate system would necessitate the employment of a team of trained and experienced personnel who are assigned solely to that project. In spite of that axiom, more systems fail or fall short of expectations because of inadequate personnel than from any other single factor. The administration simply cannot skimp on these new systems—there is no such thing as fire-sale automation.

For those reasons, an administration that seriously intends to automate serials procedures should expect to hire a professional systems analyst or at least a computer programmer well experienced in analysis. In addition, he should hire a corps of programmers that is large enough so that the loss of one or two members will not impair or wipe out the entire project. One of the most knowledgeable librarians on the staff should be relieved of all other tasks and assigned to the automation project full time to look after the library's interests. He should serve as the liaison between the project personnel and the library staff. He should be deeply involved in all of the system planning and should be sufficiently trained in systems analysis, data processing, and computer programming so that he can communicate with the analyst and programmers and understand their problems and difficulties.

This is the minimum professional personnel needed to successfully complete a serials automation system and anything less than this will result in failure or, with luck, a long drawn out project that spans a period of many years and ends with a mediocre system.

A second important area in which serials systems can easily fall short is that of planning. After creating the planning team which consists of a serials librarian and a systems analyst or at least a good programmer with experience in analysis, the proposed system must be planned. Good planning and documentation can be the difference between success and failure. If there is any chance that the library may want to automate all of its serials routines in the foreseeable future, then a complete system should be planned immediately. The entire system need not be implemented at one time, but the planning should be comprehensive enough so that nothing will be missed that could later necessitate extensive revision of the operating system. As an example, nothing is more disconcerting, to put it mildly, than to set up a check-in system and then later because of poor planning, to realize that no way was provided to determine which set of a certain serial is the subscription and which set is the gift so that the proper claim form can be sent out for missing items.

The planning should include interviews with the supervisors in the serials unit, but, even more important, exhaustive and critical inquiries with the clerical personnel into all of their daily routines must take place. These interviews should be held in a friendly and confidential atmosphere and should be intended to determine as precisely as possible how the various routines are carried out. The word "why" should be the question asked immediately after the "how" is answered. These routines should be documented and flow charted so that the work flow and work loads can be studied. Particular attention needs to be centered on the information necessary to trigger each action as these data will have to be available to the computer so that it can later make the correct decisions necessary to the operation of the machine system. Check-backs should be made frequently with the clerks working in the manual system so that accuracy is insured.

After the systems staff has a thorough understanding of the library's serials routines and of all their ramifications, the planning and the programming of the new system can begin. This usually includes the system flow charts and any necessary documentation, a time schedule for completion of various phases of the project, data preparation instruction manuals, program logic charts, etc. The documentation should be detailed enough so that a trained new person can take over the system development and/or operation completely after no more than a few days or weeks of study, depending on the complexity of the system.

The final major problem area in the adoption of a machine system is that of conversion to the new system. Briefly, this includes decisions on what phase of the new system should be converted first, establishing schedules for the change-over of the various phases, personnel orientation, completion of record conversion, determining operating procedures and completing documentation, parallel operations, etc. All of these factors apply in varying degrees to the installation of an automated serials systems.

Now that the background material concerning the development of a serials system has been briefly discussed, actual systems and their methods of operation can be examined for the major phases of an automated serials system: acquisitions and fiscal, check-in, and display. Each of these will be discussed in some detail and a few of the current methods of operations described.

The acquisitions and fiscal function usually include accounting, subscription renewal, subscription records (historical), and at least some aspects of budget control. In most libraries that have automated fiscal operations at the present time, data input is by punched card or by paper tape, but there are a few libraries that have sophisticated on-line systems, and typewriter or cathode ray tube (CRT) consoles are used. Other libraries use equipment that is off-line, but the data are transcribed directly onto magnetic tape or disc.

There is a large variety of input machines presently available on the market, and although we can discuss only a few of them, we can get a good idea of the types of equipment that are in use in libraries today. An IBM 026 keypunch is the usual method of input and by far the least expensive. When a keypunch is used, the data punched usually must be verified. This error-correcting routine requires an additional machine, a verifier, that resembles the keypunch and requires about the same amount of effort to operate. A variation of the keypunch theme is the IBM 826 typewriter-keypunch. This machine enables a clerk to type an order almost as she would on any typewriter and, as the typing takes place, the keypunch automatically produces the punched cards needed as computer input. For example, when the serial title, order number, and estimated price are typed on the order form, those data are simultaneously punched into cards. The information is then entered into the fiscal system when the cards are read by the computer. A paper tape typewriter is another of the less expensive input methods, but requires access to a computer configuration that includes a paper tape reader. A more sophisticated system of input is that of an IBM 1050 on-line typewriter terminal which enters data immediately and directly into some sort of computer storage. The most sophisticated system is that of a CRT console which operates on-line and is by far the best method for data updating. An additional method for input is the use of tape inscribers such as the Mohawk Data Recorder which, in off-line mode, records data directly onto magnetic tape.

After the data are converted to machine-readable form, the order form must be produced. Again, there are a variety of ways for doing this and they depend on the input method used. As was pointed out before, the IBM 826 typewriter-keypunch produces the order form immediately by typing. If a paper tape typewriter is used, the tape is read by the tape reader and a computer produces the order form, although it, too, can produce the order form by typing as the tape is punched. If a keypunch alone is used, the order form can be produced by reading the punched cards on an IBM 407 accounting machine which will then print the order form, or by reading the punched data on an IBM 870 document writer which will then automatically type the form. In large library situations, the order is produced by reading the card data on a computer and, as a by-product of that input function, having the computer print the order form. The computer printer produces the order form when either the IBM 1050 or the CRT console is used.

In any event, at this point the fiscal data are read into the data file and processing begins. Such data as identification number, title, date of order, estimated price, vendor, fund number, and order number are some of the elements picked up at this time. Later, after the cataloging has been completed and as subscription payments are made, additional data elements are entered into the system. These data make the production of many different kinds of output possible.

The most basic report is the budget statement that records the expenditures, encumbrances, and free balances of the library's various funds. Another primary output is the transaction report that shows each transaction that has taken place in a given fund over a certain period of time. Such a report not only includes obvious transactions, such as new encumbrances, payments, and adjusted free balances, but it also includes changes in allotments, transferals from fund to fund, and error corrections.

The report that is of most use to the serials staff is the subscription historical record. This report includes the complete record of past acitivity for each subscription. It is primarily used to prevent duplicate invoice payments by comparing dealers' or publishers' invoices with the data given on the printout. The important data elements usually supplied by the printout include entry, date of previous payments, amounts, invoice numbers, fund, source, periods of time or items paid for, and special symbols indicating added charges or multi-year payments. The symbol for added charges is included in the data so that in forecasting future costs the computer will add such charges to the year's subscription payments and not regard the added charge itself as a year's subscription. The multi-year payments are flagged as two- or three-year payments so the computer, when forecasting future budgetary needs, will charge the full amount to the correct future year and not handle the payment as an annual one. When determining average annual subscription costs, the computer will divide the multi-year payments by the number of years involved.

This historical data file enables a library to provide many worthwhile informational services. It can forecast future subscription costs based on past price activity. It can provide its branches, departmental libraries, etc., with lists of their subscriptions before renewal time, it can supply summaries of subscription costs by subject area, fund, dealer, etc., and it can produce lists of subscriptions to be renewed, if the library does not place "until forbid" subscriptions. It is obvious then that an automated acquisitions and fiscal system can provide much more than accounting data only and that it can be of great help to the administrator in his daily activity and in his planning.

The second function of a serials automated system is that of check-in. In large libraries operating under a manual system, this function is the one most in danger of hopeless disorder. It is a jumble of senseless complexity and needless frustration. A little forethought on the part of publishers could prevent a tremendous amount of difficulty for libraries and their patrons at no cost to the publishers. A simple and orderly numbering system for a serial can be adopted just as easily as a complicated, inconsistent, or muddle-headed one. A title can usually be changed just as well at the end of a volume as in the middle, and consistency in frequency of issue should not be a difficult goal to achieve. These are things that serials publishers should conform to—even down to the irresponsible and poverty-stricken "little magazines." At least they should *try* to cooperate. Since it is apparent that they will not concern themselves with library problems, libraries will have to cope with the problems themselves. Automation, it appears, is the only answer.

Since the check-in phase is the most difficult of all serials activity to control, many ways have been devised to handle it on a computer. All of them have merit, but some are more meritorious than others.

A good automated check-in system should achieve at least the following goals: 1) provide efficient inexpensive over-all control of serials receipts, 2) provide rapid check-in, 3) provide efficient and dependable retrieval of holdings information, and 4) comprise a simple operating procedure.

No check-in system, including a manual one, can meet all of these requirements. I personally consider the cathode ray tube as the most satisfactory method by far. It is, unfortunately, also the most expensive, but the results gained far surpass those gained from any other system.

Most of the automated check-in systems now operational are based on the arrival card system. This procedure was devised at the University of California at San Diego, La Jolla, in 1961.[3] Under the direction of Melvin Voigt, La Jolla was the first institution to develop a computer-based check-in system. The arrival card system is based on the prediction that a certain issue or volume of a serial will arrive in the library at an approximate date. A Hollerith card is punched by the computer in anticipation of the arrival of the next issue of each serial. (Figure 2A is an example of an arrival card.) As each issue arrives in the library, the correct card is manually pulled from the file, and after machine sorting, it is read by the computer and the record of each serial is updated. At the end of a given period, those cards remaining in the file represent issues expected, but not received. Claim forms can then be typed and mailed to the source from which the serial is received. Systems that are a little more sophisticated will produce the claims automatically when the remainder of the arrival cards are read by the computer. More advanced systems will produce the claims automatically without the use of the remaining cards and will also keep tabs on the activity of each serial so that notification will be made for serials that cease arriving altogether.

A considerable number of by-products can be had from a check-in system. For example, the computer can be programmed so that it will keep a tally of the issues received for each serial that is regularly bound. When a binding volume is complete, a binder's slip can be automatically produced along with a punched card. The slip, of course, is sent to the bindery with the issues, and the card is returned to the computer when the volume is bound so the machine record will be updated accordingly.

A variation on this idea is the system used by the San Francisco Public Library.[4] The binding card is not a punched card in that system, but a computer printed one; therefore, the serials holdings record cannot be updated automatically by returning the card to the computer when the binding routine is completed. Instead the necessary data must be keypunched as a separate operation. Nevertheless, the computer system does produce the signal that notifies the library staff that a particular serial volume is ready for binding. In addition, many instructions and informational notes are printed on the card.

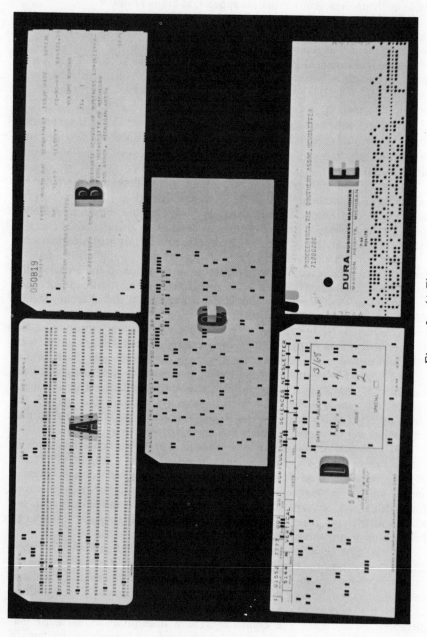

Figure 2.   (A-E).

These cards are then used to retrieve the unbound issues from the library shelves, and the issues are then processed according to the data given on the card.

Other by-products that can be provided by a serials system are routing slips for journals circulated among staff members, receipt notices for staff members who are to be notified when new issues of serials that are of special interest to them arrive in the library, lists by branch or departmental library of serials received within some certain period of time, and lists for the circulation desks of volumes at the bindery.

In spite of its many excellent advantages, the arrival card system has several very important disadvantages. Among these are: 1) the limitations of the arrival card itself, 2) the need for unit record equipment in addition to dependable computer time, 3) the need for constant "nursing" of the control codes used to forecast arrival times and used for other functions, and 4) the human error element which is of even greater significance than in a manual situation. Each of these will be discussed in detail as follows.

When a system is designed, sufficient columns on the card must be provided for "housekeeping" codes and for other necessary data. There are then usually about thirty or thirty-five columns available for entry—not nearly enough for many journal titles and particularly not satisfactory for corporate entries. The entries are, therefore, abbreviated and the check-in clerks are often faced with the problem of correct identification of a card during the check-in procedure. Libraries that have operated this type of system have devised many different ways to eliminate this problem. Some libraries partially solve the problem by using an interpreter that can print multiple lines of data on a card. Other libraries eliminate the entry from the card altogether and provide the serial's identification number in its place. Usually, in such systems, the clerk checks or circles on a printout the issue number of the new arrival and the arrival card is pulled by the identification number at the end of the day. This procedure is now being used at La Jolla in their revised system.[3]

A variation on that theme is used by the San Francisco Public Library through the use of a prenumbered IBM card.[4] In this system, each arrival card has a six digit "I.D." number preprinted and prepunched. (Figure 2B is an example of this type of card.) The cards are continuous form and are bought in numbered batches. The computer associates each serial record in the data bank with one of the card numbers. The number of each record is the only datum punched in the arrival card, but up to 2,000 characters, including the full entry and the expected volume and issue number, can be printed on the card. The cards are arranged alphabetically by entry, and are manually pulled from the file when the corresponding issue arrives in the library. The computer reads only the punched number and then updates the data file according to the volume and/or issue numbers it previously associated with that identification number. If an issue arrives for which no card is present in the file, or if the predicted data are incorrect on a card, a special form is manually filled out and the new or corrected data are later keypunched. The library averages 16 percent of such situations daily, and an average of 204 issues are checked in per day.

Another way to get around the arrival card's limitations is to eliminate that card completely and to use a printout in its place. That, however, is a complete system in its own right and will be discussed later.

A further problem caused by the lack of space on the arrival card is the impossibility to provide the check-in clerks with the improvised instructions and notes that they often record for their own use in a manual check-in file. These items include such things as "informal" cross references, discard instructions, notes concerning odd frequencies, etc. By depriving the clerks of these "crutches" their production can be affected negatively until they find a substitute.

Figure 2C shows an example of a "pseudo-arrival card" that enables the clerks to have any data they want in the system without interfering with its operation. The card contains the I.D. number (not printed on it) or the serial, the entry printed, and the clerk's note printed. The card can then be sorted and merged by machine, but it remains in the arrival file and is never read by the computer. So that it can visibly be distinguished, it is useful to use a colored card. Of course, if the printout system or the prenumbered, prepunched card system is used, this problem does not exist.

The second disadvantage of the arrival card method that was mentioned above, i.e., the need for unit record equipment, forces the large library into rental costs for machines that would probably be used very little unless automated routines in addition to the serials one are run by the library. Arrival card systems usually must have available three unit record machines—a sorter, a collator, and an interpreter, and perhaps a fourth—an IBM 407 accounting machine. Among other things, the sorter is used to sort into various orders the cards representing the serials received on a given day. If an alphabetical list by entry of the day's receipts is wanted or lists of the various departmental or branch libraries' receipts, the arrival card must be sorted accordingly. If such lists are wanted, an IBM 407 is necessary for printing purposes, otherwise that machine is not needed. If sufficient funds are available for daily computer time, the sorter and the 407 are, of course, not necessary at all since their functions can be carried out on a computer.

The collator is used to merge each newly punched group of arrival cards into the arrival file. In small libraries, the entire arrival file can be taken to the machine, thus a machine can be used that is in another location and rented by another department or agency. In libraries with a large active file, this is impossible.

The interpreter prints the information necessary for clerical check-in purposes on the newly punched arrival cards. Because of price changes and varying models, it is difficult to give a cost figure for these machines, but a reasonable total rental figure would range around $800.00 per month—about $500.00 of which is for the 407.

The third disadvantage of the arrival card system is the need for constant "nursing" of the control codes as well as other codes. These codes are not needed in manual systems, but are essential to machine systems. For example, they include codes that represent the many numbering patterns used with serials, codes that symbolize the frequency of serials, codes used to compose holdings statements, and codes used to describe the way in which indexes, title pages, and tables of contents are issued. Such codes can easily number over a hundred. In addition to the usual number of bibliographical changes in serials, the clerks have to cope with the constant changes in codes necessary with a machine system. This problem is not unique with the arrival card operation, but there are other machine systems that permit much easier updating of these housekeeping codes—on-line systems for example.

As far as the fourth arrival card disadvantage—the human error element—there are many more opportunities to "foul up" the operation under an arrival card system than there are otherwise. If only the errors are considered that can be made in the assignment and re-assignment of the internal codes necessary to operate these systems, it is obvious that the error possibilities are fabulous! These codes will be discussed in some detail subsequently.

A method of check-in that is an improvement in many ways over the arrival card procedure is the print-out system. Instead of producing the punched arrival card, the data necessary to perform the check-in function are printed out. The check-in clerk then circles or checks the correct issue number that is printed on the form. At the end of the day, the pertinent data are keypunched, or converted in whatever way is used, and the converted data are read by the computer to up-date the files.

The advantages to this system are many. For example, it eliminates all filing and card sorting; complete information about each serial can be given on the printout, including full entry, dates of past issue arrivals, claim history, etc.; the check-in clerks can write notes on the printout for later punching as problems arise; and cross references can be provided.

On the negative side, it can be argued that in a large library a lot of keypunching and verifying must be done daily. This, however, is not as serious a problem as it may seem if the punching is kept current because only the identification number, the set or copy number, the volume and/or issue number, and some housekeeping codes need be punched for each item. The work involved is no more than is necessary in an on-line mode.

It should be pointed out that this particular problem is solved (depending on the quality of the forecasting) by the La Jolla system of using the arrival card with only the I.D. number printed on it.[3] All the data needed by the computer to update the data record have been previously punched into the arrival card by the computer.

Another means to reduce the amount of daily keypunching that is necessary with the print-out method has been devised by the System Development Corporation. It is a sort of "reverse" scheme. The serials check-in portion of their LISTS system (Library Information System Time-Sharing) uses the print out method for check-in, but the serials listed on the printout are divided into two groups and printed in adjacent columns. One column includes those serials whose arrival can be predicted reasonably well, and the other column includes serials whose arrival cannot be predicted very reliably. The check-in clerk checks the numbers of the issues actually received for both groups, but those issue numbers checked are the input for the *unpredictable* group *only*. In the case of the predictable group, the issue numbers of those *not* received are the input.

This system will require very accurate forecasting for the predictable group of serials. Unless unerring forecasting is done, many claims will be made for items that arrive shortly after the claim is issued. Few serials are so dependable that their absence means they will not soon be received! Another disadvantage to this system is that failure to punch an item in the predictable group will automatically result in the incorrect check-in of that issue since the computer assumes that the numbers not punched have been received.

The system is not yet operational at the time of this writing; therefore, its effectiveness has yet to be proven. The accurate forecasting required has, however, been difficult in all other systems operated to date.

One of the major problems with all of these check-in systems, except for the CRT method, is that they require a rather exact knowledge of the publishing frequency and the numbering system of each serial. It is necessary to possess this information in order to limit the number of arrival cards on hand at any one time (or issue numbers in the case of the check-in printout) by predicting the time of arrival of each issue. Also, the frequency and numbering system needs to be known in order to provide the correct volume and issue numbers of the items expected. In short, the idea is to have the right card at the right place at the right time.

Since predicting anything in serials control is, like the stock market and horse racing, at best a very precarious business, these predictions are frequently wrong. Because of the changeability of serials, the elaborate codes assigned to each serial to identify the frequency and the numbering system must often be corrected. When a CRT is used, no forecasting is necessary because no physical files exist; hence, there is no space problem, and no numbering system codes are needed because the computer will not produce a record showing the next expected issue. The computer will show the issues already received on the CRT, and the check-in clerk will decide what issue should have been received in relation to the information on the screen and the issue at hand. She can then make any necessary changes on the CRT by keying in the correct data.

The codes that are required for arrival card or printout check-in are quite extensive. In the April 1965 issue of *American Documentation,* Bishop, Milner, and Roper published an article[5] that provides among other things, a good insight into some of the problems involved in this forecasting. In that article the authors identified twenty-six different numbering systems used by publishers. There are about the same number of frequency patterns in use. Later, in the October 1969 issue of the same journal, it was announced that through "revision and combination" the numbering systems had been reduced to eighteen different ones.[6] Regardless of which number is correct, assuming either is, the variety and instability of serials numbering patterns makes the operation of any automatic system very difficult.

One of the most used systems of coding frequency patterns is the one developed at Washington University of St. Louis, School of Medicine Library, under the direction of Estelle Brodman.[7] If a serial about to be entered into the system publishes in January, April, July, September, and October, a digit "1" is placed on a form under each of those months. A zero is placed under the remaining months. This then provides a three digit number for each quarter of the year: 100, 100, 101, 100. In order to reduce these codes to a single digit as a space saving measure, the codes are compared with a "Coding Chart" which gives single digit equivalencies for all possible three digit codes. Using the example above, 100 = 4 and 101 = 5. The frequency code which tells the computer to punch an arrival card for each of the above months at the appropriate time then is 4 4 5 4. Variations of this theme are used for weekly, semi-monthly, and other frequencies.

The system used at the New York State Library includes a "lag factor" which is calculated on the lag between the publication date of an issue and the issue's actual arrival date. This method is an attempt to forecast an exact arrival date.

In addition to all of this, the computer must know the code representing the numbering system used by each serial in the file. These are usually simple two digit codes depicting the various systems, such as 01 = volume numbering continuous, issue numbering reverts to 1; 02 = volume numbering and issue numbering continuous; 03 = volume numbering continuous, issue designation by season, etc.

The computer must also know the numbering that it punched into the last arrival card, or printed on the check-in printout, so that it will know what numbering must be provided for the next issue expected. It must also know exactly when to revert to issue number 1 when that is required. There are innumerable other details included in the mechanics of these check-in systems, but this should provide a feeling for the complexities.

Some libraries, in small situations, have adopted a simple method that eliminates all of these problems, but it is not very "automated" and it is satisfactory only in small libraries. Figure 2D shows an arrival card that has all of the necessary information punched into it except the numbering data. These data are written on the card by the check-in clerk when an issue arrives in the library and then are later punched into the card. Large libraries could not very likely afford the time required to write the data on the card and also punch it.

A system that is an interesting variation on this theme is the one used at Miami-Dade Junior College Library, Miami, Florida.[8] At that library, a file of edge-punched cards readable by a paper tape typewriter is maintained. (Figure 2E shows an example of an edge-punched card.) When a new title is entered into the system, a card is automatically punched on the paper tape typewriter as the serial's title and I.D. number are typed on a gummed label. The label is then placed on the card for visual identification and filing purposes.

When a serial issue is checked in, the corresponding card is manually pulled from the file and read by the paper tape typewriter. This action punches the serial entry and I.D. number onto a paper tape. The issue date is then typed by the operator and thereby automatically punched onto the paper tape. The tape is later read by the computer and the data file updated. Since the issue numbering data is supplied after the issue arrives in the library, no forecasting is necessary.

This system is a unique and simple one, and without question does the job well for the small library that designed it. The biggest obvious disadvantage is the manual filing of the punched cards. Usually, the elimination of such files is one of the reasons for automating. The use of paper tape requires special equipment to read it, but on the other hand, it is faster to type on a paper tape typewriter than it is to operate a keypunch and a verifier.

For a small library, or even a medium-sized one, this appears to be an excellent system. It seems to have most aspects of serials control included in it and to be well planned.

A system of check-in that is now operational in a small library, but probably could be used without difficulty in a large situation is the one used at the Pennsylvania State University, Milton S. Hershey Medical Center at Hershey.   This system uses an IBM 1050 typewriter terminal which, for check-in purposes, is off-line, and while off-line produces a punched paper tape. For visual verification purposes hard copy is also produced. As serial issues are received, the check-in clerk types the necessary identification and check-in data on the 1050 keyboard. After visual verification, the clerk directly connects the terminal with the IBM 360/67 computer at the main Pennsylvania State University campus 103 miles from Hershey. The paper tape is then read by a transmitter and the data are transmitted over telephone lines. The clerk calls in the computer programs which update the files and transfer the data to data cell storage. The storage file can also be accessed by the Hershey Medical Library.

This system gains some of the benefits of an on-line operation with something less than the high costs of that mode, and verification is easy since hard copy is supplied. In order to maintain consistently formated holdings statements, however, it would be necessary for the check-in clerk in a large library with many varied serials to go through a look-up process to determine how each holdings statement was formated previously in the system.   Any library considering the adoption of an automated check-in system should, nevertheless, look into this method if the necessary hardware is accessible.

Hopefully, this discussion of the complications and shortcomings of these systems will not scare off librarians. All of these systems except the System Development Corporation one, are being successfully operated today in libraries. In spite of the problems, their advantages over the old manual methods are legion. When well designed, they operate in many ways at an efficiency level previously unknown, and generally they afford control over serials far superior to the old manual systems. In addition, they provide a variety of output methods and formats that the manual procedures cannot even hope to match. It should be kept in mind, however, that all of these methods are steppingstones toward the ultimate serials system. That system cannot exist until librarians and publishers work together to solve serials' bibliographical problems.

The third method of automated check-in available today is that of a cathode ray tube (CRT). Referring back to Figure 1, these consoles resemble a television screen with a typewriter keyboard attached. The use of this equipment increases the efficiency of the entire serials operation because the CRT can be used for all serials procedures, not just check-in. The use of the CRT for input and update serves as an excellent system. An even better system is one that uses the CRT console for input and for public output, but to make sufficient consoles available for staff and patron use would be an expensive operation—although certainly not an innovative one.

When a CRT console is used for check-in, each serial's I.D. number is the key to entrance into the data file. It is necessary to look up the I.D. number in a listings of such numbers. The check-in clerk then keys in the number and the record for the corresponding serial appears on the CRT screen. The clerk can then make whatever changes needed—the addition of an issue or volume number, the changing of a group of issue numbers into a volume number to indicate a bound volume, the changing of a title, the addition of a history note, the correction of a spelling error, the addition of a new record as a new subscription on order, etc. When she is finished entering the data, she visually verifies the record on the screen, and if no errors exist, presses the enter key which returns the record to storage. If errors exist, she immediately corrects them on the CRT screen and then enters the data into storage.

A system much like the one just described is now in operation at Laval University in Quebec. Three IBM 2260 consoles are used, and that library has 15,000 titles and 5,000 cross references operating on the system. It has been operational since June 1968, and according to Rosario de Varennes, Director of Library Automation, has been enthusiastically accepted by the staff.

A CRT is also being used for updating serials data (but not used for check-in purposes) at the University of California at Irvine. The system is called the Serials Graphic Record Management System (SEGREMS), and it was developed under the direction of Herbert Ahn.

If it is possible to get publishers and subcription agencies to cooperate with the library, much of the I.D. number look up can be eliminated in these systems by including the serials I.D. number on the mailing label as part of the library's address. The clerk then can read the number directly off the label and key it in on the console.

Another way to accomplish the same end would be through the use of CODEN.[9] If CODEN were assigned to all serials, and if publishers would follow the lead of the American Chemical Society and print the CODEN prominently on their publications, it could serve the same function.

The CRT system provides many advantages over all other methods. As mentioned before, it is more than a means of check-in—it is a complete data update and maintenance system. It eliminates all card handling, typing, filing, etc. The data is "typed," i.e., keyed in once and all other operations stem from that one input. If consoles are provided in various places throughout the library system, the staff and patrons can determine instantly the up-to-the-minute status of any serial in the collection.

There is one other method of check-in that has been devised, but it has not yet been used as anything other than an experiment. At Los Gatos, California, the IBM Advanced Systems Development Division Laboratory has developed a method of check-in using an IBM 2760 Optical Image Unit. Figure 3 is a picture of a 2760. This machine operates on-line in a conversational mode and provides input data to a computer through the use of a translucent screen and a light-sensitive probe. The screen is composed of 120 designated response points which when touched by the light-pen, i.e., the probe, transmit electrical impulses to the computer. The data that appears on the screen are projected from a sixteen millimeter filmstrip that is contained in a cartridge and is inserted by the operator into a slot on the machine. The filmstrip is moved frame by frame in either direction by instructions from the computer or manually by the operator.

Each filmstrip contains 128 frames usable for data. The filmstrips must be produced using standard animation techniques so that the images will be registered on the film in relation to the response points on the 2760 screen. The filmstrip contains a group of "decision frames" which enable the check-in clerk to "zero-in" on the serial title required and to choose the necessary input format for the numbering system used by that serial. The only data on the filmstrip that directly pertain to each serial included in the check-in system is the title or entry.

If the clerk is checking in volume 9, number 10 or *Jet Age Planning*, she first calls for a "spin index" of title first letters. When this alphabetical index appears on the screen, she touches, with the probe, the first letter or, to narrow the field, the first two letters, of the title or entry—in this case "JE." All titles beginning with the letters "JE" appear on the screen. She then calls for another spin index, and touches the initial letter or letters of the second important word in the entry she intends to update—in this case, "A" or "AG." She continues this process until the title she seeks appears on the screen. She then calls for the decision frame which contains all possible numbering system formats, such as, volume and issue, month and year, season, month-day-year, etc. She touches the format used by the serial to be checked-in and a "keyboard image" type frame appears on the screen. This frame contains the possible numbers or dates needed to check-in the serial concerned. She then completes the check-in by touching on the screen the correct numbers or dates for the issue at hand. If the issue so checked in is not the expected one, a report is automatically typed out on the attached typewriter terminal. The decision to claim or not can be made at a later time.

To date the system has been used only for experimental purposes so its practicality has yet to be proven. It is an interesting technique and certainly a different approach than any of the others. It deserves a trial in a library where it can be studied under fire.

The final serials function that we will discuss is display. This aspect of automated serials control can take several different forms, for example, card catalogs, book catalogs, printouts, on-line terminals, or microforms.

The production of catalog cards by computer is now rather commonplace, although it is done more often for monographs than for serials. Book catalogs and printouts are the usual machine methods used to display serials data by mechanized means. The book catalog has long since proven itself a versatile tool—easily distributed wherever needed, and easily used. If it

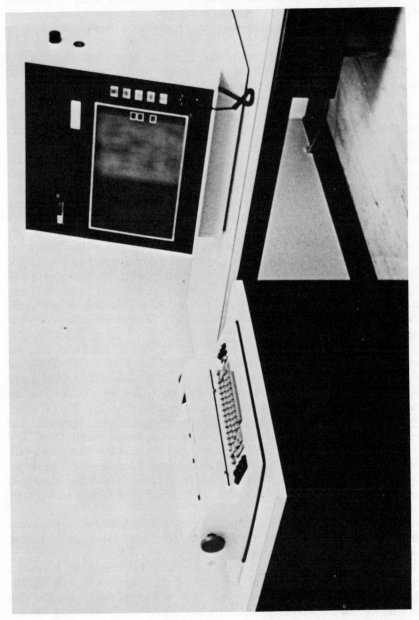

Figure 3. IBM 2760 Optical Image Unit

is simply produced, it can be frequently updated and readily replaced. It should be produced as an ephemeral document to be rapidly supplemented and soon discarded, since the data it contains is out-of-date when the mailman next arrives.

On-line terminals, whether they are typewriter or CRT, are presently the expensive way to display data, but if one wishes to query a file in a conversational mode it is the only way to do it. Even more important, it is the only way up-to-the-minute information can be made available on demand at multiple-retrieval locations.

COM, computer-output-microfilm, is the newest method of display to become commercially available.[10] It has all the advantages of any type of microform—inexpensiveness to produce, ease of reproduction, and low cost storage. Like any microform, its biggest disadvantage is the fact that special equipment is needed to read it, and even more important, most people have considerable difficulty in using that equipment. If one uses microform readers extensively, he soon joins the stiff neck, sore eyeballs club.

COM is a method of capturing computer output onto microfilm, usually, but not necessarily, through the use of cathode ray tubes. A microfilm camera is placed directly in line with a CRT, and the two are synchronized so that the CRT images are captured on film as they appear on the CRT screen. The quality of resolution is about as good as a good line printer. The first company to enter the market with this equipment was Stromberg Datagraphics (formerly Stromberg-Carlson), but there are now many companies marketing COM equipment. In addition, there are many service bureaus using COM that will commercially produce microfilm from any magnetic tape data file.

Among the advantages in the use of these machines are the inexpensiveness of their final product and their speed of output. The usual computer printer prints 1,100 lines a minute—it is claimed that COM prints 20,000 to 30,000 lines per minute, although users have been known to claim that 5,000 to 6,000 lines per minute is closer to reality. The 20,000 figure amounts to filming 300 standard-size computer pages of data a minute. The microfilm original can be produced by a commercial service bureau using COM at about 1.5 cents per page, and duplicate microfilms at less than half a cent per page. Hard copy produced from the microfilm costs about 2.5 cents per page. These costs, of course, vary from place to place. COM is now used by a commercial printer to produce the San Francisco Public Library's hard copy serials catalog.

Preprinted forms can be automatically merged with data as they are read from magnetic tape so that routine documents such as invoices, claims, overdue notices, etc., can be produced.

Another form of COM, and a newer one, is Electron Beam Recording (EBR). It was developed and is marketed by the 3M Company. It has the advantage of dry film processing by heat which provides readable film immediately. Digital magnetic tape data are converted to analog signals and those signals control an electron beam which "writes" the images onto Dry-Silver Microfilm.

Using either form of COM, a library can retain its computer output on microfilm and inexpensively produce as many duplicate films as needed, or offset masters can be made from the film and book catalogs produced.

To return to the book catalog as the most prevalent form of serials machine data display, Figure 4 is an example of a full-page three-column printout that is from the Purdue University Libraries' catalog.[11] The data elements included in the Purdue catalog are the entry, history notes, call number, library location, sublocation, compiled holdings, and special notes.

There are two ways to produce serials holdings statements for book catalogs: 1) compiled holdings statements, i.e., the computer reads coded holdings data, and then compiles the compact holdings statements from those data, and 2) by manually converting holdings statements to machine-readable form in a prescribed format, and then printing the catalog without significant change from the in-put format. This type is also known as "open-ended" because complete holdings are shown as 1- or 1+. Purdue's catalog is the compiled type.

Figure 5 is a sample of "raw" holdings data, i.e., holdings data before compilation. The printouts of raw holdings data are used by the library staff for internal purposes only. The data for each serial are printed out in matrix form and any item of datum can be located for updating or deletion through the use of coordinates. The columns of the matrix are labeled by letters and the rows by numbers. If the latest bound volume is to be added to the record, the update clerk would enter the serial's I.D. number, a code "ADDH" which tells the computer to add the new holdings data to the record, the coordinates "M5," and the new data, which in the illustration would be bound volume 65, i.e., "BOO65." The actual data prepared for keypunching would be as follows:

A50292 ADDH M5 /BOO65/

As can be seen in the illustration, each five-character word begins with a letter or a special symbol. A "B" represents a bound volume, a "U" an unbound volume, a "D" indicates date, and "X" is a bound duplicate volume, a "Y" is an unbound duplicate volume, a "K" is a volume bound out of sequence, and a "V" indicates a volume missing from a particular type of sequence. The data between slashes represent a physical piece, i.e., a physical volume or an issue. The computer reads the raw data and then compiles the familiar compact holdings statement from them.

When the raw holdings shown in the illustration are compiled into the holdings statement that would be included in the book catalog, it would appear as follows:

(1N2-4,11,13,14)2-15,17-24[1946-1955]25-64-

This statement would be read by the patron as follows: volume 1 is incomplete (indicated by the parentheses), but has numbers 2 through 4, 11, 13, and 14. The library also has volumes 2 through 15, but volume 16 is missing. It does have, however, volumes 17 through 24, and the dates, including volume 1, are 1946 through 1955. The library also has volumes 25

AMERICAN IRON AND STEEL INSTITUTE.
-STATISTICS OF THE AMERICAN AND FOREIGN
IRON TRADES.
 CEASED PUBL. WITH 1912.-
1867-71 AS REPORT OF THE SECRETARY.
SUPERSEDED BY AMERICAN IRON AND STEEL
INSTITUTE. ANNUAL STATISTICAL REPORT.
669.106 Am295
GENL 1871,1879-1887,1904-1905-

-STEEL FACTS.
669.106 Am35F
GENL 74,78,85,92,150-V15I,189'1958-65'--
 SUPPL. 154   1   1959
 SUPPL. 160   1   1960
 SUPPL. 171   1   1962
 SUPPL. 176   1   1963

-STEELWAYS.
669.106 Am35T
GENL (1945L11-1194BL14I-1949/ V6-23
 '1950-67'
669.106 Am35T
KRAN fV1n11'1963'--

-YEARBOOK.
VOL. 1, 1910 AS PROCEEDINGS.
VOLUME NUMBERING DISCONTINUED WITH
VOL. 35.
669.106 Am3Y
GENL V1-35'1910-46'/ 1947-1955-
669.106 Am3Y
KRAN V22'1932'

AMERICAN IRON ORE ASSOCIATION.
-IRON ORE.
669.106 Am33
LATEST VOL. REF.
GENL 1958-1964,1967
669.106 Am33
CALU 1965

AMERICAN IRONSMITH.
682 Am3
GENL (V6OLL-3)-164L8-12I,I7DL1-9,61-8I
'1935-57'--

AMERICAN-ISRAEL ECONOMIC HORIZONS.
330.956 I57
KRAN V2-<I7lA-7)-11'1950-59'--

AMERICAN JERSEY CATTLE CLUB.
-BUTTER TESTS OF REGISTERED JERSEY
COWS.
636.082 Am35B
LIFE V1-2'1884-86'
 NEW SERIES
 V1-4'1891-1902'

-HERD IMPROVEMENT REGISTRY OF JERSEY
CATTLE.
--CONSOLIDATED VOLUME.
636.082 Am35H
LIFE V1'1928-38'--

-HERD REGISTER OF JERSEY CATTLE.
 CEASED PUBL. WITH VOL. 117, 1931.
636.082 Am35HE
LIFE V1-117'1871-1931'--

-JERSEY PERFORMANCE REGISTER.
636.082 Am35RE
LIFE V1-13,15'1943-67'

-PRODUCTION TESTING AND TYPE
CLASSIFICATION OF JERSEY CATTLE.
636.082 Am35P
LIFE V1'1942'--

-REGISTER OF MERIT OF JERSEY CATTLE
BASED ON AUTHENTICATED DAIRY
PERFORMANCE.
636.082 Am35R
LIFE 1'1908,1911,1913,1915-1922--

--CONSOLIDATED VOLUME.
636.082 Am35RA
LIFE V1-4'1923-39'--

-TESTED SIRES AND DAMS OF THE JERSEY
BREED.
--CONSOLIDATED VOLUME.
636.082 Am35T
LIFE V1'1935'--
 SUPPL. 1950   1

AMERICAN JERSEY HERD BOOK.
 SEE
AMERICAN JERSEY CATTLE CLUB.
-HERD REGISTER OF JERSEY CATTLE.

AMERICAN JEWISH COMMITTEE.
-ANNUAL REPORT.
296 Am3
GENL V19-25,27-34'1926-41'--

AMERICAN JOURNAL OF ANATOMY.
 PAGE 98

AMERICAN JEWISH COMMITTEE.
-RESEARCH INSTITUTE ON PEACE AND
POST-WAR PROBLEMS.
--JEWS AND THE POST-WAR WORLD.
296 Am3J
GENL V1-6'1941-45'--

AMERICAN JEWISH CONFERENCE.
-PROCEEDINGS.
 CEASED PUBL. WITH NO. 4, 1947.
296 Am31P
GENL V1-2'1943-44'--

AMERICAN JEWISH JOINT DISTRIBUTION
COMMITTEE.
-ANNUAL REPORT.
296 Am32A
GENL 1949-1952,1954-1956,1962,1964,1966

AMERICAN JEWISH YEAR BOOK.
296.05 Am3
LATEST VOL. REF.
GENL V52,61-64-69'1951-68'

AMERICAN JOURNAL OF AGRICULTURAL
ECONOMICS.
630.5 J825
LIFE V1-48'1919-66'
 INDEX VOL. 1-10, IN VOL. 9-10.
 INDEX VOL. 11-20, IN VOL. 20.
630.5 J825
KRAN V1-2,4-48'1919-66'--

AMERICAN JOURNAL OF AGRICULTURE AND
SCIENCE.
630.5 Am33
LIFE V7'1948'--

AMERICAN JOURNAL OF ANATOMY.
591.05 Am3
LIFE V5'1905-6',3-V8'1908',9-V10-42
 '1910-28'-44-V45-121'1930-67'
591.05 Am3
VETS V66-118'194C-66'

Figure 4. Page from Purdue University Libraries' Catalog

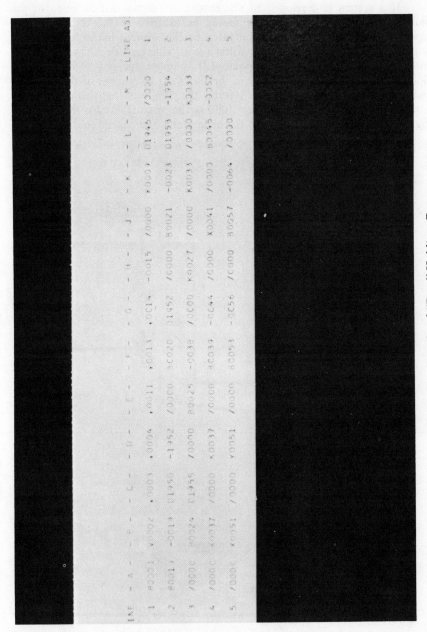

Figure 5.   Sample of "Raw" Holdings Data

through 64, and is continuing to receive the serial (indicated by the dash at the end of the statement). The dates for those volumes are unknown.

If a system is developed to this extent, it follows that as much of the mundane maintenance as possible should be assigned to the computer. One aspect of maintenance that the computer handles without human intervention is the system of cross references. When a serial changes title, the update clerk enters the new title, the appropriate I.D. number for it according to the alphabetical postion it will occupy in the file, the I.D. number of the old title, and the code "TTOX." The code informs the computer that this operation is a title change. The computer then follows the instructions for that routine. Figure 6 is a schematic drawing of the computer's title change routine.

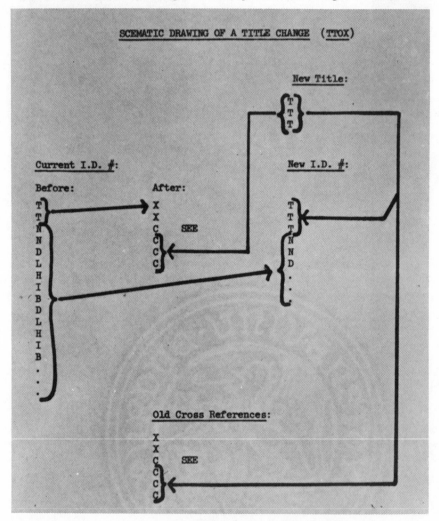

Figure 6.

Most serials catalogs are of the "convert and print" or the "open-ended" type because they are much more easily and, therefore, more inexpensively produced. Figure 7 is an example of this type and is a page from the University of Illinois's serials catalog.

The biggest disadvantage to this type of holdings record is that it does not reflect all of the detailed information about the library's serials collections that is given in the card catalog, the check-in files, etc. It is, therefore, necessary to maintain both the card catalog and the book catalog indefinitely. If an attempt is made to include all the data that are in the card catalogs and other files, the holdings statements become very complicated and difficult to read. Also, it is difficult to maintain consistency in complicated holdings statements when prepared manually. Humans tend to forget from one time to another the way in which they handled previous situations, and also they interpret circumstances differently from time to time. An additional disadvantage is that such holdings statements cannot be updated automatically by a check-in system, except perhaps by the CRT method.

The major disadvantage to the compiled type of holdings statement is that the programming logic is complicated and, because it is complicated, it does not lend itself to change very easily. It also requires more machine time to compile the holdings statements than it does just to print the open-ended type.

On the other hand, the compiled catalog enables the library to eliminate its card catalog serials records and its check-in records of bound volumes, annuals, and other occasionally received materials, since the serials raw data bank can include all of the data that such records usually contain. The compiled holdings statements can be as simple or as involved as the library wants them to be because the computer can be programmed to choose for printing only the specific data wanted at a given time. In addition, the data bank can be used for all kinds of statistical and management studies, and is much more flexible for other uses.

The decision on which type to adopt depends on what is expected from the library's automated serials system. To arrive at the correct answer to that problem, detailed study and planning are necessary. Serials, by their very nature, are too obstreperous to allow snap judgements. Libraries should control their serials collection, but unless good management is used, the reverse is more likely to be true.

This, then, brings us back to the planning of a serials system. Any library, large or small, that decides to develop an automated serials system should study the whole problem—the library's needs and wants, its financial and technical backing, and its future growth probabilities before it decides in which direction to go. In addition, studies should be made of all types of serials systems operating in other libraries so that the best one is chosen. When the homework is well done, the library can proceed on whatever course it chooses, confident that it has every chance of success and will gain maximum advantage from its automated serials program.

Figure 7. Open-ended Type of Serial Catalog

References

1. United States of American Standards Institute. *USA Standard for Periodicals: Format and Arrangement.* Sectional Committee on Library Work and Documentation, Z-39, 1967

2. American Society for Testing and Materials. Special Committee on Numerical Reference Data. *CODEN for Periodical Titles* (ASTM Data Series, DS23). Edited by L.E. Kuentzel. 2 vols. Philadelphia, American Society for Testing and Materials, 1966; *Supplement* (DS23A-S1), 1968; *Supplement* (DS23A-S2), 1969.

3. Vdovin, George, *et al. Serials Computer Project; Final Report.* La Jolla, University of California, 1964.

4. Crismond, Linda F., and Fatzer, Sylvia B. "Automated Serials Check-in and Binding Procedures at the San Francisco Public Library." *In* American Society for Information Science. *Proceedings.* Vol. 6. Washington, D.C., Cooperating Information Societies, 1969, pp. 13-20.

5. Bishop, David, *et al.* "Publication Patterns of Scientific Serials," *American Documentation,* 16:113-21, April 1965.

6. Fayollat, James and Luck, Don. "Computer Based Serials Control System, Biomedical Libary, UCLA," *American Documentation,* 20:385, Oct. 1969.

7. Pizer, Irwin H., *et al.* "Mechanization of Library Procedures in the Medium-sized Medical Library: The Serial Record," *Medical Library Association Bulletin,* 51:328-29, July 1963.

8. Eyman, Eleanor G., *et al.* "Periodicals Automation at Miami-Dade Junior College," *Library Resources & Technical Services,* 10:341-61, Summer 1966.

9. Hammer, Donald P. "A Review of the ASTM CODEN for Periodical Titles," *Library Resources & Technical Services,* 12:359-65, Summer 1968.

10. "Here Comes the C.O.M.," *Information and Records Management,* 2:45-52, Oct.-Nov. 1968.

11. Hammer, Donald P. "Reflections on the Development of an Automated Serials System," *Library Resources & Technical Services,* 9:225-30, Spring 1965.

Additional References

Curran, Ann T. "The Mechanization of the Serial Records for the Moving and Merging of the Boston Medical and Harvard Medical Serials," *Library Resources & Technical Services,* 10:362-72, Summer 1966.

Felter, Jacqueline W., and Tjoeng, Djoeng, "A Computer System for a Union Catalog: Theme and Variations," *Medical Library Association Bulletin,* 53:163-77, April 1965.

Grosch, Audrey N. *University of Minnesota Bio-medical Library Serials Control System: Comprehensive Report, Fall 1966–June 1968.* Minneapolis, Minnesota University, University Libraries, June 1968.

Srygley, Ted F. "Serials Record Instructions for a Computerized Serial System," *Library Resources & Technical Services,* 8:248-56, Summer 1964.

Thomas D. Gillies
Assistant Director
Linda Hall Library
Kansas City, Missouri

DOCUMENT SERIALS, TECHNICAL REPORTS, AND THE NATIONAL BIBLIOGRAPHY

Bibliographically, document serials. do not differ substantially from other serials. Their acquisition is largely dependent upon the use of enumerative bibliographies which identify them; their use, upon the subject bibliographies which give some measure of control over their contents. Based on local requirements, every library has its own problems to consider—storage, convenient availability, paper quality—but bibliographic access is the common need that they all share. If libraries are willing to accept Osborn's definition that "on practical grounds a serial can be defined as any item which lends itself to serial treatment in a library,"[1] then a great bulk of government document publication falls into the province of this conference. One reasonable estimate, based on a university library's receipts of documents, is that "80 percent of the material published by the United States government is serial in nature."[2] It is safe to assume that a comparable percentage pertains in most large libraries for state and foreign government acquisition.

While today there are many bibliographic aids for serials and for documents that were not available a few years ago, the acquisition librarian's and the serial records librarian's approach to document serials—whether for serial titles or for individual issues—is often far from direct or automatic. Librarians are fortunate to have *New Serial Titles* from 1950, which gives far better coverage of state, federal, and foreign documents than the *Union List Serials* did, but as with any cooperative compilation, librarians must be grateful for what they find, and philosophic about what they do not find.

The array of national bibliographies outside the United States which includes documents is impressive; and to use them well, keenness of mind, persistence of spirit, unflagging good humor, and great flexibility are needed.

146

For example, librarians must know that the *Indian National Bibliography* puts its documents in a separate section with its own index; the Soviet Union's *Knizhnaia Letopis'* includes ministry publications in the main issues, except for a few which go into a separate "Dopolnitel'nyi vypusk"; and that the *British National Bibliography* includes "certain government publications," with specific omissions which must be compensated for elsewhere. And so it goes for all the national bibliographies of which document entries must somehow be a part. In enumerating state publications, the simple virtues called for above must be enhanced by immeasurable patience and prodigious resilience in the face of frustration. The *Monthly Checklist of State Documents* is a dependable guide and an indispensable instrument for many purposes, but it is somewhat reminiscent of Carrie Nation's epitaph: "She did what she could."

These difficulties are pointed out, not to deprecate the works at hand but simply to remark the special problems of document serials. The titles of many document periodicals are included in the standard bibliographies of serials, such as *Ulrich's International Periodical Directory*. Some national bibliographies also list separate issues of both government and non-government periodicals, and of other kinds of serial publications (for example the *Deutsche Bibliographie: Zeitschriften-Verzeichnis* and *Letopis' Periodicheskikh Izdanii SSSR).* Unfortunately, we do not have this kind of a detailed bibliography in the United States for periodicals. The official bibliographies for documents are not necessarily the most economical sources for identifying government serials, because they are nearly always incomplete or partial. In our own national documents bibliography, the Government Printing Office's Price List no. 36 for "Government Periodicals and Subscription Services" is convenient, but omits many non-periodical serials; the annual "Directory of United States Government Periodicals" in the February issue of *Monthly Catalog* is helpful, but admittedly incomplete, and we are better served by Andriot's *Guide to U. S. Government Serials and Periodicals.*[3] Many document serial titles and their individual issues do not get into the *Monthly Catalog* because the Superintendent of Documents never receives a copy. This situation is not peculiar to United States document bibliography. In writing about British documents, N. G. Thompson has said:

> It has often been urged upon H.M.S.O. that it should catalogue all official material whether it publishes it or not, but whatever the distant future may hold, there is no foreseeable prospect of this Herculean—and costly—task being undertaken. The Stationery Office is equipped to do no more than catalogue what it publishes itself (some 6,000 titles a year) and the creation of a centralised cataloguing unit for material not actually published by it would present formidable administrative difficulties. This means in practice that the user of non-H.M.S.O. material must perforce turn to the individual departments and other official organizations for information and supply.[4]

So it is with other document bibliography everywhere, and so it is likely to continue to be.

The United States has tried to cope with the situation cooperatively by means of the Documents Expediting Project for non-GPO publications. By

1968, there were 142 subscribers to that Project; they received some 241,000 items. During the previous year the subscribers received "214,000 items through established channels; an additional 48,000 items were sent in response to 11,323 individual requests. Of these requests 85 percent were filled by supplying the wanted material and two percent by providing information as to the source of supply."[5] But even so, most librarians have had to pay close attention to areas of special interest and to use such wits as they have at their command to assure completeness of serial files. Even with close attention, a naturally acquisitive instinct, and a degree of clairvoyance, some librarians will have failed to complete files of such series as *Technical Memoranda* of the Waterways Experiment Station, or the *Circulars* of the U. S. Geological Survey. For serials of this sort, borrowing issues to film for collections or getting copies from personal acquaintances must often be resorted to. Ultimately, librarians live with some incomplete files; this is true for all serials but is especially apparent in irregular document serials.

The acquisition of state serial publications tends to be even more trying. In some fields the distribution is regular enough—engineering experiment stations, geological surveys, and most agricultural experiment stations. Agencies with a tradition of having their publications abstracted widely by standard services usually either accept standing orders or maintain publication announcement lists. But many state bureaus and offices do not have regular distribution programs and are not responsive to requests for regular serial distribution or for individual issues. Important as these publications are to libraries, they apparently do not seem so to the offices responsible for their preparation. Some of the distribution is on the basis of regular mailing lists; some on the basis of exchange agreements between libraries; and some apparently on the basis of an individual's memory or disposition. Research libraries should take an initiative in this area and introduce a plan for general access. This might take the form of a central collecting agency for state documents, supported by member institutions or by state governments, from which copies—either as film or photocopy—could be readily obtained. Money for such an enterprise would undoubtedly be hard to come by, but it should be possible to demonstrate that future economies would be enjoyed. Or a plan for centralization might take the form of depository collections in state libraries, which would then have a definite responsibility to compile monthly lists of all documents acquired. Such lists could be incorporated into the *Monthly Checklist,* making it a comprehensive union list showing locations for items listed. Use would depend upon good bibliography and upon the state libraries' efficient and prompt filling of request. If each state government had a sales agent for all state publications, even the higher prices necessitated by having a centralized distribution agency would be an ultimate economy to most libraries. We undoubtedly need some good studies of use of state documents, of present methods of acquisition, of current library policies, and of state laws relating to deposit or to distribution. Imposing effective bibliographic control, in the light of fair measurements of library need, is our greatest task here. If this were done, together with cooperating depositories, state documents could be much more effectively exploited.

In part because of the acquisition difficulties attendant upon the mandatory use of a multitude of catalog lists and publication notes, it has been written frequently in library literature that a separate documents collection is desirable. Like King Charles's head, the question of separate versus incorporated documents collections keeps re-appearing. For each library, the question (if there is one—some would doubt it) must be resolved by a rational compromise which would result in both a useful and an economical solution. Most government serials should be treated like other serials with title entries in the appropriate records (serials records or card catalog) and with dependence upon standard abstracts and indexes for analytics. If a serial publication of a government agency is regularly analyzed in *Engineering Index* or in *Abstracts of North American Geology*, it is wasteful to make analytics in the library's card catalog. If a library's holdings of abstracts and indexes are inadequate for this approach, decisions must be made about either adding more abstracts or selectively analyzing certain publications in the library. Usually, when appropriate abstracts are available, they will be the more economical choice. Some series—*The Bibliography on Snow, Ice and Permafrost* is an example—need full cataloging. In many cases, foreign document serials will require treatment different from that given domestic publications, again depending on available abstracts and the languages in which they are published.

Once a serial has been appraised in terms of subject access, and the serial has then been appropriately treated, its location in the documents collection, the serials collection, or some other departmental collection is of lesser importance. If an administrative economy can be effected by a separate document collection, it may be well to do so; if the library's public will be better served by integrating the serial with a subject collection, this may be the best choice. But the basis for these decisions must first be a careful appraisal of subject access to the contents of the serial, and only secondly the convenience to library administration.

In evaluating subject approach to document serials, treatment of them by the national bibliography should be of paramount significance. It our own case, the most frequently used of the national document bibliographies is the *Monthly Catalog of United States Government Publications*. Especially since the death of the *Documents Catalog* anguished and unremitting appeals for an all-inclusive monthly catalog listing both GPO and non-GPO publications have been heard. In some instances, the coverage of non-GPO publications has been improved in recent years, and chances of finding the successive numbers of serial publications are considerably better than they once were. But the likelihood of the *Monthly Catalog's* achieving a really comprehensive enumeration of all U.S. government publications is remote. There are many good departmental lists issued, as well as some comprehensive departmental indexes. Examples of these are the Geological Survey and the National Bureau of Standards. The numbers of such lists, the knowledge of their existence and the ability to use them may seem to put a burden on the acquisitions and the reference staff, but this is less of a burden than a simple professional responsibility. To hope for a *Monthly Catalog* which contains all publications issued by governmental agencies is bibliographically unrealistic. Librarians can be grateful for improved coverage, but should not waste time and effort hoping for the improbable. They should settle instead for the careful enumeration of all those items which now come to the attention of the Superintendent of Documents.

They should not, however, settle for the woeful inadequacy of the *Monthly Catalog's* index. As a subject approach to major segments of the federal publishing program, the *Monthly Catalog's* index is inefficient and ineffective in the hands of all but the fully initiated and experienced. It may be possible to train library staff, even faculty and research personnel to use the *Monthly Catalog* with a degree of certainty, but if they do so, they will be joining an almost incredibly exclusive club. The subjects entries are often made up from the individual titles at hand rather than from a standard and consistent list. The index seems to make use of the basic technique of the permuted title index, but fails to make up for the deficiencies of that device, because it rings only one change on the title. For example, if one sought the Weinberg Report published in 1963 under the title *Science, Government and Information: The Responsibilities of the Technical Community and the Government in the Transfer of Information; A Report,* he had only one chance. Under "Science" as a subject one must go to the fifth substantive work of the subtitle (which one almost certainly does not have in his reference) and arrive at ". . . Transfer of Information, Responsibilities of Technical Community and Government." As subject indexing this puts a burden of incredible persistence on the user. Most of us, of course, would simply go to *PAIS* and find it under Weinberg (whose name is not in the *Monthly Catalog* index) or under "Science and state" or "Scientific information."

Improving the index so that one could have reasonable expectations when he used it as a key to the materials listed in the *Monthly Catalog* could offer considerable economies to libraries in organization of its material. If the *Monthly Catalog* index could be brought into the mainstream of national bibliographic coverage with adequate subject headings and corporate author entries, its usefulness would be far greater, its reference function would be more available to all research workers, and document serials would be susceptible to the same reference use and control as are other serials. By using such bibliographies as *Engineering Index, Bibliography of Agriculture, Chemical Abstracts,* and *PAIS* it is possible to achieve this to some degree now. (The indexing policy that died when *Agricultural Index* changed its title was a severe blow in this respect. For libraries which have *Biological Abstracts* and *Bibliography of Agriculture,* the new *Biological and Agricultural Index* is now an expensive luxury. When it stopped indexing Agriculture Department, experiment station, and extension service publications, it forfeited its claim to real usefulness in research libraries.)

An improved index would make the *Monthly Catalog* less an instrument for the documents specialists alone. And here lies another of the major lapses in use of government serials. While all serials seem formidable to some librarians, documents sometimes seem to be totally unapproachable, if not downright evil to them. The librarian who takes this point of view does so at his peril, and so does the library school student who is seriously undertaking professional training. There are undoubtedly many reasons for this; it would scarcely be surprising to be told that a deep distaste for documents is ingested by the child with his mother's milk. It seems more likely, however, that three factors play significant roles in the popular view that documents are fugitive and difficult to use. The first is their sheer bulk and here we are helpless. The second is the inadequacy of indexing in the *Monthly Catalog.* The third is the isolation of document training in library schools. Library school curriculum committees should give serious consideration to the liquidation of courses in government documents. The content of those courses should be absorbed into other major subject areas of the curriculum—the basic bibliography of documents belongs in the study of national bibliography generally, related to it and recognized as a major part of it. The study of bibliographic access to the document literature of political science, of statistics, of economics, of international affairs belongs in the course on the literature of the social sciences. The study of the document literature of natural and physical sciences, of engineering, of medicine and public health belongs in the course on literature of the sciences and technology. Consideration of the organization of document serials belongs in the courses on administration and cataloging. Their acquisition should be studied along with the selection of other library materials. The emphasis on documents should be to put them into the mainstream of bibliography and source materials, not to put them into quarantine in a course by themselves. Such a curriculum change would charge all instructors with giving instruction in documents, but this asks no more than that they know the literature of their subjects.

A library's document serials must be related to its serials in general, and within that context the"technical report" must also be related to scientific communication in general. To determine its collecting policies, its treatment of, and its reference responsibilities for technical reports, a library must try.to see the place of the technical report in contemporary scientific literature. There is no uniform criterion for judging the significance of report literature. No two libraries will find their needs quite comparable. Scientists' attitudes toward report literature also differ from one discipline to another; generally their points of view depend upon their interest in basic science as opposed to its applications in technology.

One technical report, concerned with the role of the report in scientific and technological communication, has an appendix headed "Taxonomy of the Technical Report Literature."[6] The following descriptions of the principal types of technical reports are based largely on that summary and make use of its terminology to identify them. They are:

1. The individual author's "preprint," or processed manuscript, intended primarily for circulation among colleagues for review or comment. But these materials may also be distributed with a more formal designation, as in the Rand Corporation Papers designated as "P's," which do not represent corporate studies. Even though informally presented and distributed, they are likely to be cited or indexed. They also may be published subsequently in a journal,

but meanwhile they are in the literature and the abstracts with their first series designation—or designations, for often they are assigned series numbers by more than one agency.

2. The contract "progress report," thought to be "the most populous species of technical report in circulation." These progress reports are designed to give the sponsor periodic assessments of progress under the contract. They are also often distributed to others working in related problem areas. It is estimated that these quarterly reports (even monthly for some contracts) now number in the millions. In many cases their contents will be included or summarized in the final reports of the projects, but in some instances this is not so. It sometimes happens that the data included in the progress reports are referred to but not included in the final report.

3. The "final report" on a technical contract effort, rated "as probably the most valuable specimen in the collection." This is so in part because the final report is written with the editorial support and review of the research group of the institution as a whole. The quality and scope of such reports are widely varied, and differences in form, serial designations, distribution, and indexing can strain credulity.

4. The "separate," topical technical reports, which come closest in style and form to journal articles. These may be requested by sponsors, or may result from the researcher's simply wanting to be heard. Often they are also submitted to journals, where they are likely to appear in more carefully edited, abbreviated form. Some institutions may also give these reports, in reprint, a serial code of their own, put their own covers on them, and issue them in still another bibliographic dress.

5. The "book" in report form, likely to be a review, or survey of the state-of-the-art. Special information centers, AEC and NASA for example, generate reports of this nature, and so do such organizations as industrial laboratories.

6. Committee-type reports, which can arise from scientific advisory committees presenting their conclusions and supporting data in report format. These include Advisory Committee Reports to the President, National Academy of Science Reports, special commission reports, and so on.

These reports, with their great variation of stylistic quality, their variation from informal to institutionally refereed, also share some common characteristics. They are primarily concerned with the applied sciences—e.g., engineering, medicine, agriculture, computer technology. Often they are useful primarily because of the data which they include, and literature citations to them frequently derive from their providing an authority for such data. Arising, as they usually do, from projects having specific goals, they are strongly user-oriented and frequently concerned with use and exploitation of the techniques described. While we tend to think of technical reports as a government publication device, they are not exclusively so; their form and mode of distribution have been widely used in industry for many years. They are generally characterized by the purpose of fulfilling some sort of contractual obligation. It is estimated that "some half a million items per year fall into this technical report category."[7]

With so large and so various a body of materials, there can be no pat appraisal of its place in the literature of science and technology. But a summary of the usual forms of scientific literature may be useful to us in attempting to evaluate the technical report. Traditionally, in the western world at least, the literature of the sciences has from the first depended upon the organization of scientific societies. The academies of France and Italy, and the Royal Society of London provided for the gathering of men with inquiring minds, and then for the exchange of information through prompt journal publication. The *Philosophical Transactions* and the *Journal des Scavans* were a forum for scientific exchange and provided the prototype for what can now be called classical scientific publication. Journals grew in number, continuing for many years to be sponsored primarily by academies and professional societies. Their contents were, and are, carefully refereed; articles are edited for style and accuracy. This now also applies to many commercially published journals which have boards of editors acting as referees.

In addition to these scientific journals, there are trade journals which are more concerned with applications than with scientific discovery, and other serials reporting the work of projects, expeditions, and institutional studies. The *Monographs* and *Bulletins* of the U.S. Geological Survey are good examples of this form. The individual review or monographic study is also characteristic of scientific publications whether issued serially or independently; the many series of "Advances. . ." are examples of separate review volumes.

The scientific meeting which preceded these printed means of communication has been a significant vehicle for the exchange of information. To the bibliographer, the classical "International Congress" has now become an almost virulent form on both national and international levels and presents myriad problems of its own in connection with preprints, published proceedings, unpublished papers, reprints, and variations in meeting names. Beyond these more or less traditional forms of communication, there is also the important factor of direct personal communication, and this too is a venerable tradition. In the seventeenth century, before the Royal Society was founded, scientists met in London and called themselves the "Invisible College," a name which distinguished them from the visible Gresham College. A few years ago what were called "New Invisible Colleges," are simply called today the "invisible colleges," without the distinction of capital initial letters. These have been well defined by Derek J. de Solla Price:

> In each really active field of science today there is now in being something which we call the "New Invisible Colleges"–the group of everybody who is anybody in the field at that segment of the research front; an unofficial establishment based on fiercely competitive scientific excellence. They send each other duplicated preprints of papers yet to be published, and for big things they telephone and telegraph in advance. . . . By substituting the technology of transportation for that of publication they keep warm the seats of jet-planes and commune with each other at small select conferences and seminars throughout the world.[8]

Taken as a whole, journals and serials published as reports on exploration or experimental research, proceedings of conferences and symposia, and some research monographs comprise what has been called the "canonical" literature of the sciences, to make use of a term attributed to F. J. Weyl.[9] The rapid exchange of information in increasingly limited fields, as it is accomplished in the invisible colleges, simply brings the canonical form full circle.

Outside this canon lies the technical report, which is essentially a product of this century and has achieved, one hopes, its ultimate proliferation in the past thirty years. To the scientist or bibliographer who feels closely identified with traditional journal literature, the technical report is a bastard form—recklessly conceived, unattended at delivery, too often unregistered as a legitimate vital statistic, and either lacking a family name or having too many from which to choose. Thus it appears to be an unproper part of the scientific archive, but to research and development workers, who make up a large part of the population in technical libraries, the report is quite something else. It can provide such a worker with a prompt and timely announcement of significant technical developments (if he is on a distribution list and need not wait indexing or abstracting); it usually provides a comprehensive treatment of an application; it is more likely to include negative results than is a journal article; and its contents, if useful to him at all, can often be immediately exploited by the research and development worker. As a result reports are thus referred to in bibliographies, they are abstracted in discipline-oriented abstracts as well as in their own mission-oriented bibliographies; having been cited in papers, they are referred to in *Science Citation Abstracts;* and they are advertised for sale by the Clearinghouse for Federal Scientific and Technical Information which announces around 30,000 copies of them annually. Authors of a recent article on the source literature of plasma physics speculate on the possiblity that "there may exist a sub-culture of authors who read and cite reports."[10] In spite of what may be distaste for or ambivalence about them, librarians are forced to recognize that they are a persistent element in the exchange of technological information. As the Weinberg Report noted in 1963:

> The documentation community has taken an equivocal attitude toward informal reports; in some cases the existence of these reports is acknowledged and their content abstracted in the abstracting journals. In other cases informal reports are given no status; they are alleged to be not worth retaining as part of the permanent record unless their contents finally appear in a standard hard-copy journal. Whether this position is tenable even in the basic sciences is open to question; it certainly is no longer tenable in technological development.[11]

There is also widespread attention and interest in these reports on an international level.   A.I. Mikhailov and his colleagues at the All-Union Institute of Scientific and Technical Information (VINITI) in Moscow issued a second edition of their work on information transfer in 1968. After citing statistics from the Weinberg Report, they state that information services for technical literature must take special note of the report form because of the very important facts and data which such reports frequently contain.[12] There are also some early indications that this awareness will be further born out by VINITI's very impressive new "World Scientific and Technical Literature," which is to be a seven volume annotated list of world serial literature in the sciences and technology, relating specifically to the materials abstracted in *Referativnyi Zhurnal.* Volume 1 has recently appeared, and it too takes note of technical report literature in its description of inclusions proposed for the new list. The introduction remarks that such publications are not only difficult to obtain regularly, but also that they present special difficulties in evaluation.[13] Examples of titles included in volume 1 that would be classed as report literature in our context are the *Technical Report* of NASA, and the *Report* of the Hydro- og Aerodynamisk Laboratorium (Hydro- and Aero-dynamics Laboratory. Aerodynamics Section) in Denmark. This new list stresses evaluation and appraisal as bases for inclusion; it will be instructive to see how many additional report titles are included in those volumes devoted to the literature of technology.

Surely, no one would deny that a fairly large percentage of technical reports is at best ephemeral and at worst wasteful. Interim reports, subcontract reports, preliminary reports, and progress reports may do more to clog avenues of communication than they do to open new prospects for inquiry or to resolve specific questions. Like some journal articles, nothing would have become them so much as obscurity.

What we desperately need is a national bibliographic effort, tied to one or more national depositories of technical reports, that can provide both control and access. One possibility might be a greatly improved *U.S. Government Research and Development Reports (USGRDR)* which is better than it used to be. Before 1968, its indexes were so meagre that they were compensated for with a motley set of special, non-governmental indexes.[14] The relatively low rate of use made of *USGRDR* as compared to *Nuclear Science Abstracts (NSA), Scientific and Technical Aerospace Reports (STAR)* and *Technical Abstract Bulletin (TAB)* is evident in a study titled *Diffusion of Abstracting and Indexing Services for Government-Sponsored Research.*[15] In the survey of recipients of these indexes, 96.8 percent of the respondents subscribed to only one copy of *USGRDR*, whereas they provided their personnel with multiple copies of *NSA, STAR,* and *TAB.* This suggests that a more comprehensive and better indexed abstract service than *USGRDR* has been in the past, or possibly that more discipline-oriented abstracts, would foster better use of technical reports. The improvements in *USGRDR's* 1968 indexes make the Clearinghouse's new "Selective Dissemination of Microfiche" a much more attractive acquisition possibility. But broad bibliographic coverage and economical accessibility is needed on a much wider base.

That adequate bibliography is of paramount importance is evidenced by the success of *Nuclear Science Abstracts* and the Atomic Energy Commission's depository program. Here a large body of report literature has had order imposed upon it; appropriate indexing approaches have been provided; publication data for reports assigned numbers but not so issued are noted; format and depository information serve to locate copies; and in addition a discipline-oriented abstract service has been incorporated into a mission-oriented project. All in all, *Nuclear Science Abstracts* is an exemplary bibliographic service providing access to journal articles, translations, patents, books, and conference proceedings which have been evaluated for appropriateness to its purpose. In addition, *NSA* provides control over foreign and United States reports pertinent to work of the AEC. In 1964, it did this job for less than $600,000.[16] By 1970 this cost may be nearer one million dollars, but those who use *NSA* would surely think this money well spent. The AEC announced in July that its depository program could not be continued without cost to the participating libraries. An annual charge for the full set of microfiche will be approximately $1,650. Most depositories, I suspect, will feel that the set is well worth it, and their conclusion will rest in large measure on the bibliographic control which *Nuclear Science Abstracts* provides.

Similar efforts have already been made for the report literature of the National Aeronautics and Space Agency (NASA). The division of responsibility in this instance, between NASA for production of *Scientific and Technical Aerospace Reports (STAR)* and the American Institute of Aeronautics and Astronautics for production of *International Aerospace Abstracts (IAA)*, has both advantages and disadvantages for discipline-oriented searches. Significantly, the legal charges of NASA and AEC have served to enable them to control the literature. Some agencies are directed by law to disseminate information; among these are the Atomic Energy Commission, the National Aeronautics and Space Agency, the Department of Agriculture, and the Weather Bureau. Other agencies, although their activities and accomplishments are, one hopes, equally intended for the common good, lack any comparable statutory directives. Among these is the Department of Defense (DOD). Although that department announces in *Technical Abstract Bulletin (TAB)* those reports which enter its Defense Documentation Center (DDC), it has been estimated that DDC receives only about 40 percent of the reports generated through DOD's research and development programs.[17] Moreover, *TAB* is not available to libraries which are not "qualified" recipients by virtue of their being involved in contract work with DOD. Even libraries which qualify must deny *TAB's* use to patrons who are not similarly qualified.

While we have no single comprehensive index to technical reports, and are perhaps not likely to have, we do have at least two mission-oriented abstracts providing good control of reports, and in both cases this is coupled with a depository program making the full report available fairly easily. In the Weinberg Report, the Atomic Energy Commission's Division of Technical Information Extension (DTIE) is termed a "delegated agent" for all documents and other forms of the literature that it interprets as being related to nuclear science. In this role it has responsibility for collecting, abstracting and disseminating the literature of its discipline. Its charges go beyond the report literature, to be sure, but the coverage it gives in *NSA* to report literature is worth emulating in other areas. The concept of "delegated agent" has been carried further in the study done by the System Development Corporation for the Committee on Scientific and Technical Information

(COSATI), Recommendations for National Document Handling Systems in Science and Technology[18] in which the investigators call for a "capping agency concept" together with a "responsible .agent" concept. The capping agency would be provided by the establishment of a scientific and technical information bureau in the federal government's executive branch. It would be charged with determining the areas of information and documentation to be covered by departments and agencies. It would also have extensive responsibilities for formulating information policies, for implementing training programs, for budget control, and for establishing and encouraging us of information centers. Along with other responsibilities, it would assume a coordinating function for the various "responsible agents."

In terms of the COSATI report, these "responsible agents" might well be combinations of government and non-government agencies. In many cases, such a program would much increase some agencies' information acitivtes and would charge them with preparation of specific information services. The agents would be responsible for assuring that reports resulting from federally performed research are published. They would also be charged with broad collection responsibilities for materials in their area, for translating, for abstracting, for announcing, and for dissemination. Still this is a more ambitious program than the present responsibilities of AEC and NASA, but even its partial implementation would do a great deal to resolve many of the library's difficulties with technical report literature. Few of us could now justify compiling finding lists and cross-reference files for what may be only modest holdings of technical reports.

At the same time, libraries with large collections in science and technology can be certain that they will be called upon to identify and to provide a good many technical reports. For most in the library field responsibilities here must be determined by a compromise between the economically feasible and as good an appraisal as they can make of the value of specific reports to the patrons they serve. If they feel that the responsibility for this kind of information and data transfer should rest with a governmental agency, or at least be funded by governmental support, they may quite properly decide that the extension of their own budget to cover this responsibility is done at the expense of more pressing needs. They should, however, be able to provide good service if the bibliography were adequate and if a national depository could provide documents with dispatch.   If librarians do not have the documents in their own collections, this may mean a wait of a few hours or days. It is generally difficult for me to be convinced that this kind of delay, given the present technology of reproduction, is too serious for most users of technical reports to accomodate themselves to.

Decisions about acquisition of technical reports must necessarily be based on a careful evaluation of responsibility as compared to cost, bibliography, and individual library experience with specific requests. These will be hard decisions which each library must make on the basis of local factors. During the time that the National Science Foundation funded twelve regional depositories for technical reports, the general response indicated that use made of these reports through the depositories was not sufficiently great to warrant continued support. However, local conditions were a large factor in the use made of those regional depositories. Those libraries which were located in the midst of heavy industrial complexes where a good deal of research was going on had considerable use and in some case have continued to keep their report centers going without National Science Foundation support. Others found that local funding could not be justified, especially in view of insufficient bibliographies.

There are more hopeful elements in the present outlook than there have ever been before. The development of specialized data centers—e.g., the Thermophysical Properties Research Center (Purdue); Defense Metals Information Center (Battelle); Hibernation Information Exchange (ONR, Chicago); Chemical Propulsion Information Agency (Johns Hopkins)—may help to curtail the preparation of some contract reports in their current form. Such published compilations of data as *Thermophysical Properties of High Temperature Solid Materials,*[19] could effect a great economy for all by obviating the need to issue the information in a multitude of separate reports.

It is apparent in several ways that high levels of the government are now concerned about the problems of the transfer of scientific information on a broad front. Last April the House of Representatives held hearings on a bill which proposes "a national science and research data processing and information retrieval system" (H.R. 8809). Among the witnesses was a representative of the System Development Corporation who had done the study for COSATI referred to above. Also among the witnesses was the chairman of the Committee on Scientific and Technical Communication (SATCOM), whose report for the National Academy of Sciences—National Academy of Engineering has recently been published.[20]   This report also makes several significant comments and recommendations about the handling of technical reports. It has been sensitive to the need for a mechanism to facilitate interaction between government and non-government agencies and publishers. It has also noted the role of libraries in information transfer and has recommended the "management of *discipline-wide basic abstracting and indexing services* by appropriate scientific and technical societies and the management of other broad bibliographic services (e.g., title listings and citation indexes) by commercial organizations, national libraries, or societies, with support of these activities, when necessary, by the government agencies to whose operations they are relevant (Recommendation C1)."[21]

In its recommendations on "semiformal publications" it gives attention to the technical report and states that this kind of semiformal report should be subjected "somewhat selectively" to bibliographic control. And it defines bibliographic control for the purpose here as "orderly announcement and, in those cases that involve circulation of substantive information not scheduled for formal publication to a significant number of people, the provision of indexing, abstracting, and availability in a central depository."[22]

Especially significant from the library point of view is their request that government agencies sponsoring research and development clearly differentiate between substantive reports and those which are required by administrative and contractual needs. If this evaluation—in fact, a kind of refereeing—can be accomplished, together with an orderly bibliographic approach, then the reports in general may become a properly compelling and economically feasible resource for library acquisition. When report literature is also subject to re-processing and re-packaging into significant reviews and comprehensive summaries, then there may be reason for a sanguine look at the future in this special segment of bibliography. We can hope, with Milton, that "Our torments also may in length of time/Become our elements."

References

1. Osborn, Andrew D. *Serial Publications, their Place and Treatment in Libraries.* Chicago, ALA, 1955, pp. 16-17.
2. Lundy, Frank A. and Johnson, Eugene M. "Documents in the Divisional Library," *College & Research Libraries,* 19:465, Nov. 1958.
3. Androit, John L. *Guide to U.S. Government Serials and Periodicals.* McLean, Va., Documents Index, 1969.
4. Thompson, N.G. "H.M. Stationery Office as Publisher."*In* Ronald Staveley and Mary Piggott, eds., *Goverment Information and the Research Worker.* 2d rev. ed. London, Library Association, 1965, p. 10.
5. U.S. Library of Congress. *Annual Report of the Librarian of Congress for the Fiscal Year Ending June 30, 1967.* Washington, D.C., The Library of Congress, 1968, p. 43.
6. U.S. Federal Council for Science and Technology. Committee on Scientific and Technical Information. *The Role of the Technical Report in Scientific and Technological Communication.* Washington, D.C., Department of Commerce, National Bureau of Standards, 1968.
7. *Ibid.,* column 26.
8. de Solla Price, Derek J. "The Scientific Foundations of Science Policy," *Nature,* 206:236, April 17, 1965.
9. U.S. Federal Council for Science and Technology. *The Role of...,* op. cit., column 15.
10. East, H. and Weyman, A. "A Study in the Source Literature of Plasma Physics," *Aslib Proceedings,* 21:168, April 1969.
11. U.S. President's Science Advisory Committee. *Science, Government, and Information: The Responsibilities of the Technical Community and the Government in the Transfer of Information; A Report.* Washington, D.C., U.S.G.P.O., 1963, p. 19.
12. Mikhailov, Aleksandr Ivanovich, *et al. Osnovy informatiki.* Moscow, Nauka, 1968, p. 105.
13. *Mirovaia nauchnaia i tekhnicheskaia literatura.* Vol. 1. Moscow, Akademiia Nauk SSSR, Institut Nauchnoi Informastsii, 1968, p. 6.
14. For an indication of the frustrating history of its indexes see: Boylan, Nancy G. "Identifying Technical Reports through U.S. Government Research Reports and Its Published Indexes," *College & Research Libraries,* 28:175-83, May 1967.
15. Klempner, Irving M. *Diffusion of Abstracting and Indexing Services for Government-Sponsored Research.* Metuchen, N.J., Scarecrow Press, 1968.

16. U.S. Federal Council for Science and Technology. Committee on Scientific and Technical Information. *Recommendations for National Document Handling Systems in Science and Technology.* Washington, D.C., U.S. Department of Commerce, National Bureau of Standards, Institute for Applied Technology, 1965, p. 6/82.

17. U.S. President's Science Advisory Commission, *op. cit.,* p. 41.

18. First issued as PB 168,267, the report was subsequently issued as *National Document-Handling Systems for Science and Technology* (Information Sciences Series). System Development Corporation, New York, Wiley, 1967.

19. Purdue University, Lafayette, Ind. Thermophysical Property Research Center. *Thermophysical Properties of High Temperature Solid Materials.* Y. S. Touloukian, ed. New York, Macmillan, 1967.

20. National Academy of Sciences, Committee on Scientific and Technical Communication. *Scientific and Technical Communication, A Pressing National Problem and Recommendations for its Solution; A Report* (National Academy of Sciences Publication 1707). Washington, D.C., National Academy of Sciences, 1969.

21. *Ibid.,* p. 15.

22. *Ibid.,* pp. 71-72.

Bill M. Woods
Executive Director
Engineering Index, Inc.

BIBLIOGRAPHIC CONTROL
OF SERIAL PUBLICATIONS

An important problem with serials is bibliographic control. What good does it do for libraries to select, acquire, record, catalog, and bind large holdings of serial publications if the contents of those serials remain a mystery to all except the few who have the opportunity to examine selected journals of continuing personal interest and have discovered some magic way of retaining the gist of the contents? Bibliographic control is the indexing and abstracting of the contents or guts of what is included in the serials. It is this control, provided by secondary publishing services, which this article will discuss.

Just as there are problems with serials in general, there are some easily identifiable problems connected with their bibliographic control including: volume, overlap, costs, elements and methods, and a few other miscellaneous considerations. Some history of bibliographic control will also put the current problems in a helpful perspective. Hereafter "bibliographic control" will be designated by the term "abstracting and indexing," one of these alone, or the shorter "a & i." (I do distinguish between abstracting and indexing and believe that they are *not* in order of importance and difficulty.) Although a & i do provide bibliographic control, this paper will not discuss cataloging, tables of contents, back-of-the-book indexes, year-end indexes, cumulative indexes, lists of advertisers, or bibliographies.

If there is to be control, there must always be indexing. Abstracting is a short cut, a convenience, and perhaps a bibliographic luxury which may be now, or is fast becoming, too rich, in light of other factors to be discussed, for library blood and for the users of libraries—especially for the users of indexes who may not depend upon the library interface. Abstracting, though, provides a desirable control, and one which will continue to be advocated.

161

Engineering Index (EI) is a medium-large service, although dwarfed both
by *Biological Abstracts* and *Chemical Abstracts*. There are many medium-small
abstracting services, and many which handle only a few hundred .or a few
thousand items each year. To the extent possible in this article, I will make
reference to the full range of services as to size and subjects covered, although
I will include almost no coverage of "social-consciousness" literature.

VOLUME

To the usual observer there seems to be a plethora of a & i services. A
directory[1] published in 1960 by NFSAIS (National Federation of Science
Abstracting and Indexing Services)—the trade association of the
field—described 500 U.S. published services in science and technology only. A
second directory[2] issued in 1963, also by NFSAIS, identified 1,855 services
published in forty countries; 365 were U.S. services. Greater selectivity was
shown in this issue, for the total number examined and considered was 3,155
with only 56 percent qualifying for inclusion.

FID (Fédération Internationale de Documentation) published a·revised
edition of its 1965 directory, *Abstracting Services in Science, Technology,
Medicine, Agriculture, Social Sciences, Humanities.*[3] Abstracting services only
are included, and there are approximately 1,300 in volume one, which covers
science, technology, medicine and agriculture. Surprisingly, 200 items will be
covered in the second volume for the social sciences and humanities. (A total
of 800 items was described in 1965.) Had the FID inventory included
indexing services in addition, the total would have been substantially larger.
Plans for a revised and continuing service are being discussed by FID and
NFSAIS.

Bibliographic control by services described in these directories is
provided in a wide variety of forms. Many a & i services are separately
published in bulletins which are printed periodically, e.g., *Tobacco Abstracts,
Abstracts of Photographic Science and Engineering Literature;* others are
issued in card form only, such as *Polymers Digest* and the several services of
Lowry-Cocroft; some appear as a regular feature in a journal, such as the
coverage of plastics patents in each issue of the *SPE Journal* (Society of
Plastics Engineers); some services are issued in a multiplicity of forms—printed
bulletins, cards, magnetic tape, or microfilm, as are *Biological Abstracts* and
Engineering Index (EI). EI further cumulates monthly issues into annual
bound volumes. As far as I can determine, no continuing service is offered on
magnetic tape only, yet this is both an economic and technical possibility
(EI's CITE-Electrical/Electronics has been an exception in 1968-1969);
searching of merged data bases from several services is also a new phenomena.

Many services have had their genesis in a journal editor's good intentions
of calling to attention some pertinent articles, patents, reports, or books
published elsewhere but of interest to his readership. For example *Information
Science Abstracts* had its genesis in the minds of several individuals,
particularly Claire Schultz, a past president of the American Documentation
Institute. In the early 1960s (November 1962), the National Science

Foundation (NSF) called to the attention of a roomful of representatives of the information community that the field of documentation and librarianship was suffering from the lack of a single comprehensive a & i service, and that much of the relevant literature was not indexed at all. At this time someone at NSF identified nearly fifty publications which attempted to provide a partial indexing of literature of the field. *Library Literature* ignored almost completely the expanding field of documentation, indexed few reports and did not carry abstracts. *Library Science Abstracts* provided a minimum number of items and timeliness was a problem.

A few years went by and in April 1965, the time seemed right for some of the duplications to stop and improvement to be instituted. In Philadelphia a meeting attended by Arthur Elias (of ADI which in *American Documentation* had included a section "Literature Notes" and had decided to issue it as a separate supplement), Herman Skolnik (of the Division of Chemical Literature of the American Chemical Society, which had felt an obligation to provide an "Annotated Bibliography" in *Chemical Literature)* and this writer (then of Special Libraries Association, which, in several publications indexed and/or abstracted pertinent items relating to librarianship and documentation), *Documentation Abstracts* was conceived and a plan was written. The first issue was dated March 1966. In the meantime, the expansion of *Library Science Abstracts* based on a study of nineteen services made by H. Allan Whatley has resulted in an expanded and renamed, *Library and Information Science Abstracts* which began publication with a January-February 1969 issue. *Library Literature* has not expanded its scope.

That there is some duplication in coverage of journal titles by a & i services cannot be denied. That they differ significantly usually will be determined on closer examination, if such a study is done. A specific case study will be reported later. The broadly based services provide a coverage which inevitably will be duplicated by more specialized services. The wholesale role of the large services needs to be developed further.

The pattern of growth and proliferation is a familiar one. The broader services such as *Biological Abstracts (BA), Chemical Abstracts (CA), EI, Bibliography of Agriculture,* and *Index Medicus* are the oldest. As the need for a greater in-depth coverage of a specialized field or inter- or cross-disciplinary service is identified, or as the general service is unable to respond to a special need, or as the literature becomes too bulky to be found (or to retain an identity and be found) in the larger service, or as the price of the larger service becomes too great for the individual, or as a special service is needed to cover foreign, highly technical, difficult to acquire, or esoteric material, then other bibliographic services will likely come into being.

Just as *Information Science Abstracts* illustrates an attempt at coordination, other cooperative efforts have evolved and have improved the picture. Anglo-American interests have joined forces to improve the three-part *Science Abstracts* by forming separate parts for electricity and electronics, computer and control, and physics. *Review of Metal Literature* and *Metals Abstracts* have merged using the latter name. A merger of two publications in the photographic field is being discussed. A unique international network is found in the field of chemistry, with Chemical Abstracts Service as the principal; there is British involvement, and most significantly, the German *Chemisches Zentralblatt,* produced since 1830, was discontinued at the end of 1969 with its efforts now merged in the larger groups. The *Bibliography of Agriculture* is studying how it might handle inputs from other services having like interests. There are other fields—education, computers and plastics to name three—which are saturated with bibliographic control titles.

NATIONAL FEDERATION OF SCIENCE ABSTRACTING AND INDEXING SERVICES

Coordination between the scientific and technical abstracting and indexing services in the United States was long overdue. At an informal meeting in December 1957, a number of a & i services met to organize for their mutual advantage and for the ultimate advantage of the users of the services. A conference held January 1958, in Philadelphia organized the National Federation of Science Abstracting and Indexing Services (NFSAIS), by unanimous action and on April 29 of that year the Federation was incorporated with headquarters in Washington, D.C. Offices were moved to Philadelphia in December 1967, and since July 1968 Stella Keenan has served as executive director.

NFSAIS has as a basic objective the coordinating of cooperative work of the member services (eighteen as of this writing) and the seeking of new ways to improve them. The ultimate goal of the Federation is to improve communication among scientists through the documentation (abstracting, indexing, and analyzing) of the international scientific literature.

Among its activities are an annual conference, a publications program (newsletters, directories, and technical reports), a collection of statistics and scope of coverage of members, the sponsorship of seminars for members and for user groups, and the conducting of studies to assist and improve the work of member services. It further cooperates with other organizations dedicated to improved information handling.

HISTORY

Undoubtedly the best summary of the development of the indexing and abstracting services up to the time of its publication is an article provided by Verner W. Clapp in a 1954 issue of *Library Trends.*[4]

Among the earliest attempts to provide control over the periodical literature was the alphabetical table to the *Philosophical Transactions* of the Royal Society and the indexes which accompanied the *Tatler, Spectator,* and *Guardian.* Subsequently, general indexes were issued such as the one of 1757 which indexed all three periodicals, or the cumulative indexes to the *Philosophical Transactions* which covered volumes 1-12, 12-17, and 1-70. This kind of control is a common one and generally is not what is being discussed in this paper, although in 1942 some 4,000 cumulative indexes were identified.

The next stage of development was the combined index to more than one periodical. The first of its kind was probably Jeremias David Reuss's *Repertorium*, which for the period 1801 to 1821 indexed in a classified arrangement, with author and title entries, contents of the publications of the academic societies of letters.

A few more specialized indexing publications came into being in the decades that followed. American entry, according to Clapp, was centered at Yale and in the work of the librarians of the Brothers in Unity, a literary society. In 1847 John Edmonds issued a small pamphlet, *Subjects for Debate, with References to Authorities*. In 1848, William Frederick Poole produced his first index, *An Alphabetical Index to Subjects Treated in the Reviews, and Other Periodicals, to which No Indexes have been Published: Prepared for the Library of the Brothers In Unity, Yale College;* an expanded edition appeared in 1853. Poole's efforts continued, with cooperation of a number of major libraries, and in 1882 a 1,492 page work indexing the contents of 6,245 volumes of 232 serials dated from 1802 to 1881 appeared. Supplements were issued in 1888, 1893, 1897, 1903, and 1908.

The indefatigable H. W. Wilson Company began its interest in bibliographical services in 1900, and fifty-three years later when H.W. Wilson retired as president, the company was issuing thirty current periodical and other indexing services. Its products continue to be the best known in the field.

Other major indexing projects of the period were the Royal Society's *Catalogue of Scientific Papers, 1800-1914, Index-Catalogue of the Library of the Surgeon General's Office, Index Medicus, Engineering Index, Zoological Record*, and numerous others.

Although my background in science and technology may bias me, the importance of journal literature in these fields has meant that more and larger collections of technical publications exist and that the need for indexes is more critical. Such ventures share a greater chance for fiscal success and for perpetuity.

Typical of indexes which trace their origin from twentieth century dates are *Chemical Abstracts*, 1907; *Biological Abstracts*, 1926; *Index to Legal Periodical Literature*, 1909; *and the New York Times Index* which began in 1913.

OVERLAP

Like the words of the spiritual "Everyone's Talking about Heaven ain't Agoing There," there is a lot of talk about eliminating overlap, but getting there is another thing. It is easy for a librarian, for instance, to be concerned that 67 percent of titles indexed in one service are also indexed elsewhere, or that 53.4 percent of the journals indexed by one major service are also indexed by another major service. Although unnecessary or duplicative overlap should not be condoned, such superficial comparison is faulty and dangerous. Any overlap is reason for concern, because duplication of effort is a great waste when many journals are not indexed in any source.

This vicious circle of serials not being indexed, so libraries do not acquire them or of libraries not acquiring a certain serial, so it is not indexed, reminds me of the words of that old gospel song, "Will the Circle be Unbroken?" I cannot vouch for the regular practice of libraries, but I doubt that the other half of this circle applies other than to the Wilson indexes. Most other indexing services are rather independent, yet responsive to the needs of libraries. *CA,* for example, says it tries to cover "everything the chemist needs." I do not know the total number of journals indexed nor the number unindexed, although the number of those indexed is obviously a much smaller number. A NFSAIS inventory for ten services in 1961 counted 17,036 titles indexed.[5]

There exists a mistaken idea that overlap of titles indexed means a duplication or overlap of effort and approach. This is far from the real situation. Described below is a recent brief study of two services in the field of plastics (at least fifteen specialized services in the field are known). Compared were *Plastics Monthly (PM),* published by Engineering Index, and *POST-J (Polymer Science and Technology-Journals),* published by Chemical Abstracts Service. Four hundred and seventy-nine journals were handled by *POST-J;* 390 by *PM;* 134 were duplicated. Occasional articles from other journals were also indexed—185 journals in 1969 by *EI.* The most revealing information concerns the depth of coverage and the indexing approach applied to the duplicated titles.

The lists of journals can be divided into five types—hard core plastics titles covered in depth by both services and which produce a large number of items; applications titles (a particular strength of EI); hard core engineering (which CAS leaves alone); hard core chemistry (which EI would not touch with a ten foot pole); and a final category of hard core foreign titles (where CAS shows greater strength, particularly in Russian and Japanese).

Invariably the indexing approach is different—CAS stresses the chemistry (the monomers and the polymers) of plastics, while EI emphasizes the processing, the equipment, the final product and its use. Indexing terminology assigned also reflects this poles-apart interest.

Another example of diversity is evidenced in the depth of coverage. In one sampling of eighteen journal issues (excluding hard core chemistry) which contained 205 papers, EI indexed 135 for *PM,* while CAS indexed only forty-four in *POST-J.* If hard core chemistry titles were sampled, the balance in numbers would likely be similar and the difference in coverage would be reemphasized (in other words, relatively little real overlap).

The description above is not intended as a rationalization for what goes on, or as a claim that no overlap exists. Each time abstracters-indexers in Columbus, Philadephia, San Antonio, Metals Park, New York, Washington, D.C., or wherever, pick up the same journal, scan or read the same article, write a similar abstract, and assign a variety of indexing terms, duplication of effort is taking place. There is concern about this from managers of the services, user groups, funding agencies, and everyone else involved in the problem.

In 1968, 759,488 items were published by NFSAIS member services; 844,500 were projected for 1969. Some of these are certain to be the result of duplicative effort. NFSAIS is concerned with this and has established a coverage study committee. Some of the a & i services are independently looking at the problem. The National Science Foundation more than once has sponsored overlap studies, such as the *CA-Nuclear Science Abstracts* comparison, and has expressed interest in sponsoring others.

SATCOM (Committe on Scientific and Technical Communication of the National Academy of Sciences) expressed its concern this way: "Ideally, efficient production of abstracts should be done but once—at least for a single broad field of coverage and a single language of abstracting—and the author should have no choice as to the basic abstracting journal that will cover a particular paper.[6]

Abstracting at source (i.e., by the author or in the author-referee-editor cycle) should be encouraged and thereby prevent major duplication of effort. Such efforts as those by the Engineers Joint Council (EJC)[7] need greater push, support, and acceptance. The EJC has urged with some, but minimal, success, the inclusion of well written abstracts along with descriptors or other indexing terms with each article appearing in a primary journal or conference proceedings. These would be used as input into secondary services and other information systems. Although they have been discussed elsewhere and are primarily tangential here, the CAS's ACCESS program, the National Serials Data Program, and the National Serials Service all have contributions to make to the elimination of unnecessary and costly overlap.

ELEMENTS AND METHODS

Standardization and/or compatibility have long been concerns of purchasers, and to a lesser degree, users of indexing services. We are led to believe that standardization is possible and desirable. Various attempts at standardization have been tried, and current efforts are particularly aggressive. The American National Standards Institute (formerly the United States of America Standards Institute and American Standards Association) Standards Committee Z39 on library work, documentation, and related publishing practices, is presently working in twenty-three different areas. Many of its deliberations and the standards which will be developed should be of direct concern in bibliographic control. Z39 is just beginning an effort on thesaurus rules and conventions. Drafts of standards on proof corrections and bibliographic references have been circulated for comment. A draft of a standard for the writing of abstracts (the third try in the last half-dozen years) has just been distributed. A revision of the standard for periodical title abbreviations was approved earlier this year.

Manipulation of bibliographic data by electronic and optical devices has introduced a new problem. A machine, unlike a human, is less adaptable to the different ways the same thing may be done. A lack of standardization either in the data base, its format, the software, or the hardware can make it costly to use machine-readable data. Z39 has produced a standard for bibliographic information interchange on magnetic tape which due to a technicality has not yet become a standard. At the same time, an informal group, JAG (Joint Agreements Group) is also developing standards in this field. A late comer and mystery-shrouded group, UNISIST, jointly organized by UNESCO and ICSU-AB (International Council of Scientific Unions-Abstracting Board) is studying the problems of information exchange. WFEO (World Federation of Engineering Organizations) is still organizing, although information is receiving fairly high priority as a candidate for international cooperation. As can be seen from the above, efforts toward cooperation are receiving attention.

A particularly pertinent controversy is that of a periodical coding system for use in machine control: CODEN vs. SSN (Standard Serial Number). CODEN, although it has been around since the early 1950s did not attract the attention of librarians and bibliographers until about 1962. Three volumes of assigned codes (five capital letters and a possible additional check digit) have been published by the American Society for Testing and Materials (ASTM), and a current assignment service is offered through Franklin Institute.

Only the fields of science and technology are covered by CODEN with assignment made to some 80,000 journals. By February 1970, between 100,000 and 105,000 will be assigned with publication of a new volume scheduled for August 1970. Between 12,000 and 18,000 more journals are estimated to require CODEN and will be included. The Standard Serial Number (seven numbers and a check digit) would be a universal, all subject assignment, and would, in fact, include conversion from CODEN to SSN. There are perhaps three million to three-and-a-half million journals totally, giving an idea of the scope of SSN assignments necessary. In spite of its heavy use it is unfortunate that CODEN has not become a standard, and whether the choice is CODEN or SSN, there will be extra expense involved, particularly if the present draft of a SSN standard is approved. While CODEN has been acceded to be of interest primarily to the scientific community, the recent substitution of SSN for CODEN as a desirable magnetic tape element in a chemical information system is an interesting turn of events. There is a choice to be made between alpha and a numeric coding system.

An informal comparison made of three major a & i services, BA, CA, and EI, considered editorial aspects of seven elements: title, authors, author address or affiliation, journal citation, language, abstract body, and abstract signature. In the twenty-element breakdown only one similar practice was discovered—the German umlaut is converted to the vowel followed by "e" by each of the three services.

Earlier efforts to encourage author-written abstracts were discussed. Most services describe the type of abstract they write—indicative, informative, critical, selective, or some other designation. That there is really a difference has yet to be proven. More important is the success of the author in telling his story or the success of the abstracter (a staff member of the indexing service or less expensive but slower-producing specialist) in giving the gist of the contents, filtered through his knowledge of the technical content of the original piece, within the style and length restrictions imposed and with his skill in the right choice of words to describe it. Who, incidentally, is training such personnel?

Indexing methodology and language will be considered briefly. Index approaches vary. Should all concepts, ideas, facts, materials, methods, uses, and processes be represented by the assignment of terms or should only a single main idea be brought out? Simple subject headings and subheadings may be assigned; descriptors chosen from a controlled thesaurus may be used; free-language indexing with terms selected from the text being indexed may be permitted; coordinate indexing or links and roles may·be applied; citation indexing or the use of citation trails may be the instruction. The depth of indexing and the number and kind of terms may condition the success of the indexing. Recently a search of an EI tape service produced hits with over 80 percent relevancy as compared to 40 percent with another data base.

The form of the indexing may take many guises: an alphabetical array by subject, a classified arrangement using terms or numbers or both, a permuted index using KWIC, KWOC, WADEX (word-author index), AKWIC (author plus KWIC), or any number of other tried or untried systems. Author, area, compound, formula, patent, and ring systems may all be separate indexes. Most a & i services have prepared instructions for abstracters; most are available if one should want to discover for himself the point of view and form which a service hopes to present.

Manual methods may be the sole means of manipulation with some indexes, while in other instances input and output may be produced and controlled by data processing or computing equipment. Machine indexing may become a reality in the future and solve many of the current problems. As the computer comes into greater use for keyboarding, merging, storing, and compositing, standardization becomes increasingly important. The choice and sequence of elements is important as are abbreviation, punctuation, and codings. The possibilities of merging inputs in machine-readable form from several sources, and the creation of new products as a subset of a larger data base are a reality. There are unrealized problems which will demand attention and answers.

OTHER MISCELLANEOUS CONSIDERATIONS

Pertinent to the success of any bibliographic control system are such matters as frequency, timeliness, intent of the service and how well this intent is satisfied, access to the service or the system, and access to the material being indexed.

Design of the a & i service may take on two, or at least two, characteristics. It is designed as a current awareness service, a shopping guide, or is it primarily a retrospective searching tool? Form and frequency then become important. Magnetic tape is of little value if a computer, systems and interface staff, the necessary dollars, and the need to have this kind of sophisticated service are lacking. Microforms also have both their advantages and limitations, and must be kept in mind.

Frequency of publication may suggest the intent and kind of use. Obviously a daily, weekly, or an on-line service accessible by remote terminals is intended for an environment where the value of information has been determined and the necessary dollar investment has been made to support the cost of the service. Annual publication obviously is intended for retrospective searching.

Most users of a & i services cannot receive their indexes too soon. Promptness costs money and is usually a major concern of most services. Time lag (or the coefficient of topicality) and particularly public time lag (the time which elapses between the actual date of publication as opposed to the date printed on the publication) must be distinguished from internal lag. Internal lag is something over which the service can provide some control—the time it takes to record receipt, abstract, index, edit, keyboard, proofread, compose, print, bind, and mail.

All a & i services are concerned about time lag and are trying to reduce it whenever possible. In a study conducted by EI two years ago on 1966 and 1967 issues, the public time lag was found to be 10.9 months for the *Monthly* and 9.8 months for *Plastics Monthly (PM)*. The range was two to fifty months for the *Monthly* and two to twenty-six for *PM*. Internal lag, however, was 8.26 and 4.33 months respectively. A later analysis of the March 1968 *PM* produced these results:

All journal literature	5.4 months
All journals and proceedings	7.1 months
U.S. journals assigned to *PM*	3.4 months
U.S. journals referred to *PM*	8.1 months
Foreign journals assigned to *PM*	6.6 months
Foreign journals referred to *PM*	13.4 months

For both publications, the lag between the date of the issue and the actual publication date ranged from 1.25 to 2 months. This lag has been controlled, and extensive controls to reduce the over-all internal lag and to eliminate the upper extremes have been instituted.

Nothing is more frustrating to a potential user than to learn that the article listed in an index is not available to him. It is not enough for an a & i service to index an article, but it must assure the user that he can examine a copy somewhere or receive a copy for his own files. A complete information service includes this feature. *Applied Mechanics Review* indexed items are available in the Linda Hall Library, *BA* items from the John Crerar Library, and *EI* items from the Engineering Societies Library. The Center for Research Libraries, Chicago, also has a program to provide copies of all items indexed by *BA* and by *CA*, and *CA* tries to provide all non-copyright (that is, Russian) items.

VALUE AND COSTS

Indexes have been called the "magic key" that helps librarians to pluck quickly the precise information "needle" from the giant and rapidly growing "haystack" of miscellaneous data being heaped all about them. If these indexes were not available, the cost to duplicate them or the service they provide would be prohibitive, and the service of all libraries would be severely handicapped.

There are still many individuals around who remember the year (1955) when *Chemical Abstracts* raised its price from $80 to $500 (or when *Review of Metals Literature* went from $35 to $500); there are librarians who object to the service-basis method of charge practiced by the H.W. Wilson Company; there must be those who object to a flat rate charged to all libraries; and most assuredly, all must express concern at the rising prices for a & i services.

During the past decade numerous a & i services have had substantial government funding to create new services or to maintain or upgrade existing services. Libraries and researchers, too, have benefited from this same support. Generally the day of heavy federal government support—particularly by the National Science Foundation—is past, and many services operated by not-for-profit organizations are being required to become self-supporting, a requirement which the information companies have always faced, through the sale of publications and services.

The price trend for abstracting and indexing services has been upward for some time. A major percentage increase for serial services for 1969 was reported.[8] The average price index for 1,031 services, excluding eleven Wilson indexes, was 198.0 compared to a 1957-1959 base of 100.0. Although all classifications showed an index increase, the range varies from a low of 5.0 for business services to a high of 111.4 for science and technology—a percentage increase of more than 23 percent in dollars. (The price of the EI *Annual* increased 167 percent during that same ten-year period.)

All a & i services have been keenly aware of increasing expenses and increased costs for their publications. In fact, NFSAIS has established in the past year, a cost study committee which is studying the problems, how comparisons might be made, and norms or bases established. There is also in early stages of discussion a proposal to develop guidelines for decision making in abstracting and indexing services based on cost/performance/benefits performance. Is it possible?

Other recent studies have looked at the costs of producing secondary services. System Development Corporation in a COSATI-sponsored study[9] on indexing and abstracting collected extensive information on costs, but this material or any conclusions were conspicuously missing from the final report. SATCOM considered the dollar situation of a & i services and the need to find the necessary support:

> It is already feasible, and the need is urgent, to provide specialized access to information for professional groups of this size [a thousand or so] with common information requirements.[10]

> We dare not depend on support of information transfer exclusively on the part of users to produce a system that is in over-all economic balance.[11]

Government support of operating deficits was identified as a possible solution. Two situations, in fact, must exist and must provide a balance of nature in the ecology of information. Profit-oriented companies must be

Average Prices and Cost Index
U.S. Serial Services 1969
(Based on 1957-1959 prices)

Year	Number of Services	Average Price	Index
Business			
1957-1959	544	$ 78.75	100.0
1968	214	119.35	151.6
1969	231	123.31	156.6
Law			
1957-1959	353	$ 28.46	100.0
1968	133	57.65	202.6
1969	147	68.86	242.0
Science and Technology			
1957-1959	469	$ 13.50	100.0
1968	224	64.02	474.2
1969	224	79.05	585.6
Miscellaneous			
1957-1959	165	$ 23.80	100.0
1968	108	45.65	191.8
1969	110	49.84	209.4
U.S. Documents			
1957-1959	123	$ 17.51	100.0
1968	144	18.40	105.1
1969	145	21.35	122.0
Soviet Translations			
1957-1959	149	$ 43.38	100.0
1968	164	90.39	208.4
1969	174	93.93	216.5
Wilson Index			
1957-1959	32	$143.50	100.0
1968	11	257.00	179.1
1969	11	268.91	187.4
Combined (excluding Wilson Index)			
1957-1959	1,803	$ 39.80	100.0
1968	987	70.87	178.1
1969	1,031	78.79	198.0

permitted to make a profit on self-supporting services; other organizations must be permitted sufficient grant or contract support to assure that useful, but unprofitable, services are established or kept in existence.

One table produced by SATCOM is of special interest. Subscription percentage increases between 1963 and 1968 for twelve major services and the percentage increase in price per entry are given. The subscriptions have increased from a low of 11 percent for *Nuclear Science Abstracts* (*NSA*, a federal government service published by AEC) to a high of 1,030 percent for *Physics Abstracts* published by a technical society in London. (A decrease of 45 percent was noted for *International Aerospace Abstracts (IAA)*, a privately produced but NASA-funded service.) Increases per entry varied from a low of 0 percent for *Chemical Abstracts* to a high of 236 percent for *Physics Abstracts*. *Psychological Abstracts*, *IAA*, and *NSA* all reported a decrease in price per entry.[12]

At best, the pricing picture is cloudy and confused. One service, *Bibliography and Index of Geology*, published by the Geological Society of America in cooperation with the American Geological Institute, in January 1969 discontinued abstracting in order to increase the number of items indexed and to live within fiscal realities. Substitution of a published abstract in a secondary service in lieu of full publication in a primary journal is contemplated by some organizations as a way to reduce over-all publication costs. Will such actions become necessary for other services?

Various seers and sages have predicted the demise of the kind of old-fashioned bibliographic control described here. Not a demise due to lack of dollars (some way will be found to continue support), but a demise because the abstract is out of date and can never be a satisfactory surrogate for the original, so why bother. There is question, however, that anyone reading this article should be concerned. Attention, though, must be given to the improvement of bibliographic control. The creation of machine-readable data bases, of regional information dissemination centers, and a trend toward more centralization will all have a bearing. Bibliographic control of the future is in the minds of the practical genius.

References

1. U.S. Library of Congress. Science and Technology Division. *A Guide to U.S. Indexing and Abstracting Services in Science and Technology.* (National Federation of Science Abstracting and Indexing Services Report No. 101). Washington, D.C., 1960.

2. U.S. Library of Congress. Science and Technology Division. *A Guide to the World's Abstracting and Indexing Services in Science and Technology* (National Federation of Science Abstracting and Indexing Services Report No. 102). Washington, D.C., 1963.

3. International Federation for Documentation. *Abstracting Services in Science, Technology, Medicine, Agriculture, Social Sciences, Humanities.* Rev. ed. Paris, Fédération Internationale de Documentation, 1969.

4. Clapp, Verner W. "Indexing and Abstracting Services for Serial Literature," *Library Trends,* 2:509-21, April 1954.

5. National Federation of Science Abstracting and Indexing Services. *A List of Serials Covered by Members of the NFSAIS.* 2 vols. Washington, D.C., 1962.

6. Committee on Scientific and Technical Communication. *Scientific and Technical Communication, A Pressing National Problem and Recommendations for Its Solution.* Washington, D.C., National Academy of Sciences, 1969, p. 54.

7. Engineers Joint Council. *Guide for Source Indexing and Abstracting of the Engineering Literature.* Frank Y. Speigth, ed. New York, Engineers Joint Council, 1967.

8. Huff, William H. and Brown, Norman B. "Price Indexes for 1969, Serials Services," *Library Journal,* 94:2572-73, July 1969.

9. System Development Corporation, Santa Monica, Calif. *A System Study of Abstracting and Indexing in the United States.* Falls Church, Va., 1966.

10. Committee on Scientific and Technical Communication, *op. cit.,* p. 10.

11. *Ibid.,* p. 17.

12. *Ibid.,* p. 159.

Warren B. Kuhn
Director
Iowa State University Library
Ames, Iowa

SERVICE

In ancient Greece King Augeas was the ruler of Elis who had difficulties with his housekeeping. By skillful attention to an acquisition program with his bulls zestfully engaged in their own activities, he had managed to accumulate immense herds, but somehow never got around to cleaning his stables. By the time Hercules was given the task of policing the area, the Augean establishment was overflowing with thirty years of deposit collections.

Good King Augeas and his stables kept returning to mind as I considered my topic for this paper: the problems of arranging and servicing a large serial collection. Even more than other aspects of libraries, the serial and periodical collections present a vast and seemingly immmovable presence. Once processed, our busy attention to them, like that of Augeas, has often been diverted elsewhere. Unfortunately, while Hercules had the River Alpheus to help him cleanse the stables, our torrent of proliferating periodicals and serials pours in at a new flood level each year—and never runs out again!

Being no Hercules, I have concentrated on only a few considerations of serial service in our Augean establishments that seem to me to warrant special attention.

First, let me try to assuage the feelings of those who have already reacted to my implication that librarians have not been handling periodicals as well as they might. I have no doubt librarians' hearts are Herculean in the desire to be of service, but their attempts have, *as yet,* not been overly effective. I say *as yet* because there are current developments which promise help, some of which librarians have initiated, and many of which they must begin to more actively investigate and try.

Librarians have only begun, for instance, to learn how research users approach serial and periodical materials. This is a standard criticism, but a valid one. Librarians know even less of how research users become acquainted

175

with sources of information in general. The library profession has provided subject access to books and a proportion of the symposiums and published conference proceedings, but despite the signicant advances in indexing and abstracting services, it has not provided anywhere near the simple and direct access to *all* journal articles that is needed. Are there any new arrangements in periodical display that can be tried? What is being done with the problem of "current awareness"? What is happening with circulation?

In this paper I would like to discuss a number of the points I have just mentioned and draw some subjective and personal conclusions. Patterns of use of periodicals by the reader would seem an appropriate place to begin. There have been some studies of this, primarily on information requirements by scientists, but obviously more of this type of investigation is necessary. This is an area in which library schools might do more, but their studies would not release us from specific local investigations in how faculty, students and other users approach large collections. There is a particular need to determine the comparative importance of the different means used by the researcher in locating information. I refer here not to evaluations of abstracting journals and indexes or to lists of the most cited journals in specific fields. Instead I refer to the type of study cited by Melvin Voigt in his monograph, "Scientists' Approaches to Information." *How much* of the literature "is located by regular reading, by recommendations of colleagues, by references in other publications,"[1] or by other means?

Voigt reports that:

> More printed information sources than were obtained by any other means, probably one third or slightly more, were obtained or used *without any bibliographical reference.* That is, they were come upon, and read or used, as part of a regular or irregular practice of browsing through or reading the most important journals in the immediate field of interest.[1] (Italics added.)

Abstracts and indexes supplied only from 4 to 7 percent of the references used by scientists. These and other means of surveying the literature become more important at the beginning of an experimental program or when a researcher prepares the results of his work for publication.[2] In any case, these needs occur relatively infrequently in comparison with the total time spent by scientists using current, or what Voigt terms "everyday," approaches to the literature.

A Case Institute study of physicists and chemists concluded that slightly more than 50 percent of their total reading was undirected browsing—only 10 percent of it done in the library. Another study found that industrial technologists sought material apparently more for stimulation than for reference.[3]

It is not my purpose to explore this aspect too deeply here, but it does point out the reliance of at least the scientific researcher upon regular browsing through a limited number of the most important journals in his field. Some librarians have attempted to meet this need by routing the most current or next to most current issue of certain journals to the faculty. The benefits of this sort of service are appreciable as a personal convenience, but short of very heavy duplication it can lead to undue harrassment of other faculty as well as of the student community.

At my own institution we have just terminated a routing service that had been in effect for many years. Previously, we had been circulating more than 485 journal titles to approximately forty-seven departments. On a small campus this may be sufferable; on our large campus it had reached the point where substantial difficulties were being constantly encountered. Many faculty and departments would return journals quickly; others were retaining issues for as long as two months because of genuine interest and internal circulating practices of their own. Fines had some effect, but were becoming onerous only to the individual departmental representative who had been assigned as the point of contact.

The librarian, at the present stage of technology and funding, is thus placed on the horns of a very severe dilemma. Can there be a substitute for the routing practice, one that will in its own way serve, if not a similar purpose, a more limited fulfillment of needs? I should add here that we have had little or no substantial reaction to the cessation of our routing. Some of the reasons for this may be that it was stopped just as we opened a new library addition with more room and facilities for in-building use, and because we contemplate offering some substitute services.

One such substitution might be the introduction of a "table-of-contents" service tailored to a specific university campus. This could be made available to all departments, not the scientific departments alone, that at least in our case, made the heaviest use of the actual journal routing service. The titles of an initial maximum of approximately fifteen journals considered most important by that department's faculty could be solicited from each major teaching department or administrative unit. A single photocopy of the contents pages from these journals could then be regularly distributed to each department for "current awareness" purposes. A certain amount of flexibility could be exercised based upon demand, the number of journals in a given field, the size of department and other factors. Correlation of demand could also be used statistically to determine where we might duplicate subscriptions within the main collection or even within departmental collections.

The purchase of multiple copies of the various "Current Contents" publications could be a more expensive variation of this service. There are now some six of these weekly pocket-size guides, covering journals mostly in the sciences. Two recent ones cover agriculture - food - veterinary sciences, and engineering - technology. Such guides do not presently cover all academic fields, but they do range widely and extensively in many pure and applied fields. Use of multiple subscriptions to "Current Contents" publications of course, could continue to supplement and expand the local departmental coverage; we could begin by making available whenever possible the core offered by them and then concentrate on the peripheral titles and those fields not yet available in commercial publications.

A second variation might be a canvassing of the publishers of heavily used periodicals to see what reprint service they offer and making more of the faculty aware of these so they would have an opportunity to secure desirable reprints at a reasonable cost on their own. The current contents publications provide alphabetical listings of authors and their current addresses to facilitate reprint requests.

While these services may be of particular help to the scientist and engineer, it is not certain whether it would have the same applicability to the humanist and the social scientist. The "current awareness" aspect, however, should certainly be tempting to any department, and would represent the library as going "out" to the reader as it should, rather than waiting for the reader to come "in" to it. Such a program would allow us to provide the core of the routing arrangement, permit us to assist faculty, especially scientific faculty, in regularizing their browsing habits, and still retain the actual periodicals centrally for the greatest number of users.

One foreseeable user objection to this might be that article titles are often not sufficiently descriptive to give the user a true indication of what the article itself is about. Ultimately the real answer would seem to lie in the selective dissemination of information approach via user profiles and magnetic tapes. In the meantime, the "table-of-contents" service might be a workable substitute, expanding on the base of what is presently available.

Beyond the need of the researcher for current materials is his need for older serial sets. For librarians this is the problem of conventional shelving as opposed to storage for periodical back sets, and of knowing where the break can legitimately be made within a set to divide active volumes as opposed to those lesser used. Prediction of use has been explored by Fussler and Simon,[4] but the fact that more libraries are restricting circulation of periodicals poses problems of ascertaining recorded use.

One approach we might take is to accumulate fresh and reliable "citation-of-use" lists of journals similar to the American College and Research Libraries' study done a decade and a half ago by Charles Harvey Brown.[5] Special libraries have done some of this, but there is a positive need for a study of the differences between, for instance, the stable disciplines, the literature which becomes obsolete more slowly, and those disciplines dependent on fresh data because of new problems (such as the applied fields). We can readily agree that removing to storage the important works of humanists on the basis of frequency of use would render humanistic libraries ineffective and seriously hinder historians of science. However, the same is clearly true of the comparative sciences that accumulate durable references and remain more stable over longer periods of time. In this we can include back sets in such fields as mathematics, economics, geology, chemistry, botany and parasitology. Burton in his study of the "half-life" of scientific literatures and their rates of obsolescence also notes that it is quite possible for certain journals even within less stable disciplines to contain larger proportions of what he terms "classic" references and to be retained for longer active use than might be supposed from the activity of the field itself.[6]

Further, an investigation of patterns in these areas must include studies of intralibrary use in depth—studies of shelf-return tallies, data on serial units handled by photocopy, interlibrary loans and supplementary interviews of users (although the latter is always a tough one to handle). Raisig suggests that a real start might be made in this by choosing the first few hundred serials ranked in a valid citation list. These most valuable and most used items could be thoroughly analyzed for not only out-of-building use or interlibrary loan use, but also for comparision of intralibrary use, even to the degree of attempting to identify frustrated *wants* and how these were handled.[7]

Reports on student use of periodicals have been especially rare, but when they are published, they do seem to offer some clues to improving serial services to this group. A recent study of 338 graduate students and their use of periodical literature at the University of Michigan reveals, as we would suspect, substantial use. Peterson reports that 84 percent of the students surveyed attested to use of periodicals during the given school term.[8] Sixty percent reported use at least once weekly, and periodical use was almost as heavy in non-science libraries as in science libraries. He also notes that students using periodicals at least once weekly comprised 79 percent of all users of science libraries, and 68 percent of all users of non-science libraries. The interesting point is that the subject approach was the primary one used by graduate students. They located their material mainly through indexes or abstracting services, and far less frequently consulted serials by publishing society, country, language or even age of periodical. An overwhelming number, Peterson reports, came well prepared to find the article they needed, and the majority used periodical literature for research purposes.

While this heavier and encouragingly self-sufficient reliance on indexes and abstracting tools centers on the graduate student, there is an indication that undergraduates are making use of the more common of these same tools. This would seem to be evidenced by the increasing number of newer undergraduate facilities that are adding back sets of the more usual periodical indexes. Actual use has not yet been reported, but libraries are attempting to provide increased opportunity for use of indexes by duplicating sets for undergraduates. Stanford's Meyer Library for undergraduates has a collection of general indexes near its reference center and more specialized subject indexes on its upper floors in reference alcoves which serve as entryways to the subject collections. Maryland will provide in its new undergraduate library a small reference collection with considerable duplication at each service desk, including major bibliographic tools and indexes. In its undergraduate service area, Iowa State duplicates selected back sets of major indexes. Apparently this effort is being made by these libraries so that students may* have the proper references in hand when they go on to use the backup resources of the main library research collection. A secondary benefit is the chance to teach the use of these indexes to undergraduates when they are motivated by a definite inquiry.

This increased use of indexing aids suggests an attractive possibility for better periodical service in the larger collection itself. Especially frustrating to a student, and indeed to anyone, is finding himself on a stack floor, seemingly miles from the periodical indexes and abstracts usually housed only in the reference or periodical room. To compound this sense of loss, add the injury of a student suddenly discovering that his periodical reference is erroneous or incomplete, or that the one article for which he has a reference and which he has found has set him off on a brand-new search for other articles on other topics.

Why could we not provide selected, duplicate sets of indexes and major abstracting services in what might be called "index stations" strategically located throughout the library? For a start, these might consist of only a five or ten-year file within reasonable distance of appropriate periodical back files, reasonable being defined as back sets no further away than a maximum of one or two floors. As an added convenience, we might even add several dictionaries, both in English and foreign languages, an atlas or two, and a few other basic reference tools. Naturally, this means duplication and expense, but think of the time saved for the user and the elimination of frustrations, to say nothing of the succor of inspiration otherwise discouragingly nipped in the bud. If we are concerned about the "wandering" index that might grow mysterious feet and disappear, it is conceivable that these volumes might be fastened into a clamping rack similar to those used in telephone centers to hold large out-of-town directories.

Obviously, this sort of help is suited to the library where periodicals are classified and distributed throughout the collection, but there well may be some value in trying a number of "reference and abstract stations" in a very large monographic collection.

Since we have broached the perennial subject of classified versus unclassified collections, let us discuss it briefly. Is there a "best" shelving arrangement for periodicals through one or the other of these methods? This is a question well calculated to raise the hackles of many otherwise mellow librarians. Any proper answer, of course, depends as always on the library's avowed purposes and objectives. Unfortunately, as with choosing one's ancestors, the decision to classify or alphabetize has probably been decided long ago for the individual librarian.

Nevertheless, some situations do arise when there is a chance to break the mold, or at least review the possibilities of change. Such occasions might be the establishment of a new library, or the occupying of a new building or addition. Conceivably, we could institute a self-generated local review of whether to classify or alphabetize even without a new building or addition, but, admittedly, to the librarian of a large institution any major change in arranging the bulk of his periodical collection would seem to assume the semblance of rebuilding the Great Wall of China.

A thoughtful article by Joseph Borden[9] presents a good view of both sides of the fence. From the reader's viewpoint, which is the one in which I assume librarians are interested, Borden describes the classified collection as one that distributes the periodicals, generally the bound volumes, by subject throughout the stacks. Thus the reader finds his periodicals for a given subject located relatively close to one another; there is a greater possibility of back files being shelved together despite title changes, transactions and proceedings of the same organization can better be kept together, and non-indexed periodicals are somewhat more accessible. However, the reader must also first search out a call number, and if he is concerned only with periodical references, he will find his potential sources more widely scattered among the books of the library.

In the alphabetical arrangement, the user has a more direct approach. The periodical collection is usually maintained in one centralized area, and materials can be located by title without further preliminary checking. If his interest is in periodicals alone, he can ignore the rest of the collection. The disadvantage of transactions and proceedings being shelved apart can be corrected by shelving under corporate author, but this may tend to work against the journal-oriented scholar not searching for the name of the issuing organization.

These are some of the physical advantages and disadvantages of classification, but the intellectual level of the collection also affects its use. In the case of the research library, I think librarians could agree that the greater the number of scholarly periodicals, the greater the percentage of periodicals capable of fairly specific classification and thus capable of being shelved closer together. This is suggested by Pierson who also notes the probability that in the larger library there will be a greater number of periodicals not indexed in the currently available indexing media.[10] Relevant also is that the larger the research collection, the greater the number of other serials which would already have been classified. For these reasons the user of the research library will probably find the collection more serviceable if it is classified.

Pierson says the reverse might also be true. He asks: Why not alphabetize the undergraduate collection which would be smaller and less scholarly-oriented? He also points out that for undergraduates it may be more important, however, to appeal to interest levels and subject motivation, thus requiring classification even for the undergraduate library. Another point that must be made is that if the research library classifies, then probably so should the undergraduate library in order that a student may more easily transfer his search for a given periodical from one library to the other. This is especially pertinent for undergraduate collections since their periodical back files are normally at a minimum with the research library forming the main resource.

We cannot really resolve this question of the two systems, but a survey conducted several years ago indicates a degree of preference for classifed systems. Of sixteen large university libraries selected, twelve had classified periodical collections, two classified some periodicals, and two did not classify any. Most of those classifying periodicals used the same classification scheme for the remainder of the research collection.[11]

We have said nothing so far of the shelving problems of current issues as distinguished from bound back sets. A common arrangement is that the central periodical room is used for current numbers with back sets shelved elsewhere. Some libraries have shelved the most recent bound volumes near their current issues, with older sets in still another location. This type of "third" location has some undesirable features, yet the increasing number of storage facilities makes some version of this inevitable as older and lesser-used titles are transferred out of the "active" library entirely. Some of the onus, incidentally, could be removed from extramural storage if a "browsing capability" of some sort were retained at the "inactive" location. Still another version has the most heavily-used current unbound titles maintained in a separate periodical area while lesser-used unbound issues are shelved beside bound back sets in the stacks.

Would it be desirable to shelve all current issues and their back files together, perhaps via a pamphlet box at the end of each title? From a reference standpoint this has some advantages, but it immediately destroys the possibility of a general periodical display, as well as scattering issues and providing no security for the more popular and fast-disappearing titles. Some compromise has been suggested by shelving current issues facing reading areas with back files in adjacent ranges. The variance in shelving requirements for individual back runs, however, would prohibit any systematic or economical consecutive shelving under this arrangement.[12]

The divisional plan does permit some retention of current issues close to back files, but there are many titles of an interdisciplinary nature that could fit one place as well as another. This underlines in part the continuing need of a common periodical room for *generalia*.[13]

Aside from keeping all current issues in a central periodical room, is there some way that libraries can combine the positive assets of current issue display with reasonable proximity to back files? I am, of course, assuming in my answer that librarians are in favor of displaying important periodicals, that they have classified their periodical collection, that they have open shelves, and that they are not on the divisional plan. These assumptions could describe a good proportion of our larger libraries. Normally, the current periodical area and the bound periodical collection are some distance removed from each other. In the completely classified collection the bound volumes are quite scattered in relation to a central current issue display.

What if libraries divided current issues by broad subjects and established smaller versions of a periodical room throughout the stack collection? How would such a system work?

Librarians could first select those periodicals in the significant disciplines which receive the heaviest use, or are considered worthy of being seen regularly by those who work within that discipline. For display, stack areas could be adapted into periodical alcoves with sufficient lounge and small table seating for comfortable browsing. We would not have an alcove on every floor, but we might plan a sufficient number to accommodate subject periodicals in fair proximity to five or six of the largest subject divisions of the collection. We could have, for instance, a literature alcove near the language and literature collection, or one for life sciences close to monographs and bound volumes in botany, biology, zoology and bacteriology.

In each alcove could be maintained the "index station" already mentioned, as well as a small working reference collection. Presumably, only those indexes with applicability to the titles on display and/or the bound volumes on that floor or nearby floors would be duplicated.

Control would demand attention, but current issues wander discouragingly in any case. Since some central periodical room for more general periodicals, including the most popular ones, would have to be retained, it could also house those journals most interdisciplinary in scope or which experience shows come under such heavy use as to require a more controlled arrangement. In either the LC or Dewey classifications, the general periodical room would still concentrate on the AP's or the 050's, leaving more specific subjects dispersed. In the case of the central periodical room there would be the advantages of display; the removal of the barrier of form (present arrangements in effect, say, to the user that he must read only current periodicals *here* and bound volumes *there*); it promotes the subject cohesiveness of the collection; and it might even seduce some students into reading journals which they may never have read before.

There are ready arguments against such a system, the most damning the one of control. Libraries are, however, already utilizing some aspects of this dispersed arrangement in departmental collections or divisional plans. Why should the subject-oriented person be diverted to several locations simply because of the form in which material appears? For the same reason, I am also a firm believer in dispersed microtext collections for the reader's benefit, decentralizing them on the basis of alliance—newspapers and periodicals on microfilm, for instance, close to the newspaper and general periodical collection and not in some distant basement room. After all, is the centralized current issue periodical area with its raggedly filled shelves the only way of attacking this old problem?

So that it may be known that I am practicing what I preach, we are experimenting with just this sort of arrangement at Iowa State. We utilize periodical alcoves on three open floors and on three alternate levels of a new multi-tier stack, seven alcoves in all. To form these alcoves which allow us to display approximately 120 current titles, we have sacrificed four double-faced sections on the end of five stack ranges and four single-faced sections on the inward site of two additional ranges; on the open floors devoted to the humanities and social sciences we have utilized three bays at corridor entrances on two floors to accommodate lounge seating, tables and display shelving for several hundred current titles. Two smaller alcoves are intended for our topmost floor. Directories indicate what is shelved in each alcove, and copies of a computer-produced current serials list distributed around the building also list the periodical alcove locations for these titles. We still maintain a general periodical and newspaper room, but we now shelve within it our entire Library of Congress "A" classification. This permits us to have both current issues and all back sets to the most popular periodicals, which seem to fall within this classification, in a suitable reading room under supervision. Thus our most heavily-used periodicals are controlled, are given at least some on-the-spot reference service, and the heavy traffic they generate is kept to one location.

If the experiment fails, it is simple enough to retreat in the tiers by adding more stack supports and by reshelving with regular shelves, and by using the display shelves from both tiers and open floors elsewhere. As for the displayed periodicals, we can also easily expand the current issue display within the general periodical room which we have retained.

Restrictions on periodical circulation come as close to blasphemy on the university campus as anything can. A librarian tampering with long-established and liberal circulation practices for periodicals assumes the appearance of Beelzebub tampering with Holy Writ. And yet, there is indication that more libraries are limiting periodical circulation, or at least considering it more seriously, than ever before.

Among fourteen midwestern university libraries of large size which we surveyed recently, there was almost unanimous agreement on building use only for unbound issues, with the exceptions permitting only overnight circulation. For bound volumes, eight of the fourteen libraries restricted circulation to either the building or overnight borrowing. Faculty members received somewhat more liberal treatment in six institutions, with one library offering extended loan, one a one-month loan, and four ranging downward from two weeks to two days. Among graduate students, two weeks was the longest period of loan for bound volumes, and this only for older periodicals at one institution. Undergraduates were allowed two weeks for the same journals at the same university, but ten libraries restricted circulation to two days or less. Or those institutions that permitted limited circulation, the stress was on older volumes, usually those older than five years or with publication dates before 1960. One library restricted science loans for faculty and graduate students to three days for volumes from 1955 to date. Another recent and wider survey of smaller-sized academic libraries reported that forty-five state and private universities did not allow periodicals out of the library for more than three days, while a fair proportion indicated only overnight circulation was permitted.[14] Some librarians contacted personally admitted with reluctance that the time had just about come when something had to be done to keep the periodical collection as consistently available as the reference collection.

There is a tendency to assume that departmental libraries or other subject collections outside the main building are more liberal in their circulation practices. Conversations with library administrators at various universities indicate that this may not really be true any longer. At Princeton, for example, the science libraries tend to be much more restrictive in journal circulation than the main library. With minor exceptions none of the departmental libraries circulate journals, bound or unbound, at all. The exceptions are mathematics-physics, which permits overnight use only, and geology, which has a one-month rule. In the past ten years, Princeton reports that all of the science and technology libraries have tightened their rules dramatically.[15]

Two reasons why restrictions may be working in some departmental collections are a reliance on greater duplication of heavily used titles and the availability of photocopy. Princeton, in addition, has been working on a system of coordinated binding so that at least one copy of each duplicated journal is available somewhere all the time. An important assist to such restrictions are pressures from graduate students and a growing number of faculty who want periodicals available on a more regular basis within the library.

After a considerable period of quite liberal loans at Iowa State University, we have recently restricted periodical circulation of both bound and unbound issues to overnight use only. This was accomplished at the same time we opened a new addition to the building which provided vastly larger and more comfortable in-building facilities. Our reasoning was based on the increasing problem of recalling materials and on the ever-rising criticism of the earlier, more liberal system by both faculty and graduate students. After several months, we have had relatively few problems with the change and a significant amount of support. We do, of course, try to remain flexible in individual situations to answer urgent needs.

As an indication of faculty support for this change, I would like to quote from a memorandum from the chairman of an important science department on the campus. He writes:

> I find (as do most of my colleagues) that the occasional inconvenience of not being able to remove a volume from the Library is trivial compared with the frustration of not being able to *find* a volume in the Library. Even limited (24-hour or 3-day) circulation would restore the frustration in many cases.
>
> I realize that others may have different requirements, and that it may some day be necessary to modify these restrictions. If that day comes, you will have my support if you give ground very grudgingly!

Restrictions on periodical circulation in the main library as well as in the departmental library place renewed demands on fast copy service. Coin-operated machines offer effective answers as long as copies are procurable at a low cost, and machines are in sufficient supply and on a constant maintenance schedule. Partial subsidies of coin-operated machines might well be encouraged so that a maximum number are available throughout the library proper and at other locations.

Photocopy is particularly advantageous to the science researcher since scientific and technological articles tend to be shorter and simpler to copy. Lucker suggest that, "scientists tend, in general, to write shorter articles and more of them."[15] Humanistic articles, on the other hand, tend to be longer and more costly to copy, which may be another reason why the humanist argues that he needs a periodical loan period of greater duration than the scientist. Unfortunately, the science researcher often has some fund support to pay his photocopy bills, whereas the humanist is in the position of a perennial Mother Hubbard. Where the path lies that will lead us from this dilemma is hard to predict, short of free photocopying, which would send everyone into panic.

Photocopying in the case of mutilations and missing issues is now also an accepted practice, as is the photocopying of articles for interlibrary loan. Bound volume lending for interlibrary loan has almost ceased entirely. It may even be that mutilation is less serious today than it was ten years ago simply because of the advance of the copying machine. More libraries are resorting to copying out-of-print single issues to complete volumes for binding since the search for single issues through the second-hand market is so time consuming and costly, even provided they can be found.

A growing development which has been adopted by several libraries and which may offer some real assistance to others is the location or relocation of the serials staff closer to public access and reorganization of them into a collecting, processing *and* reference unit. In his new book on planning library buildings, Ellsworth refers to the duplication found in work and record keeping by both the processing and public service departments, and to the fact that some libraries are not only combining the public records into a central serial record, but also placing this public office close to the reference desk.[16] The University of Iowa has a serials information window adjacent to its reference desk, and Louisiana State University has placed its public serials records just off an entrance lobby and close to the catalog and bibliography area. Princeton is contemplating a relocation of its serials division staff and combining it with a new single collection of all general periodicals now held within its main library. Stanford has long had a serials information desk adjacent to both its circulation and reference desks. The basic idea for all is to centralize receiving, acquisition *and* a point of reference service.

In terms of the computer, the current serials printout in use at a good many libraries provides valuable reference help by duplicating an alphabetical list of current serials, together with call numbers, locations and holdings, and maintaining these at strategic building locations. The old and cumbersome visible public card files, annoying to use and difficult to maintain, are thus reproduced in book form, greatly expanded to include all current titles and not just a sampling, and made available in several locations rather than in only one. Some institutions have printed annual or biennial compilations from the same format. Such individual serial lists, if programmed compatibly from the beginning, provide a natural source for state or regional union serial lists, as well as later incorporation into local or regional data banks.

In addition to the list of titles for the public, the computer can also produce a serials shelflist printout if the original input is comprehensive enough. Important elements that can be included in these are cost, frequency, source, and country of origin. The resulting dividend allows not only many copies of a master list of titles, but individual lists by subject, jobber, location or any other permutation, for collection evaluation, desiderata lists and other similar aids.

A brief word about microforms. These certainly have charms to soothe the savage growth of serial collections in matters of space, handling and duplication, if not necessarily in cost. They offer libraries vast opportunities to fill retrospective gaps and acquire basic back sets. Their latest development, color, has intriguing aspects for the fields of fine arts, architecture, interior design, and even entomology and botany, to say nothing of the potent possibilities for the undergraduate now that *Playboy* is available in living color on microfilm.

For the infrequently-used serial or periodical the microtext is not only highly practical but the only possible way many newly-established libraries or re-emerging institutions can provide for comprehensive collections. The older, larger libraries have, however, already found it cheaper to store the old, bound volume than to convert it all to microfilm, at least against that day when the micro-image can be placed in the reader's hand by the computer. Proper indexing tools, or the lack of them, is a service problem for many microform areas, and adequate service must still depend heavily on the skilled reference librarian. Let us also insist that our architects play fair to readers in the microtext reading room by allowing sufficient outlets to accommodate individual reading lights, some tables designed for typewriters, if desired, and some partitioning to give the user some opportunity for privacy. At the moment our microfilm rooms look very much like the Bijou on Saturday afternoon, without the popcorn.

Also the ability of microtext to duplicate a back set in little space offers possibilities toward increasing the comprehensiveness of the departmental library. This edges librarians again, though, toward studies of obsolescence, and the question of when would it be wiser to simply deliver a microform from the main library? If departmental libraries are limited, as they probably should be in most cases, to current and frequently-used materials, the hard copy subscription will undoubtedly predominate except where materials are available in no other way than microform. If a two-to-four-year period is the range of current interest for many periodicals within departmental collections, is there any imperative to binding these if at least one complete set is available in the main library in hard copy or on microform? Why not retain unbound issues until the microtext is available for the volume year and then discard, or return them to the main library as duplicates? Certain selected sets could continue to be bound, but the greater majority would not. There will always be those readers for whom microtext is anathema and who insist on bound volumes. Hopefully, with motorized film-drives, improved optics and better resolution of image, our present undergraduates, who will become our next generation of researchers, may turn to microtext as a daily tool as readily as our bibliothecal ancestors pushed aside their papyri rolls when the codex became commonplace.

Mere provision of duplicate copies in microtext may, nevertheless, not always be the successful answer. In theory, the duplication of popular titles on microfilm for use by undergraduates who are aware of the delights of technology sounds quite workable. In actuality, I would like to report the disappointing results of one experiment at Iowa State. We attempted to provide back files of several general periodicals on microfilm for use in a distant men's residence hall library. Fifteen periodicals of the *Time-Life* variety, heavily used by undergraduates in the main building, were purchased and maintained with back sets of approximately two or three years each, immediately adjacent to a microfilm reader and publicized through on-duty staff. Current, unbound issues of the same titles were also provided. After two years we are removing both the reading machine and the microfilm since its use by undergraduates as a resource tool was too slight to be worth continuing. Some good has arisen from this since we have simply transferred these duplicate sets of popular titles to our general periodical room.

The computer search services and SDI (selective dissemination of information) has, I believe, the most significant potential for improving serial service of anything that has come along in years. There is undeniable benefit for users in the computer's ability to search a file of 5,500 items a week and to pick out specific articles on a reader's "interest profile." For librarians it permits extension of highly specialized, direct services in a manner that has been beyond their previous economic capabilities.

SDI allows the computer to browse the literature for the reader and match articles, titles and abstracts with words selected by the reader that describe his specific areas of interest, his "interest profile." Of considerable importance in the SDI system is that many publication sources are included, rather than only the core journals which most researchers in a field read regularly anyway. Sources in allied or dissimilar fields, peripheral areas, or obscure materials can thus be searched with a greater sense of confidence that what has been published has been covered than a reader could expect in our libraries using the conventional limited indexing and abstracting media. Users can be thus made aware of a far wider spectrum of publication and, by continually modifying their profiles, keep the program tailored to their new interests as these occur. Periodically a personal bibliography can be provided for the individual user, which lists in chronological sequence everything selected that was of interest. One commercial service prepares bibliographies on a three-month basis, including in this a subject bibliography, an author index and a key word (KWOC) index.

Problems so far have usually been ones of cost and the availability of data. The advantage at present lies heavily on "current awareness" aspects, but as more materials come to reside on magnetic tape, the retrospective search possibilities will become increasingly more important.

Certainly in the scientific disciplines the variety and quality of magnetic tape services being offered to the serial user are diverse and increasing. There are available, among others, the following: Chemical Abstract Condensates, Biological Abstracts, the Plastics Engineering and Electrical/Electronics Engineering tapes from Engineering Index, MEDLARS, NASA and the very large Institure of Scientific Information and the Pandex Service magnetic tape files. A copy of magnetic tape containing the material included in the document resumés printed in *Research in Education* is also now available on a two-week loan basis without cost from ERIC.

Many universities through their computer centers are already participating in these services, but it is still the library with its major files of periodicals that provides the basic resource for the largest proportion of these. At the moment the emphasis is on science and technology, but sooner or later the humanists and social scientists will be opening their doors to this through such programs as those being studied by the American Council of Learned Societies and the National Foundation for the Humanities. When these are actualities, libraries must be ready to tap into them so that their enormous serial collections can be utilized to the fullest extent, far more then they are now being used.

In terms of specific cost and service, perhaps a brief look at the Ames SDI system may be helpful. This current-awareness literature retrieval system was first developed at the Ames Laboratory of the Atomic Energy Commission and is now being offered to all faculty at Iowa State on a cost-sharing basis through the Iowa State University Computation Center. The search tapes are subscribed from a magnetic tape service giving access to the literature of science, technology and medicine. The approximate cost is $50 to $100 per year per profile and the service is available to individuals at cost or through departmental funds. There is a charge of $2 per quarter for profile change; the user is free to use those terms which best describe his interests in preparing his profile which is to be matched against the spectrum of journal articles on tape; the cost per word in the profile is ten cents. There is every expectation that there will be an increased load on library photoduplication services for reproducing these articles for SDI users. Some 2,100 to 2,300 domestic and foreign scientific journals are searched via this system, with approximately 75 percent of these available currently and in back sets in the Library.

In summary, I have been urging a fresh sense of attention and as much unfettered experimentation as possible in arranging periodical and serial collections and providing service for them. Efficiency in technical processing, reducing costs and getting extensive masses of serial material ready for the reader are vital, of course, but libraries also need to employ an enlarged sensitivity to the way they make available periodicals to people. In the words of Daniel Bergen, we must establish "library conditions that are psychically satisfying to users."[17]

The library's Augean stables are obviously going to be around for some time to come, even with the Age of Armchair Availability presumably just around the corner. The immediate task is to provide a more reader-oriented type of serial service—one that reaches out imaginatively and experimentally even if the cost is higher.

There is always danger of beating a metaphor to death, but I trust you will bear with me when I say the Old Paint, the periodical, is still the workhorse of the library's stables. The thoroughbred monographs can make easier bids for attention, and even the permutated indexes are infinitely more glamorous, but they are only the racetrack around the farm. Old Paint's form may change, he may become just a ghostly image on ultramicrofiche or a flash in the computer, but he is still essential component in the larger library. Despite his unprepossessing appearance, he is indeed a horse of another color, and a pretty faithful one at that. Libraries owe him every chance at a new pasture.

References

1. Voigt, Melvin J. "Scientists' Approaches to Information," *ACRL Monographs* (No. 24), 1961, p. 5.

2. *Ibid.*, pp. 29-30.

3. Marron, Harvey. "Science Libraries: Consolidated Departmental?" *Physics Today,* 16:34-36+, July 1963.

4. Fussler, Herman H., and Simon, Julian L. *Patterns in the Use of Books in Large Research Libraries.* Chicago, University of Chicago Library, 1961.

5. Brown, Charles Harvey. "Scientific Serials," *ACRL Monographs* (No. 16), 1956.

6. Burton, R.E. and Kebler, R.W. "The Half-Life of Some Scientific and Technical Literatures," *American Documentation,* 11:18-22, Jan. 1960.

7. Raisig, L. Miles. "The Circulation Analysis of Serial Use: Numbers Games or Key to Service?" *Medical Library Association Bulletin,* 55:399-407, Oct. 1967.

8. Peterson, Stephen L. "Patterns of Use of Periodical Literature," *College & Research Libraries,* 30:422-30, Sept. 1969.

9. Borden, Joseph C. "The Advantages and Disadvantages of a Classified Periodicals Collection," *Library Resources & Technical Services,* 9:122-26, Winter 1965.

10. Pierson, Robert M. "Where Shall We Shelve Bound Periodicals? Further Notes," *Library Resources & Technical Services,* 10:290-94, Summer 1966.

11. Whetstone, Gloria. "Serial Practices in Selected College and University Libraries," *Library Resources & Technical Services,* 5:284-90, Fall 1961.

12. Pierson, *op. cit.,* p. 291.

13. *Ibid.,* p. 293.

14. Under *News* "Survey Finds Reluctance to Circulate Mags," *Library Journal,* 94:2391, June 15, 1969.

15. Lucker, Jay K. Letter dated Oct. 8, 1969.

16. Ellsworth, Ralph E. *Planning the College and University Library Building.* 2d ed. Boulder, Colorado, Pruett Press, 1968, p. 69.

17. Bergen, Daniel. "Socio-Psychological Research on College Environments," *College & Research Libraries,* 23:478, Nov. 1962.

INDEX